THE STATE OF SECULARISM

T0366687

THE STATE OF SECULARISM

Religion, Tradition and Democracy in South Africa

Dhammamegha Annie Leatt

WITS UNIVERSITY PRESS

Published in South Africa by:

Wits University Press
1 Jan Smuts Avenue
Johannesburg 2001

www.witspress.co.za

978-1-77614-057-2 (Print)
978-1-77614-102-9 (Web PDF)
978-1-77614-103-6 (EPUB)

The manuscript for this book, *The State of Secularism: Religion, tradition and democracy in South Africa*, won the University of the Witwatersrand Research Committee Publication Award in 2016.

Copyeditor: Pat Tucker
Proofreader: Elsabé Birkenmayer
Indexer: Mirié van Rooyen
Cover design: Naadira Patel

CONTENTS

Abbreviations and acronyms

ACDP	African Christian Democratic Party
AIC	African Independent Church
ANC	African National Congress
AWB	Afrikaner Weerstandsbeweging (Afrikaner Resistance Movement)
CA	Constitutional Assembly
CLARA	Communal Land Rights Act
Codesa	Convention for a Democratic South Africa
Contralesa	Congress of Traditional Leaders of South Africa
Cope	Congress of the People
COSAG	Concerned South Africans Group
Cosatu	Congress of South African Trade Unions
CP	Conservative Party
DA	Democratic Alliance
DP	Democratic Party
DRC	Dutch Reformed Church (see NGK)
EFF	Economic Freedom Fighters
FF	Freedom Front
Gear	Growth, Employment and Redistribution
GNU	Government of national unity
HSRC	Human Sciences Research Council
IFP	Inkatha Freedom Party
KZN	KwaZulu-Natal
LMS	London Missionary Society
MPL	Muslim Personal Law
MPNP	Multiparty Negotiations Process
NGK	Nederduits Gereformeerde Kerk (see DRC)
NGO	Non-governmental organisation
NILC	National Interfaith Leadership Council
NP	National Party

NRLF	National Religious Leaders Forum
PAC	Pan Africanist Congress of Azania
RCMA	Recognition of Customary Marriages Act of 1998
RDP	Reconstruction and Development Programme
SACC	South African Council of Churches
SACP	South African Communist Party
SALC	South African Law Commission
SANNC	South African Native National Congress (precursor to the ANC)
SAPS	South African Police Services
SYC	Shatale Youth Congress
TBVC	Transkei, Bophuthatswana, Venda and Ciskei
TC1	Theme Committee One
TC4	Technical Committee on Fundamental Rights during the Transition
TRC	Truth and Reconciliation Commission
UDF	United Democratic Front
UDM	United Democratic Movement
WCRP	World Conference on Religion and Peace
WCPCC	Western Cape Provincial Council of Churches
ZCC	Zion Christian Church

Glossary

amabutho	warriors
amakhosi	plural of *inkhosi*; also *magoshi* or *bagoshi*
baruti	plural of *moruti*
bogadi	see ilobola
imbizo	a traditional council meeting, now designating any conference
imbongi	praise poet of praise singer
inkhosi/inkosi/nkosi	a chief or ruler; God
ilobola/lobola	the payment made from a groom to a bride's family before marriage
moruti	minister of religion
Nkosi sikelel' iAfrika	God bless Africa (South Africa's national anthem)
sangoma	traditional healer, particularly a diviner rather than a herbalist
sjambok	a leather whip
talaq	divorce by repudiation in Muslim personal law
ubuntu	from a phrase common to the Nguni languages of South Africa, which translates as 'a human is only human because of other humans'; it has become shorthand for a philosophy of African humanism that stresses interdependence
ulama	Muslim legal scholars
umma	the community of Muslims
volkekunde	folk studies; apartheid's state-sponsored ethnography
volkstaat	independent Afrikaner state or homeland
volksfront	people's front

Preface

For readers who are interested in ideas about secularism, the first chapter is the place to start this book. There you will find a model of political secularism that I have used to understand religion and tradition in South Africa's transition. I suggest that secularism is a normative account of the place of religion in society and government and a way of ensuring that religion is held in that place. As background to this account the first chapter details something of the history of secularism, what forms it has taken around the world and what it means for religion in different contexts. Here I introduce the ideas of differentiation, separation and relationship between the religious and the political as the key operations of secularism.

I also extend some ways of thinking about secularism to traditional and customary authority and law, something that is rather unusual in writings about secularism. I've become convinced that there are large areas of overlap between the religious and the customary in relation to power, authority and everyday practices of social reproduction. I hope this approach, and the form of analysis it offers, helps towards an understanding of other postcolonial contexts and situations where Christianity is not the only or main religion.

For those who are less interested in the concepts and want to go straight to South Africa and its history, the second chapter is a good place to start. There I offer what I call a morality tale – reflections on the ways religion and traditional authority were entangled in or against racialised rule in South Africa's past. The argument in this chapter is that secularism was impossible before democracy because there could be no normative place for religion or tradition. Instead, various forms of white government tried to annex or use living traditions to authorise white rule and deny moral or political community between rulers and ruled.

For those whose main interest lies in the negotiations, the next three chapters look at the great, slow drama that was the constitutional negotiations and the political transition. Amid violence, competing interests and the minutiae of diverse technical and legal processes, a consensus and a Constitution were born together. It was not an easy birth. In fact, it was far more difficult than most South Africans now remember. It was more violent, more arbitrary and more technical.

In these chapters, 3 to 5, I have sought to shed light on what was at stake in often painstaking debates about the law and the future. There were not just one or two people who had it in their power to decide how things would turn out. Instead, there were many players with diverse interests and perspectives, who sometimes misunderstood each other, who often disagreed and who, at times, held similar positions for very different reasons. What they cobbled together as relationship, political culture and a Constitution has had far-reaching consequences.

Chapter 3 looks closely at the ways religious groups influenced the negotiations about a future place for religion. It explores political parties' perspectives on religion and the way these were particularly influenced by an ecumenical interfaith movement. The chapter tracks the beginning of negotiations and the drafting of a right to religion. I show that almost everyone at the negotiations thought that religion was important and acknowledged its place in the lives of most South Africans. Turning that consensus into a legal framework raised interesting questions about conscience and community and about what sort of place religion should occupy in the public and schools, hospitals and prisons.

Chapter 4 looks more closely at the story of how traditional leaders – many of whom were in precarious situations in homelands in the 1980s – came to be in a position to ensure that traditional leadership and customary law were recognised in a postapartheid dispensation. How that happened turns on the relationships between the African National Congress (ANC) and the Inkatha Freedom Party (IFP), both inside and outside the negotiating chambers. And it is a story of intergenerational conflict and aspirations to either succession or the making of a single unified polity after apartheid. With all its twists and turns, I suggest that the new government's relationship with traditional authority can be understood as a failed attempt at secularisation. However we understand its genesis, it is true that the result is multiple and ambivalent forms of government and administration, particularly at local level.

Chapter 5 explores the dimension of secularism concerned with how a state founds its authority. The chapter traces an evangelical Christian story of transition that includes race reconciliation on the one hand and, on the other, an attempt to preserve socially conservative sexual morality, a moral majoritarian interpretation of the Constitution and recognition of God's sovereignty over the nation. This went hand in hand with the promotion by traditional leaders and the white right of strong cultural pluralism. Against this, the process of negotiation and the founding of the new nation were largely secular in terms of rituals, the valorisation of law itself and nationalism.

Chapter 6 does a slightly different job. The negotiations anticipated an idealised future for which many people were preparing. The chapter traces some of the ways in which the Constitution and the settlements that were made during the negotiations have fared in the past two decades. Taking stock of the social, economic and political fate of postapartheid South Africa, the chapter examines changing relationships between churches and an increasingly struggling and bankrupt ANC. It looks at the increasing influence of traditional leaders and evangelical Christians in an antiliberal alliance. And, looking at the development of marriage legislation in the past 20 years, it explores some of the contradictions of the legal framing of religion and tradition in the Constitution.

Friends and readers ask me how, as a practising Buddhist, I came to write a book about political secularism. This project has been ten years in the making. It was started as a PhD in 2007 at the University of the Witwatersrand (Wits) Institute for Social and Economic Research (WiSER). After graduating, I taught in the Religious Studies Department at the University of Cape Town before moving back to Wits, where I worked for the Johannesburg Workshop in Theory and Criticism (JWTC). In these roles I had a chance to look at religion from a political perspective. I asked what kind of relevance religion has for politics. In what ways are politics and its legal, institutional and state dimensions consequential for religion? And, of course, what is secularism? During those same ten years I was in training for ordination in the Triratna Buddhist Order. I was ordained in 2013 and given the name Dhammamegha, which means 'she who has a cloud of the truth' or 'she who rains down the truth that brings freedom'. I have since moved country to live and practise in a Buddhist community, stepping away from university life.

There are mutual threads in these two decade-long projects that have been conditioned by my upbringing and an enduring fascination with religious studies. I grew up around the Methodist Church where, when I was a small child, my father, Jim Leatt, was a minister. When I was very young our family moved to the Eastern Cape to be part of the staff of the Federal Theological Seminary. It was an ecumenical black liberation theology seminary where I had a happy and unusual childhood for a white South African. There the threads of faith, of pastoral care and of politics and liberation joined seamlessly.

Leaving the seminary, we moved back to Cape Town where I went to an all-white government school and a suburban church where the same faith expressed its politics very differently. In a way, this move picked apart the seamlessness of right and authority and love.

In both situations my place as a girl in the church ran its river between God and me. As a teenager I discovered meditation and the Dharma and found ways of imagining a life for myself and others, free from hypocrisy. I found the tools of Buddhist practice and friendship fertile and inspiring then and continue to do so now.

When it came to going to university, it was Religious Studies that captured my imagination. It was a way to study Buddhism. And I was fascinated that in one discipline you could examine everything from the most interior and intimate encounters of faith and the phenomenology of the mind to world historical trajectories of economics, symbolism and political culture.

Seemingly private moments of communing and encountering what it means to be fully human as an individual and in community become linked through relationships and views that motivate engagement in the world. And we are born into a horizon of views, institutions, practices and forces that think they are right, pass laws, act and have enduring effects. How that all hangs together and co-creates the worlds we live in continues to fascinate me.

There is a reason why books have so many thanks and acknowledge-ments. Writing one is definitely a collective endeavour. The main body of research for the book was done as part of that PhD at WiSER from 2007 to 2010. They did something very innovative there, introducing a four-year cohort PhD model that aimed to synthesise the best parts of North American and English postgraduate study.

One part of the model was having a supervision committee. The mem-bers of mine were Deborah Posel, Achille Mbembe and Jonathan Klaaren. Debbie did a penetrating and critical reading of the work in all its stages, and offered her fascination with the institutions of the negotiations and endless curiosity about what motivates people. Achille has been pro-foundly trusting of my intellectual judgement and brought a generous curiosity to the project. His astute and poetic reading of black and African philosophy and political culture deeply influenced the intellectual culture at WiSER. Jonathan gave his deep understanding of law-making processes, timely suggestions and was willing to take over as chair of the committee in its last year. Najibha and Adila Deshmukh are amazing in their work as administrator and financial administrator, respectively, looking after gen-erations of students and visiting scholars.

WiSER provided a rich and unique public intellectual space with an emphasis on global and southern intellectual citizenship. Staff and inter-national colleagues provided an enormously stimulating space for intellec-tual exchange and friendship. Irma du Plessis was a great confidante and reader. Jonathan Hyslop, Pamila Gupta, Sarah Nuttall and Liz Gunner all took the time to discuss my project, read sections of it and host events that have shed new light on what it attempts to do. Many other colleagues and friends indulged me in long explorations and discussion, particularly Natasha Erlank, Susan van Zyl, Alison Moultrie, Sharad Chari and Lynne Slominsky (Slo).

It was exhilarating to be part of the JWTC during its years of experimentation. At different times Eric Worby, Kelly Gillespie, Achille Mbembe, Leigh-Ann Naidoo, Julia Hornberger, Zen Marie and Juan Orrantia asked vital questions and convened brilliant and thoughtful exchanges. I also owe a special debt of gratitude to my previous teachers, the late John Cumpsty, David Chidester and Allan Grapard. Sa'diyya Shaikh nurtured the best kinds of questions and a sisterhood of study.

José Casanova, Winnifred Sullivan and Peter Hudson all generously reviewed my PhD and pointed out errors and possibilities that shaped the book. A series of anonymous reviewers for Wits University Press pointed to new avenues and helped with facts and understanding.

It is not only intellectual support that gives life to a project like this. Tim and Ilse Wilson made a wonderful home for Rebecca and me in Johannesburg. Madelaine Fullard and her cats hosted me generously in Pretoria (Tshwane), where I spent long days at the national archives. Vajrasakhi and Ratnadharini were lights on the horizon. Thank you for your wise friendship and, Ratnadharini, for ordaining me.

I am most grateful to the Wits Research Office for granting me a publication award. Pat Tucker edited so skilfully and efficiently that I barely noticed the cuts. If the book is readable, it's because of her labours. Thank you to my editor, Roshan Cader, who believed in the project and guided it all so well.

To my Freeth family – John, Jilly and Timo – thank you for being behind me all the way guys! To Rebecca Freeth, who has been a friend and companion most of my adult life, thank you for sticking with me through the lovely and the rough bits, and then for letting me go. Your integrity, skilful communication, friendship and sense of justice have inspired and shaped me. I appreciate your love and all kinds of support over the years.

To my parents, Jim and Jenny Leatt, no thanks are adequate for your open-handed generosity all along this project and the many years before. You read each draft each time, baked delicious snacks, fed me vegetarian food, kept me warm, edited and edited, made great suggestions and propped me up and encouraged me each step of the way.

I take full responsibility for all errors and lack of understanding you might find in these pages.

Dhammamegha Annie Leatt
2017

1

THINKING SECULARISM FROM SOUTH AFRICA

This project began with a few simple questions. Is contemporary South Africa secular? What does it mean to be secular? What kind of secularism does it have? I asked them because religion has been so saturated by politics in South Africa's past, and politics so saturated by religion. The historical importance of religion and tradition to South African governance raises the question of whether and how it is possible for a new postapartheid state to found itself without their authority. Why did the churches give up so much of their political role in the transition? How can we think about tradition and the customary in relation to secularism? How can we not? Why do we have traditional leaders and customary law in a dispensation of democratic secular liberal constitutionalism? These are the questions that animate this book.

The African National Congress (ANC), religious groups, press and political commentators all say that democratic South Africa is secular. But religion and things that look a lot like religion continue to be important and visible in South African politics and public life. Traditional leaders wield state power in rural areas, *sangomas* and praise singers are found at inaugurations and public rallies, and the Truth and Reconciliation Commission (TRC) employed overt theology. Statecraft includes a 'Moral Regeneration Movement' that calls on religious partners, and Jacob Zuma likens himself to Jesus.

With the exception of the TRC, very little of this has been adequately researched or conceptualised. So what is to be made of the public and political presence of religion and tradition in postapartheid South Africa? And what is secularism if it is not the absence of religion? Charles Taylor (2007:15) said about the study of secularism: 'It seems obvious before you start thinking about it, but as soon as you do, all sorts of problems arise.' This is true. 'What is secularism?' has to be the biggest problem.

The forms and attributes of political secularism have often been settled at times of political transition and state formation. There is a double meaning in the title of this book, *The State of Secularism*. On the one hand, secularism is a mode of state. The second meaning opens an evaluation of the state secularism is in today. The book uses a framework developed here to characterise South Africa's postapartheid secularism and understand how it came to be. My hope is that this framework will also prove useful in analysing other situations, particularly in the many other places in which Christianity has not been dominant, or where colonialism was the vehicle for the introduction of secularism.

WHAT IS POLITICAL SECULARISM?

A cluster of concepts – such as state, politics, religion, secular, church–state relations, differentiation and establishment – are essential to the notion of secularism, but they are difficult and ambiguous. They are complicated by the variety of ways in which they have been used normatively, descriptively and at different times, and by the fact that many of their usages are currently being challenged. To add to the complexity of understanding the relationship between religion and secularism, an investigation of this area in South Africa also requires attention to African traditions and the customary.

A polity, an individual, a form of subjectivity, an epistemology, a tradition, a text or a mode of reasoning can all be secular. And historically as well as normatively, the various objects of the secular are deeply intertwined.

A number of authors have sought to articulate the nature and characteristics of political secularism. Talal Asad, for example, in his influential *Formations of the Secular*, distinguishes between the secular, secularism and secularisation, referring to the secular as 'an epistemic category' (2003:1). Secularism, on the other hand, he conceives of as a political doctrine. In his analysis, secularisation is the application of this epistemic category and political doctrine to other forms of social and political life, a process he investigates in relation to Muslim and colonial law in British Colonial Egypt, among other systems. His principal object is secular political rationality and its effects on subjectivity, power and sociality.

José Casanova, in the book *Public Religions in the Modern World*, differentiates among three versions of secularisation theory. The first, he suggests, is the 'differentiation and secularisation of society' – the emergence of autonomous spheres of state, market and religion (1994:21). The second is 'the decline of religion'. The third is what he calls the 'privatisation thesis', which posits a marginalisation and interiorisation of religion in the modern world. By separating out these three meanings, he is able to assert the validity of the first while questioning the second and third and positing a contemporary 'deprivatisation' of religion (1994:211). His principal object is the wave of recent Christian movements that seek to reoccupy the public realm, and he develops a normative argument for their validity.

Any discussion of the relationship between religion and politics must identify the basis on which the two can be distinguished from one another. For example, by what signs are we to know that Archbishop Desmond Tutu is a religious leader and Nelson Mandela a political leader, especially when Tutu is engaged in political critique and Mandela is understood to be a miracle and source of transformation? Without this distinction, secularism is impossible.

The roots of the secular differentiation between religion and politics lie within Christianity. Political secularisms of all kinds developed in predominantly Christian contexts and it is impossible to narrate the emergence of the secular without taking Christian history into account.

To plot it rather crudely, Christianity started off as a Jewish messianic cult. Originally, Christianity was separate from and persecuted by Rome. It was, to quote Mark Lilla (2007:43), an 'apocalyptic sect in a pagan empire'. After the death of Jesus and under the authority of the Apostle Paul, the early church split from Judaism and asserted itself as a vehicle for universal salvation. This transformation took place in its spread to the many non-Jewish groups in the Roman Empire; the communities to which Paul wrote his Epistles. It was only with the conversion of Constantine and many of the Roman elite in the fourth century that Christianity was Hellenised, became a state religion, acquired its empire and thus became Christendom (Lilla, 2007).

In Western Europe the traces of the earlier differentiation between a messianic cult of Jesus and the politics and culture of the Roman Empire can be mapped in tensions between the Christological Kingdom of God, the papal realm of church authority and the monarchs. Relations of power and authority between the church and the princes were both administratively and theologically contested. As Casanova (1994) puts it:

> The theocratic claims of the church and spiritual rulers to possess
> primacy over the temporal rulers and, thus, ultimate supremacy and
> the right to rule over temporal affairs as well, were met with the

caesarapopist claims of kings to embody sacred sovereignty by divine right and by the attempts of temporal rulers to incorporate the spiritual sphere into their temporal patrimony and vassalage.

While there were clearly differentiations between prince and cardinal in Western Europe until the seventeenth century, the exact terms and location of this differentiation between religion and politics were contested.

One of the ways in which to trace a history of secularisation is through changes in the meaning of the words that refer to it within Christian Europe. The etymological root of the terms 'secular' and 'secularism' – the Latin word *saeculum* – means time or age. As a theological term it designates the time from Jesus's incarnation until his second coming (Casanova, 1994; Lilla, 2007). Paradoxically, therefore, it refers to a time without the Son of God; a worldly time, but within the context of a broader theological narrative and cosmology.

In the Canon Law of the Middle Ages, *sarcularisatio* came to designate the release of a cleric from the obligations of his order and into the status of a secular priest in order to work 'in the world' (Asad, 1999; Blumenberg, 1966; Casanova, 1994). This 'world' was nonetheless thoroughly Christian. Once again the term had the double meaning of a worldliness that was asserted from an ecclesiastical point of view. Unlike the temporal meaning mentioned above, this one has a spatial dimension that refers to the worldliness beyond the monasteries' walls and religious participation in that worldliness or laity.

This secularisation as laicisation was part of the major upheaval in medieval Christianity. The medieval Catholic Church sought, as Asad (1993:37) suggests, the 'subjection of all practice to a unified authority' that could discern truth and falsehood. This authority was policed by accusations of heresy and excommunication, tantamount to social and political as well as religious banishment. Heresy was not only about incorrect belief; it was also about a refusal to cede to the church the power to authorise truth. A manual for inquisitors in 1248 refers to a heretic as 'he who believed in the errors of heretics and is proved still to believe them and because, when examined or when convicted and confessing, he flatly refused to be recalled and to give full obedience to the mandates of the Church' (Lopez, 1998:25).

The diocesan borders of the medieval church marked both polity and population. Its functions and privileges included 'the allocation of administration of judicial matters, education, the documentation of life cycle events (such as birth, marriage, death) and social welfare responsibilities' (Casanova, quoted in Gill and Keshavarzian, 1999:460). In practical terms, the parish was the functional mode of tax collection (Taylor, 2007).

It had, in other words, what would now be considered a wide range of governmental functions and roles.

Between 1450 and 1640 a fire of religious reformation swept through the Catholic world, eventually leading to the emergence of Protestantism. During this period a series of reformers attempted to raise 'the quality of spirituality of the masses', as Taylor (2007:65) puts it, by focusing increasingly on the Passion of Christ and on pilgrimage. The gap between the laity and the priesthood was breached and what had previously been an elite theological concern over divine judgement, for example, became laicised.

Among these Catholic movements were various attempts at institutional as well as dogmatic reform. These included the founding of new orders such as the Jesuits in 1534, the intensification of practices of individual piety that began with the medieval mystics, and church approval for the study of Greek, Latin and Hebrew texts (Lilla, 2007) that had been preserved by Muslim scholars through the Christian Dark Ages.

Many writers have identified the origins of both modern political thought and modern interiorised subjectivity in these developments. The rediscovery of the classics animated the Enlightenment. Michel Foucault (1986), for example, examined the laicisation of confession practices, their intensification and spread, locating the reflexive subjectivity that authorised the novel and psychology's talking cures in these forms of discipline. The seeds of church reform were to bear fruit in the emergence of secular modern subjectivities.

The late fifteenth century also saw the development of the natural sciences and the invention of the microscope and telescope. Geological sciences cut away at the biblical foundations of creationism and the early modern states engaged in exploration and early mercantile colonialism (Anderson, 1991). Expanded trade routes became a source of information that was hard to reconcile with biblical narratives. China, for example, proved to be verifiably 'older than any civilisation mentioned in the Bible' (Lilla, 2007:60). All these developments undermined the authority of the church as purveyor of truth about God and nature and gave authority to newer sources of knowledge. They also led to the historically unprecedented emergence of atheism, the possibility of no belief or relation to God, along with a profound scepticism about religion as institution and mode of knowledge.

THE POLITICS OF CHRISTIAN PLURALISM

The Reformation was launched when Martin Luther pinned his 95 theses to the door of Wittenberg Cathedral in 1517. His was the first heretical movement the Catholic Church was unable to suppress and it led to a split in Latin Christendom. The complex monopoly of the Roman Church was broken (Casanova, 1994). For the first time Western Europe became the site of Christian pluralism, a split that was to have far-reaching consequences.

The Reformation was to liberate the spheres of economy, society, science and politics from religious control by breaking the monopoly of the Catholic Church. As Louis Dumont argues, 'medieval religion was a great cloak. Once it became an individual affair, it lost its all-embracing capacity and became one among other apparently equal considerations, of which the political was the first born' (Quoted in Asad, 1993:27).

In the thinking of Luther and John Calvin and under the later Enlightenment critiques of religion, the centre of gravity in Christian practice moved from sacraments and rituals and other collective practice to inner transformation or salvation through 'personal faith'. In Luther's fiery movement it was only the inner realm that could guarantee freedom and the possibility of salvation. The outer person was subject to systems of worldly power that could only corrupt it (Casanova, 1994). Many sacraments, the doctrine of intercession by saints, and celibate priesthood were abandoned.

Much of the Enlightenment's conceptualisation of freedom, maturity and rationalism comes from the anti-Catholic polemics of Protestant reformers. But the critique of Catholicism was not only ideological or theological; it was also a reaction against the Roman See's political role and the consequent weakness of the republican princes. According to Anthony Gill (2008:77):

> When Luther nailed up his theses, the north-western German princes and electors had no legal power to staunch the flow of funds to Rome or to limit the expansion of Church lands ... By turning Protestant and confiscating church property and income, as Luther advocated, they reversed their unfavourable situation vis-à-vis the church ...

Until the Reformation, Western European religious and political communities and territories had been almost entirely coterminous. As a consequence, the split in the church had violent repercussions. The wars that broke out after the Reformation were fought not only over individual souls or the rights of conscience and confession, but also over the affiliation of polities and territories. France, for example, suffered a series of civil wars from 1562 to 1598 over this matter. Religious conflicts fed into the English Civil War of 1642 to 1651. All across Western Europe, the Vatican, the princes and the new Calvinist and later Congregationalist, Quaker and Lutheran reformers sought to assert their truth and power over territories and subjects as well as souls. Unlike the Catholic Church, Protestantism was profoundly fissiparous: continually splitting and founding new denominations that were in competition with each other as much as with the Catholic Church (Weber, 1978).

There were a number of attempts to pacify the violence. The Netherlands supported religious tolerance after its independence in 1579, becoming a haven for Protestant dissidents from across Europe. The Dutch Declaration of Independence asserted that 'no man may be molested or questioned on the subject of divine worship' (Gill, 2008:81). In 1598 King Henry IV of France signed the Edict of Nantes, giving Huguenots, the minority French Protestants, 'a guarantee of non-persecution for their faith' (Gill, 2008:1). Almost a century later Louis XIV rescinded the edict, unleashing a wave of violence against the Huguenots that resulted in the emigration of nearly 400 000 people to elsewhere in Europe, North America and later to what was to become South Africa. In England in 1689 the Crown passed the Act of Toleration as the dissenting Anabaptists, Presbyterians and Quakers increased in number.

Out of the resolution of religious war was born the modern notion of individual religious liberty (Gill, 2008). By granting individuals the right to practise religion, thereby separating religious from political affiliation, religious pluralism could be tolerated and neutralised in the state. Individual religious choice and freedom of conscience was a political necessity and a secular right.

In order to bring peace to a seventeenth-century Western Europe ravaged by the Thirty Years' War, a peace treaty was signed between the Vatican, the princes and some representatives of the Reformation churches. In settling this Peace of Westphalia in 1648, the nascent early modern state was founded on the boundaries of the earlier principalities. Still under the control of monarchs, they gained autonomy from the Vatican and had the capacity to decide the religious affiliation of the polity. It was possible, in other words, for them to establish either a Protestant or the Catholic Church as their official religion, while granting 'tolerance' to other denominations. This is the source of the modern establishment of official religions.

The Peace of Westphalia granted individuals 'the liberty of conscience' and 'freedom of religion'. While not granting equality of citizenship, it did provide some protection for religious dissidents. John Stuart Mill, writing his *On Liberty* in the late 1850s, explains the development:

> Those who first broke the yoke of what called itself the Universal Church, were in general as little willing to permit difference of religious opinion as the church itself. But when the heat of the conflict was over, without giving a complete victory to any party, and each church or sect was reduced to limit its hopes to retaining possession of the

ground it already occupied; minorities, seeing that they had no chance of becoming majorities, were under the necessity of pleading to those whom they could not convert, for permission to differ. It is accordingly on this battle-field, almost solely, that the rights of the individual against society to exercise authority over dissentients openly controverted. (2002[1859]:6)

The emerging early modern states appropriated monasteries, land and other fixed property as well as a vast network of social and governmental functions including, gradually, the collection of taxes, education and welfare (Blumenberg, 1966). As a result, the term 'secularisation' gained a new meaning after the Reformation (Arendt, 1958; Casanova, 1994). Not only did it mark the strengthening of the state through the appropriation of the powers, resources and property of religion, but it also came to signify 'the transfer of ecclesiastical real property to laypersons, that is, the "freeing" of property from church hands into the hands of private owners, and thence into market circulation' (Asad, 1999:186). This became an important economic driver of mercantilism and industry.

Although the term 'secularism' is often taken to mean 'without religion', political secularism is only possible in the presence of religion or in an attempt to absent it. It is a designation for a certain kind of relationship between politics and religion. Secularism challenged religion as a contender for 'worldly' power. The question of political secularism is the question of what place religion should occupy in the polity and how it should come to take that place. The question of what the state ought to do about religion therefore remains a vital one in a secular polity.

Secularisation literature attends in great detail to the relationships among God, faith, belief and rationality, for example, as well as to political theology. It is all too often engaged in a long and rather tedious debate between Western Europe and North America about which mode of secularism is properly normative. It also increasingly attends to the Christian inheritance embedded in secular epistemologies, political rationalities and imaginaries (see, for example, Asad, 1993; Baudrillard, 1983; De Vries and Sullivan, 2006; Derrida, 2002; Gauchet, 1997; Jäger, 2007; Lefort, 2006; Schmitt, 1985; Taylor, 2007; Vattimo, 2005; Žižek, 2002).

As interest turns to the status and forms of political and pietist Islam, these same debates are extended to secularisation in the context of Allah, the Qur'an and modes of Islamic reasoning and scriptural interpretation. The more challenging task is to understand the processes and effects of secularisation beyond monotheism in contexts of diverse and institutionally varied cosmologies of power and worldliness in Africa and Asia.

POLITICAL SECULARISM

Secularism, as the 'ism' suggests, is an ideology; a coherent, normative account of what place religion should have in a nation-state. This normative account is paired with interventions by political and religious actors to achieve this place or to contest it. I propose that a variety of possibilities are secular in as much as religion becomes appropriated and subordinated to the state and the nation and does not compete for political power. But the form political secularism takes depends strongly on the conditions of the state, the religious groups and the theologies involved. It depends on whether there is a single dominant religion or religious pluralism in a territory or polity. It depends on the forms of religion and their political theologies. And it depends on the ambitions of the state according to its liberal or socialist ideologies.

SECULAR INSTITUTIONAL RELATIONS

This dimension of political secularism refers to institutional configurations and normative relationships between church and state, or, more inclusively, between religious and state institutions. There are varied forms of political secularism, but all of them involve the political management of relationships between the institutions of state and religion, legislation on the place of religion that sets it apart from government and administrative interventions in the affairs of religion. It is possible to identify four historical formations of political secularism that emerged in Europe and North America. In order of appearance they are: Establishment secularism, American First Amendment secularism, *Laïcité*, and communist atheist secularism. Each of these constitutes a sort of template or political map, a model or practical norm for other countries in their formation and consolidation, particularly after colonialism.

ESTABLISHMENT SECULARISM

During the Middle Ages Christian Europe was ruled by the Austro-Hungarian, Russian and British empires. On its border lay the Ottoman Empire. In these areas of Christendom populations were ethnically and linguistically diverse. Rule was monarchic and dynastic and there were at least three centres of power: feudal lords, the monarchy and the church. Law-making was shared between the monarchs and the church. Control over the means of violence was shared between the monarchs and the lords.

The massive changes of the late Middle Ages and early modern period, of which the Reformation was an essential part, gave rise to the increasing centralisation of powers under the monarchs, who defeated or co-opted other sources of power within their territories, including the churches and lesser nobility. With the end of the monopoly of the Catholic Church, lands and other resources were appropriated to these early modern states. In addition, the boundaries between states became increasingly delineated and movements of nationalism and cultural homogenisation sought to create nations (Anderson, 1991). There were increasingly centralised and bureaucratic forms of monarchical rule in the seventeenth and eighteenth centuries.

Establishment secularism was the earliest modern attempt to resolve the tension between the centralising and consolidating powers of the state and Christian religious pluralism. Monarchs adopted official religions which were an important part of the legitimation of their sovereignty (Anderson, 1991). However, at the same time subjects were granted a certain degree of civil freedom and the right to practise their religious choice or conscience independent of that official religion. The right to religious freedom was, in other words, the first individual political right. And the political communities of these early modern nation-states came to include believers and unbelievers, Protestants and Catholics. Establishment secularism asserted a separation between the public or national sanctioning role of religion and the constitution of a multireligious or -denominational political community.

Much of Western Europe still practises Establishment secularism and some of the establishments constituted at the Peace of Westphalia remain in place today. In England and Denmark, for example, the monarch is head of both the state and the church in ceremonial terms. In the latter, evangelical Lutheranism is the state religion; in the former, the Church of England.

Parliaments would later replace monarchs as the holders of political authority, but in many cases the older link between monarchical sovereignty and religious sanction was maintained (Foucault, 1997). As a remnant of an earlier form of political authorisation, Establishment secularism has, Casanova (1994) suggests, done religion no favours. He maintains that the Establishment churches are in the unenviable position of being almost completely unable to adapt to new social realities and that their membership has fallen dramatically. In fact, he writes, 'One might say that it was the very attempt to preserve and prolong Christendom in every nation-state and thus resist modern functional differentiation that nearly destroyed the churches in Europe' (Casanova, 1994:29). Levels of individual religiosity in Europe are extraordinarily low; a planetary anomaly.

The second half of the 1700s ushered in the age of revolution based on the ideas of the Enlightenment. First were the American and French revolutions, later the Russian. Each of these resulted in a new formation of political secularism. Each sought to exclude religion from participating in the state or exercising political power. But they used divergent strategies and differing degrees of violence or co-option to achieve this.

In terms of institutional relations there was one very significant change – the centre of power shifted from the monarchs as the holders of political right to 'the people' as rights bearers in modern states. In all three revolutions monarchy and Establishment were eradicated and states gained new political controllers and a new logic of legitimacy. The state, which became authorised either by democratic means or by popular or revolutionary overthrow, became legitimated through social contracts expressed in constitutions, elections and the mediation of political parties, or, in the case of communism, in the leadership of the party.

Relationships between religious and political institutions in early modernity had been forged between the church and the monarch as both the head of state and the titular head of the official church. Since the revolutions, new relationships have been forged between religious institutions as members of civil society and governments. These are usually framed in law at some point in the formation of modern states, becoming a significant element of their political culture. This is why a study of secularisation in South Africa requires a close reading of the constitutional negotiations and the processes of democratic state formation, for they are the main sites of those secularising processes.

AMERICAN FIRST AMENDMENT SECULARISM

The Congregational puritans who founded the American colonies in the 1600s modelled their relationship with the colonial government on that between the Church of England and the monarchical state. 'They [Congregationalist churches] expected the state to support public worship and suppress heresy' (Gill, 2008:64) and made laws that impinged on the religious freedom of Anglicans and Quakers, restricting the franchise to church members.

As waves of Catholic and other immigrants arrived in the colonies, Congregational churches attempted to assert a monopoly over state religion. In 1646, for example, a Massachusetts law required all inhabitants to attend church. Baptists and Quakers were regularly arrested and beaten and some were tortured and killed. In Virginia the Church of England was officially established and supported by citizen taxes. Preachers of the First Great Awakening in the late 1700s were barred from founding churches and holding political office.

Between 1775 and 1783 the American colonies fought a war of independence from England and the Crown and in the aftermath the founding fathers articulated a new regime for relations between religions and the state, inspired by the Virginia Statute. This was a political necessity driven by the pluralism of Protestant religious affiliation and the inability of any one denomination to establish a religious monopoly. It was also informed by John Locke's liberalism.

The First Amendment of the American Constitution, ratified in 1788, begins: 'Congress shall make no law respecting an establishment of religion or prohibiting the free exercise thereof' (Quoted in Sullivan, 2002:390). The foundation of modern American secularism is Thomas Jefferson's 'wall of separation' or disestablishment. There was to be no official religion in America – an historical first – and the government was forbidden to legislate about religion. In addition, the 'free exercise' clause granted religion a high level of autonomy.

The First Amendment has been an enduring feature of American public life and political culture since then. Religion is not allowed in the government itself, at least not administratively and legally. School prayers and Bible classes are not allowed in state schools and the US census bureau is not allowed to ask about religious affiliation.

In contrast, American public and political rhetoric, culture and nationalism are awash with religiosity. The assertion of political secularism and disestablishment did not lead to a reduction in levels of individual religiosity or in the visibility of religion in the public, as it did in Europe. There are high levels of individual religiosity and very strong legal protections for the rights to religion and conscience and their free exercise.

The free exercise clause means that there are few grounds on which the state can criticise or curtail religion. Religion is understood to be a positive social contributor to what Robert Bellah and Phillip Hammond (1980) call the development of Republican virtues, and a political and legal framework for the flourishing of religion is supported. Because of the enabling framework for religious organisations, the appearance of 'bad' religion is very threatening, whether it emerges in the form of Jim Jones, the Branch Davidians, George Bush or political Islam. State and society have few means other than violence to limit the scope of religious activities. Perhaps the country closest to this American model is India, with its pluralistic religious communities, high levels of religiosity and strong legal protections for the right to religion. Like South Africa, India engages with customary law in parallel to religion.

LAÏCITÉ

Inspired by its American predecessor, the French Revolution was the most radical version of the eradication of a European monarchy and its alliance with Rome. The French Catholic Church and its Marianist Counter-Reformation was very powerful and the battle between proponents of a secular republic and the church was fierce (Harris, 1999), leading to outright violence against church buildings and against the clergy. Anticlerical laws were passed in many Catholic states, banning religious orders, religious education, the wearing of clerical robes and prohibiting the clergy from either voting or criticising government officials (Burleigh, 2006).

Unlike in majority Protestant countries where these processes were more diffuse, in France the revolution ripped social, juridical and material resources from the hands of the church (Leatt, 2008). In 1789 it was announced in the Revolutionary National Assembly that 'all ecclesiastical goods were at the disposal of the nation' (Madan, 1987:748).

This arrangement has been consolidated in France under the name of *Laïcité*. In this system religious groups, including the Catholic Church, are under strict administrative control by the government and in law. There is an extensive registration process that discriminates against small and new religious institutions and the state is involved in sanctioning religious education curricula. It also pressures religious groups to 'organise themselves into a single centralised church-like institutional structure that can be regulated and serve as interlocutor to the state, following the traditional model of the concordat with the Catholic Church' (Casanova, 2007:2).

Laïcité is characterised by strong sanctions against public religion and a very circumscribed zone of privacy in which religious practice is tolerated. Even the surface of the body is not considered sufficiently private for displays of religiosity, as the recent and uneven banning of veils, crosses and other religious attire attests. While the right to religion or religious liberty is affirmed, heavy limitations are placed on its practice so only the most hidden and interior elements of religiosity are tolerated or sanctioned. Where religion appears in public, as it does in the built environment and the historical churches, the state maintains very tight administrative control and, in many cases, ownership.

Revolutionary Turkey modelled its relations with Islam along the same lines and adopted the policy of *Laïcité*. From 1938 it passed a series of secularising laws which banned the use of Arabic script, the call to prayer, higher religious education, Shari'a law and the Islamic brotherhoods. Polygamy was banned and veiling strongly discouraged. As is the case in France, Turkey's population became less observant and less religious in the wake of these secularising policies (Keddie, 1997). French *Laïcité* is under pressure to make a more inclusive public place for Muslims and Islam. And in Turkey, the government of President Recep Tayyip Erdoğan has launched a violent campaign to Islamise education and oust secularists.

ATHEIST MARXISTS, LENINISTS AND MAOISTS

Communist ideologues went even further in levels of state aggression against religion. When the Bolsheviks seized power in the Russian Revolution in 1917, they immediately set about crushing the Russian Orthodox Church. An official state church since 988 CE, it ran the country's parish primary schools and, until 1905, leaving the church was an offence punishable by state law (Gill, 2008). No less a figure than Leon Trotsky was given the job of cracking down on religion. The church was disestablished and, according to Gill, more than 25 000 religious buildings were closed in two decades, assets were seized and publications banned. Under Joseph Stalin, priests were among those most often executed on political grounds. By 1940 there were ninety per cent fewer priests than there had been at the time of the revolution. Other religious groups, such as Jehovah's Witnesses and Seventh-Day Adventists, were even more vociferously persecuted under a regime of state-sponsored atheism (Gill, 2008).

In some respects the Marxist formation of secularism is similar to *Laïcité* in its disdain for religion, its strong political culture of secularism and the removal of religion from the public sphere. But the Marxist critique of religion as false consciousness and as opiate of the masses added another layer. Religion was not only policed in the public sphere – there were also attempts to eradicate it from the private sphere and those zones of conscience that were recognised as the locus of religious freedom in post-Reformation thought. Perhaps, to be more accurate, the Jacobin aspiration to totally remake society made privacy impossible, and the state sought to saturate society in the making of new men and women.

In extreme manifestations, Soviet and Maoist communists conceived of the possibility of the total eradication of religion and a reliance on the state for the creation of an ideal society and individual happiness. Socialist utopias, while themselves mimicking some of the structures of religious language and imagination, promised a future free from religion, in which human development could be entirely self-motivated (Leatt, 2008).

Communist ideology sparked a series of further revolutions. Most significant was Mao Zedong's 1949 revolution in China, when almost all institutions of state and society, religious institutions and property were destroyed and Confucianism, Taoism and Buddhism banned. The height of this destruction came during the Cultural Revolution. A number of anti-colonial independence movements across Asia and Africa took this communist secularism as their model. Of these, only North Korea has retained this totalitarianism. In Southern Africa, both Mozambique and Angola instituted communist anticolonial revolutions and sought to destroy or nationalise the institutions of religion as well as traditional leadership

(Haynes, 1996). With the fall of the Berlin Wall in 1989 and the collapse of the Marxist polarity of the old world order, Jacobin-style suppressions of religion are decreasing (Casanova, 1994). Much of the former Soviet world has seen waves of religious revival since 1989. These include the return of old traditional religions such as Buddhism in Mongolia and China as well as the rapid spread of Pentecostal Christianity.

ADMINISTRATIVE INTERVENTIONS

While there are various forms of secularism as political ideology and practice, they all share some common administrative strategies. As Saba Mahmood (2005:77) puts it, 'secularism has entailed the legal and administrative intervention into religious life so as to construct religion; its spatial entailments, in its worldly aspirations, and the scope of its reasoning along certain lines'. There are legal, administrative and regulatory restrictions on practising religion in all modern states, whether explicitly secular or not, and regardless of whether religion is viewed positively or negatively in ideological terms.

These include limitations on what are considered to be undesirable sects, such as Christian Science in France or Snake Handling churches in the USA. In many countries religious groups must register, giving governments the power to grant legitimacy to religious organisations. Tax exemptions, the registration of ownership of property and access to chaplaincy positions in state institutions such as prisons, army, police and hospitals may be dependent on such registration (Gill, 2008). In some places holding public office may be officially restricted by religious affiliation. Legislation rather than religious texts or religious authorities now arbitrates religion in public disputes (Sullivan, 2005).

On the other hand, the state can grant preferential endorsements to selected religious groups through financial subsidies to welfare and education services, the payment of clerical salaries and the maintenance of religious buildings, as is the case in France and Turkey and was the case in many parts of Latin America in the nineteenth century. Where there is an established church, such as in Germany or the United Kingdom, mandatory taxes finance the public functions of these institutions (Gill, 2008).

Secular states ban religious practices such as wearing the veil (France and Turkey), snake handling (USA), caste and untouchability (India), the use of peyote or marijuana (USA, South Africa) and the use of religious language or script (Turkey). Some practices are banned outright, while others are discouraged through zoning laws, taxation and a bevy of industry, health and public morality regulations.

THE STATE OF SECULARISM

The common ground of this dimension of political secularism is, therefore, that the state is able, through some combination of law, violence and administrative intervention, to discipline religious groups and practices. Some of this discipline is relatively benign, more co-option than compulsion. This is particularly the case in the North American model, in which religion is considered to be a basis for social and civic good. The Jacobin and Marxist models show this discipline in its most violent and coercive forms.

The presence or visibility of religion in the public or political sphere is not, per se, an indication that there is no secularism. Instead, to determine the presence of political secularism is to evaluate the ends to which religion is participating, to identify who is setting the agenda and to delineate who is framing the terms in which such presence is realised.

The second dimension of political secularism deals with the legal and ideological foundations of the legitimacy of modern states. It involves two closely related arenas. The first is Enlightenment political thought and the foundation it provides for political authority and government. The second is nationalism and, in some cases, civil religion.

ENLIGHTENMENT FOUNDATIONS OF POLITICAL THEORY

Enlightenment thinkers provided the rationale for the antimonarchic democratic revolutions of the late eighteenth century, reintroducing political concepts from classical Greece and Rome into European philosophy and political thought.

Inspired by such political concepts, Thomas Hobbes provided a route out of Christian political theology. His book *Leviathan*, first published in 1651, posited a state of nature that politics could constrain through a combination of violence and political rationality without any detour through religious institutions or dogmas. The 'world', in Hobbes's work, is given to us individually and through bodily sensation and perception. Common life is not guided by any transcendent principle or design or purpose; not by providence and not by natural law.

'Hereby it is manifest,' he wrote, 'that during the time men live without a common power to keep them all in awe, they are in that condition which is called war; and such a war is of every man, against every man' (Hobbes, 2006[1651]:84). Violence is therefore the primary condition of the political in Hobbes's conception. Where there is no common power, he thought, there can be no peace, no justice, no culture, no law. This is a state in which each 'man' has a natural right to commit violence. And this is a right that he [sic] will willingly and rationally lay down in the interests of peace, prosperity, a long life and protection.

In order to avoid realising this implicit state of war, Hobbes recommended that a person or assembly be granted total sovereignty so that each individual may be protected and flourish. In this common power the religious would be subsumed by the sovereign in the total control of members of the polity. He suggested, in other words, that religion could and should be completely incorporated into the sovereign political principle: 'The sovereign would have total monopoly over ecclesiastical matters, including prophecy, miracles, and the interpretation of scripture. He would also declare that the only requirement for salvation was complete obedience to himself' (Lilla, 2007:86).

Locke's work is the next decisive step in the basic genealogy of secular humanist political thought. Instead of arguing that the state of nature is war, Locke suggested a basic human goodness that could be cemented through a contract based on individual liberty that respects the liberty of all others. Sovereignty was not, therefore, to be maximised in one person but rather to be distributed among all within a social contract which, he hoped, would supplant violence as the foundation of common life (Gill, 2008).

In his influential 1689 'Letter Concerning Toleration'[1] Locke made a case for the disestablishment of state religion on this basis. He proposed that respect for individual rights and the defence of property, liberty and life would be improved in a state with widely distributed authority and an elected representative body. In this model, which forms the foundation of modern liberalism, religion is a matter of individual good, a right to be exercised in private and in such a manner that the social contract can secure a common good.

The shift between early modern and modern political forms of government involved replacing monarchs with representative or parliamentary democracy. In parallel, as Carl Schmitt (1985, 2007) suggests, Niccolò Machiavelli and Hobbes sought to replace theistic and transcendent conceptions of power and state with theories of violence and interest. At first the object of this governance was territory and national economy. But this shifted in the modern period to a new object, the population. This is the other side of 'the people' who provide the legitimacy for rule.

In this process new political rationalities and techniques of statecraft were developed, including statistics, bureaucracy and public administration (Herzfeld, 1992), which further strengthened and centralised political power. Social contract theories that legitimated the power of modern states were developed through theories of the representation of society as the basis for political legitimacy, mediated through political parties and then, later, deliberative consensus in the public sphere and civil society (Habermas, 2002; Lefort, 1988; Mouffe, 2000, 2005). In this process new imaginaries of political freedom developed – civil society, democracy, elections, the will of the people and representative government. These foundations of modern political thought are captured in a cluster of civil and political rights and have since become normative in the formal constitution of modern states and the stated logic of the international community.

The Enlightenment asserted a political ethic independent of religious convictions and a political community independent of religious affiliation (Taylor, 2007). The revolutionary states were inaugurated by people inspired by this political imaginary and the modern state became the guarantor of these ideals of secular politics. This is why, if we are to look for normative secular authority, it is to the formation of the modern state we must turn and the political principles it claims to embody. And if we are to assert that a polity is secular it has to be founded on political principles that do not depend on the authority or divine right or sanction of God or tradition or on a chosen people, a religious franchise, the church or some other religious institution. In practice, however, violence and discrimination against some citizens are often applied on racial or religious grounds. The dynamics of nationalism is one of the forms this takes.

ROMANTIC FOUNDATIONS OF NATIONALISM AND CIVIL RELIGION

Enlightenment political thought is not the only inheritance of the modern secular state. Nationalism and its twin, civil religion, link population and territory. Though in practice the two principles are often at odds, they both drink at that other stream of Western philosophical thought, Romanticism.

The Romantics, who critiqued the rationality of the Enlightenment (Campbell, 1987; Jäger, 2007), sought to reintroduce a degree of enchantment into what they saw as an increasingly mechanistic, rational and rule-bound world. Isaac Newton, with his mechanistic natural laws, was a particular target. Romantic writers said he had 'clipped an angel's wings, disenchanting the world and reducing all life to the status of a machine' (Campbell, 1987:181).

Jean-Jacques Rousseau, the movement's foundational thinker, wrote that the Enlightenment's rejection of religion would fail to account for what was best in human beings and would thus encourage baseness (Lilla, 2007). Rousseau did not defend revealed faith but 'man's' religious instincts. Human capacity for goodness, morality, conscience, charity and the like was not dependent on revelation or, as Immanuel Kant would have it, on rationality. Instead, Rousseau suggested, it is dependent on sentiment, on subjective feelings that are an assertion of human freedom.

Romanticism was not so much a counter-philosophy as an aesthetic: a vision of freedom and heroism and a sentiment. It was not only a critique of rationalism; it was also a resistance to the levelling or conformity of the social and the Enlightenment principles of equality and exceptionlessness through tropes of heroism and genius (Arendt, 1958).

This aesthetic was applied to nations as well as individuals. Monarchical rule of the early modern states was legitimated by transcendental concepts and close links with church institutions and leaders. The object of divine sanction was the king and his political rights, or at least the political rights of his office. The Enlightenment revolution changed the subject of political rights from the monarch to 'the people' and the land. New objects were sanctified under secularism, particularly territory and population.

The relationship between religion and nationalism is complex, ambiguous and historically variable. Benedict Anderson (1991:12), for instance, wrote:

> I am not claiming that the appearance of nationalism towards the end of the eighteenth century was 'produced' by the erosion of religious certainties, or that this erosion does not itself require a complex explanation. Nor am I suggesting that somehow nationalism historically 'supersedes' religion. What I am proposing is that nationalism has to be understood by aligning it, not with self-consciously held political ideologies, but with the large cultural systems that preceded it, out of which – as well as against which – it came into being.

In Europe, the cultural systems from and against which nationalism was asserted were monarchical and religious. In nationalism, feelings and imaginaries that have religious roots are read through Romanticism, appropriated by political powers and used to seek to bind citizens to each other and the nation. But these affects and imaginaries are secular, in as much as they are no longer connected with religious salvation or religious specialists. Nationalism seeks to create and strengthen a bond between people within a nation and between 'the people' and some sacralised and idealised essence of that nation, often through either exclusion or war.

Technological and economic changes made these bonds possible. Anderson, for example, identified media through which people could experience themselves as part of an imagined community. Foremost among these were newspapers, other print media and novels – all of which proliferated through new printing technologies as well as the introduction of more universal education and literacy. In addition, national languages were standardised, reducing cultural and linguistic heterogeneity. They became a medium of widespread communication and also of affection and identification (Anderson, 1991).

There are two sides to the political imaginary of nationalism. On the one hand, nationalism stimulates and channels connection, bond, identification, love and self-sacrifice. It is political love of a homeland, motherland, national community and its many symbols. This form is best seen in Romantic poetry about the nation, the singing of national anthems and national events of collective significance. This affect is collected around national symbols and moments of heightened awareness and ritualisation of the bonds between people in the nation.

On the other hand, nationalism is thanatocratic and has led to exclusions, death and racism on a scale unimaginable in premodern times. The nation and its mystical bond are, above all, something to defend and to die for if necessary. Nobody can embody the national subject better than the war dead; those who have sacrificed everything for the fatherland and the *volk*. In this, nationalism concerns itself with the human's place in the cosmos, with species being and with contingency (Anderson, 1991:10). Its racism was found, in Europe at least, in the concern to homogenise the people of a nation and its 'spirit' and therefore exclude those who failed to correspond with the national subject.

Many of nationalism's forms were derived from medieval religion and particularly those elements of Catholic practice that were rejected by Protestants. Temporal cycles of the ritual calendar were appropriated as national holidays. Sites of pilgrimage, usually sites of violence, were adopted as national monuments. Hymns were adopted as anthems and coronations as inaugurations.

Some forms of secular nationalism explicitly exclude religious content; others draw on an overt repertoire of religious beliefs. Both Establishment and American First Amendment secularism have included religious content in nationalism, developing what has been called a civil religion. *Laïcité* and Jacobin communist forms have political cultures that exclude religious content, even as they often mimic it.

The most extreme version of civil religion in an Establishment state developed in twentieth-century Germany, articulated in German Idealism. Georg Wilhelm Friedrich Hegel, for example, argued that religion motivates and creates society and that its vital power lies in the shared spirit of a people. Like the Enlightenment thinkers before him, Hegel ranked the quality of the spirit of the people on a hierarchy of progress, asserting that some forms are closer to the deepest truths, to 'absolute knowledge' (Lilla, 2007). It was in deist Christianity that universal or historical destiny was to be found. Kant, too, thought that Christianity was the most universal, most reasonable, most moral religion; the true universal church. The problem with it, he suggested, was Judaism, 'which should be removed from

Christianity to reveal its genuine universalism'. Prefiguring a thick seam of anti-Semitism and racism in secular versions of Christendom, he called this 'the euthanasia of Judaism' (Quoted in Lilla, 2007:157).

For Hegel, the final and consummating phase of human history would take place within Christendom and through Protestantism in the German nation. The latter, he wrote, 'perfected the principle of freedom that was implicit in the Christian Incarnation and that would take rational form in modern thought – the principle that "freedom is for itself the goal to be achieved and the only goal of the spirit"' (Quoted in Lilla, 2007:197). He was intolerant of other religious groups whose faith, he suggested, 'may make it impossible for them to fully take part in the political life of the state' (Lilla, 2007:205). He proposed a complete abdication of religious autonomy and the loss of institutional control over religion by the church in its subordination to the state. This, in turn, divinised the modern state as the bearer of the spirit of the German people, thus providing the ideological rationale and the sentimental attachments that were later exploited by Adolf Hitler's anti-Semitism.

The carnage of the world wars and the Holocaust reduced the likelihood of Establishment states engaging in this kind of Christian nationalist rhetoric after the war. But this logic is again being reasserted in relation to Muslim migrants and a Christian autochthony in Europe today.

The USA is the second major example of nationalism with an explicitly religious content. Bellah and Hammond (1980:xi) refer to civil religion as '[t]he possibility that a distinct set of religious symbols and practices may arise that address the issues of political legitimacy and political ethics but that are not fused with either church or state'. Elements of US civil religion include 'a widespread acceptance by Americans of a few religiopolitical tenets regarding their nation's history and destiny' (1980:41). These include that God's will can be known through democratic procedures and that America is God's primary agent in history, giving it a special mission, a notion alluded to by Sidney Mead (1965) in his description of America as a 'Nation with the Soul of a Church'. There are similarities between America and India with respect to civil religion. In both countries powerful formations of political religion – conservative Protestantism in the USA and Hindutva in India – have challenged and reappropriated the powers of the modern state.

In the other two formations, *Laïcité* and communist, the content of nationalism explicitly excludes religion. More than this, they positively incorporate elements of secularism as a political culture and a national identity. The difference between the religious and non-religious content of nationalism is the ruling political ideology about religion and the ruling political culture of secularism.

COLONIAL AND IMPERIAL ADMINISTRATION

The history of secularism has often been written as a European story about Europe and as the story of universal truth emerging in Europe from the darkness of dogmatic clerics, liberating the universal human and its capacity for technological progress and self-founded self-mastery. Secular modernity is said to have emerged from 'a more primitive, religious, caste-and-kin-bound, inegalitarian, unemancipated, bloody, unenlightened and stateless time' (Brown, 2001:6). It is told as a story of political freedom spread around the world in its liberal free-enterprise or socialist versions. It is a story, in other words, of progress.

But this story is both partial and flawed. It leaves out the colonial, imperial and European others on whose land, bodies and practices the idea of secular Europe was built. Despite the fact that Enlightenment and European thought viewed colonial inhabitants as remnants of the past, the history of mercantile expansion, colonialism and imperialism is utterly entwined and historically coterminous with the process of European secularisation and the formation and consolidation of modern states. The colonised world experienced the Enlightenment 'in an indirect manner' through colonialism, imperialism and mission (Ellis and Ter Haar, 2004:16). It has been estimated that by 1930 'colonies or ex-colonies covered 84.6% of the land surface of the globe' (Ellis and Ter Haar, 2004:5). The colonial stories of secularism are not marginal, either historically or in the present. And they are largely missing from the academic study of secularism.

There are two issues at stake in thinking about secularism and colonialism together: the relationship between politics and religion in the colonies, and the forms and powers of colonial states.

It is possible to identify three broad kinds of relationship between politics and religion in the colonies. These relationships were conditioned by the strength and forms of colonial government and the kinds of religious life and organisation the colonists encountered. French, Spanish and British colonialism imposed differing cultures of contact and strategies of subordination and extraction. The first relationship was one of outright destruction and the near eradication of indigenes. Genocides were conducted against indigenous Americans, aboriginal Australians and the Khoisan in South Africa. These genocides were legitimated by claims that these people were like animals, didn't deserve the lands they inhabited and had no religion. This 'lack' of religion was often coupled in European imaginings to a lack of other defining characteristics such as law, a state, political organisation, morality, marriage and language (Chidester, 1996; Lopez, 1998; Masuzawa, 2005).

In the second instance, indigenes were ascribed religion, but one that was declared to be 'primitive' or communal rather than individual; religion that was non-universal and preliterate. In the European imagination this religion was a mark of the strange and the backward. This second relationship between colonising powers and people to whom this kind of religion was ascribed was an attempt to destroy that religion and culture rather than the people themselves. This destruction, or attempted destruction, came under many names: assimilation, civilisation, conversion.

Colonial administration was raw and contested. It was, as Karen Fields (1982:572) puts it, a situation in which 'a distinct group of rulers consciously impose their own law and order against the interests and heard objections of a subject population, lately sovereign'. This was not a model of rational or bureaucratic rule. Other images that better describe it include those provided by Achille Mbembe (2001:14), who identifies colonialism as a mode of phallic power; desiring, rapacious and brutalising. Despite much of its ideology, the process of civilising, converting or assimilating retained servitude and racial hierarchy. Indigenes were groomed, experimented on and allowed into a joint world, but they could almost never be equal (Mbembe, 2001).

Colonialism often presented two faces: the administrator and the missionary. In doing so it displayed an institutional separation between church and government. Governmental and religious elements of colonialism with a 'civilising' or assimilationist ambition brought different tools of subordination and extraction, but they often shared a view of those they colonised, particularly those without the religions of the Book (particularly Islam) or salvation religions (such as Buddhism).

As Stephen Ellis and Gerrie Ter Haar (2004:190) suggest, 'European administrators, operating within Western precepts of order and governance, sought to confine religion to a private sphere within the ambit of cultures that colonial officials tended to regard as discrete systems.' But to do this it was necessary to introduce into the traditions of those they sought to rule a differentiation between religion and politics and between public and private (Asad, 2003).

However, the colonialists encountered forms of religion in which the relatively well-established differentiation within Christendom simply did not exist, directly or by analogy. Traditional Islam, for example, recognises no clergy, and the Muslim *umma* is simultaneously a religious and a cultural community. Processes of destruction, assimilation and indirect rule therefore had extremely complex implications for those religious traditions (Ali, 2002; Asad, 2003; Tayob, 2009).

Where colonial agents encountered forms of authority that they recognised as being institutionally or theologically powerful enough to contest colonial rule, a form of differentiation and secularism was attempted. In such cases, colonialism performed a partial secularisation. These attempts at secularising the religions of colonial subjects definitely had some institutional success, but in many cases indigenous imaginaries of legitimacy and understandings of power and morality were not severed from their religious or cultural embeddedness.

Colonial rulers were simply not strong enough to subordinate religion in the colonies entirely. Nor, of course, did they seek fully to institute the second condition of secular political foundations. It was certainly against the perceived economic, political and strategic interests of colonial powers to sponsor Enlightenment ideals of democracy, universal franchise or representative government, and incomplete processes of political secularism were often abandoned in favour of indirect rule. This is the third kind of relationship between politics and religion in the colonies.

Where colonial administrations could not rule directly, they annexed a wide range of local political powers, including both religious and traditional leaders, in indirect rule (Fields, 1982:586). In doing so they almost always sought out the most conservative renditions of religion or culture in subject populations, and conservative local elites used indirect government as a way to assert control over heterogeneous traditions and create a bulwark against social and economic change.

Though undoubtedly modern, colonial and imperial rule bore many resemblances to premodern forms of political government. Anderson (1991:159) argues, for example, that colonial racism was 'pseudo aristocratic' in its solidarity amongst whites and against a racialised underclass. Justifications of colonial rule also regularly invoked transcendence, including racialised political theologies. These forms of rule were the very antithesis of a 'moral community between rulers and ruled' (Fields, 1982).

Colonialism introduced political secularism across the globe, but it did so in incomplete, contested, ambivalent and hypocritical forms. Only some aspects of secularism were exported, particularly its institutional relations. And colonial rule was simply not strong enough, on the whole, to saturate the political and social spaces. For this, the colonialists annexed other modes of political and social governance and leadership, modes that came with non-secular metaphysics of legitimation.

POLITICAL SECULARISM TODAY

Political secularism is a normative account of the place of religion in politics and society and a series of disciplinary interventions to ensure that religion is put and kept in its place. It was developed in the context of modern centralising states in a time of intense religious conflict and pluralism, and formed and consolidated across the Christian transatlantic world. Its application, and the introduction of the logics of secularism across the world, was part of another configuration of power. Colonial rule introduced some of its elements and ignored others, sometimes attempting and failing to implement its institutional terms, often ignoring or supplementing its ideological core.

But many of the nationalist movements that sought independence from colonial rule in the twentieth century took formations of political secularism as models for modern government and as ways to manage relationships with religion and tradition within newly independent countries. Through such processes political secularism has become part of a globally hegemonic ideal of national rule and constitutionalism.

But there can be little doubt that the conditions for national rule in the late twentieth and early twenty-first centuries are very different from those of the ambitious consolidating and centralising states of Europe in the eighteenth and nineteenth centuries. Political secularism developed amid a revolution in Christian institutions and practice, one that led to religion's interiorisation, privatisation, deregulation and fissiparity. Many contemporary religious movements are becoming increasingly public and transnational. It is apparent that the ideological and administrative ambitions of political secularism are being countered by a wide range of religious forms and aspirations in the transatlantic and postcolonial worlds. The conditions under which states can serve their citizens and assert authority over religion in the political space are increasingly hard to assert and maintain.

The Iranian revolution in 1979 was the first indication that political secularisation was not as inevitable or natural as had been assumed. Then the 1980s saw not only the tandem rise of political Islam and the Christian religious right, but also of Solidarity in Poland, Catholic involvement in the Sandinista revolution and other Latin American conflicts, liberation theology and all the conflicts that had lines of religious fracture: the Middle East, Northern Ireland, Yugoslavia, India and the Soviet Union (Casanova, 1994). Evangelical Protestantism affected presidential elections in Columbia, Guatemala and Peru (Gill and Keshavarzian, 1999) and Christian centre-right parties became increasingly prominent in Europe.

It is impossible to pick up a newspaper anywhere in the world without encountering some version of the political return of religion: 9/11 and the so-called 'war on terror', destabilisation in Afghanistan and Pakistan, ISIS (Islamic State in Iraq and Syria) or Boko Haram, and increasingly contested zones of encounter between Christians and Muslims in North Africa. But in none of these cases is the designation 'political religion' really helpful. It is a compound term, dependent on the opposition of the terms that these events, in their different ways, are disputing.

The ongoing conditions for political secularism are dependent on developments in three areas. The first is the capacity, power and ambition of late modern states. Will they be strong enough to govern in a way that excludes or incorporates religion institutionally and ideologically? The second is the public and political aspirations of new religious movements, institutions and theologies. Will they value the separation of their institutions from the state and allow their theologies to be excluded or appropriated by political actors? The third is the fate of the differentiation between politics and religion, both in philosophy and in the context of religious traditions that have had this form of differentiation applied to them. Will it be possible to continue to differentiate between politics and religion in a way that allows for their separation? The various formations of political secularism are all being tested and contested by late modern social, economic, political, religious and philosophical developments. Globally, some religious movements are contesting the right to hold political power, and religion is politicised in violent conflicts.

The past 60 years have also seen a growth in what Casanova calls public religions. He argues that there has been a 'deprivatisation' of religion. 'Social movements have appeared which either are religious in nature or are challenging in the name of religion the legitimacy and autonomy of the primary secular spheres, the state and the market economy' (Casanova, 1994:5).

Public religion does not necessarily contest political power as a competitor to the state, but it does seek to alter the terms on which politics is founded through a contestation around morality and ethics. These can focus on issues of the family and sexuality or, in the context of corruption, on political virtues and the possibility of political principle as a restraint to a politics of power as its own end (Casanova, 1994). Such movements are not restricted to the better-known examples of the American right. The rapidly expanding pietist movements studied by Mahmood in Egypt, for example, challenge the 'process by which religion is relegated to its own differentiated sphere' (Mahmood, 2005:48).

The consequences of the return of religion are variable and as yet incompletely worked out. The current public debate tends to be divided between those who interpret some forms of religious involvement in public and political life as a long-awaited return of morality and principle to a public politics that has degenerated into nothing other than a principle of power (Casanova, 1994; Madan, 1987; Taylor, 2007). Others suggest that a return of religion to political life is a return to a dark age of irrationality and violence (Harris, 2006; Huntington, 2002; Rorty, 2003). What is certain is that the conditions for political secularism and the techniques through which it is maintained are deeply contested in the late modern period. In the postcolonial and neoliberal world, the conditions under which the state can institute authority over religion in political space are increasingly challenged.

2

A SOUTH AFRICAN MORALITY TALE: RELIGION, TRADITION AND RACIALISED RULE

The natives must be made clearly to understand and to realise that the presence and predominance of the White race will be preserved at all hazards, and that all attempts to destroy its hegemony, whether overt or covert, such as the Ethiopian propaganda, will be promptly punished, instead of being disdainfully treated, as in the past.
Natal Native Affairs Commission 1907 (Sundkler, 1948:69)

South Africa has a long and complex history of entanglement between religion, tradition and political rule. Until the political transition in the 1990s, governance was not secular. Despite their many differences, successive regimes made use of Christian political theologies and what I will call here 'things African', a phrase introduced by John and Jean Comaroff (2004), to secure rule without democratic legitimacy. They attempted a subordination of black interests to white rule by instrumentalising traditional leadership, customary law, Christianity, violence and duplicitous forms of legality. The apartheid government claimed explicitly that South Africa was a Christian country, ruled, however perversely, in terms of Christian values.

The country was not secular prior to 1994, in a variety of ways. From the establishment of a national state in 1910, South African governments consistently espoused a political theology to legitimate white rule. The state instituted a variety of relationships with religious institutions, sometimes appropriating church resources, sometimes drawing close to churches for political legitimation and sometimes harassing and unleashing violence upon religious groups and leaders. Aspects of modern statecraft were turned towards the antidemocratic politics of white rule.

Writing in these areas requires the uncomfortable but necessary reproduction of the racist language of racial governance. Some of this chapter refers to primary materials of the colonial administration, missionaries and apartheid bureaucrats. The language of these documents is often offensive, referring to 'Kaffirs', 'heathens', 'natives', 'Bantu' and the like. They are referenced in this chapter because it was on these terms that religion and culture were racially marked across time; authorising violence, exclusions and techniques of subjugation.

DIFFERENTIATION AND SEPARATION

Religious Studies scholarship has repeatedly pointed out that the concept of religion as a universal category of human life is, in fact, modern (see, for example, Masuzawa, 2005) and the distinction between religion and other domains, such as politics, economy and culture, is a product of secularism (Jäger, 2007).

Colonialism and then imperial and apartheid rule performed a partial and ambivalent secularisation of the indigenous traditions of Southern Africa. This was not the result of a coherent strategy; it was produced by a range of sometimes contradictory interventions. But it did have systematic effects. Some of the most important have been on the political imaginary and institutional locus of chieftainship and the codification of what came to be called customary law.

For the first nearly 150 years of European occupation after 1652 there was little intention to engage 'the natives', also referred to as 'heathens', beyond the need for trade in meat and other supplies, the elimination of those who were understood to be a threat to the settlers and the incorporation of those who could become labour in the emerging colony. When settlers first moved north in search of grazing and land, neither they nor African polities were able to exert full control over one another. This led to a range of early interactions, some of which were relatively egalitarian. Others, though, were coercive and genocidal, particularly on the early northern frontier with the San and Khoi (Giliomee, 1988; Legassick, 1980; Penn, 2005). But across the board '[t]he Colonists carried with them to the frontier a set of attitudes, most important of which was the notion that as "Christians" they were culturally superior to the "heathens" who they associated with crudeness, conflict and treachery' (Giliomee, 1988:433).

It was the missionary movement that led to an intimacy and intensification of interactions between colonists and Africans. A combination of the French Revolution, Romanticism, British evangelical revivals and a Protestant reaction against Calvinism gave birth to the evangelical missionary societies that promised liberation to the human masses through the gospel. They took their biblical mandate from Mark 16:15, in which Jesus said, 'Go into all the world and preach the good news to all creation. Whoever believes and is baptised will be saved, but whoever does not believe will be condemned.'[1]

Between 1799 and 1857 missions were rapidly established across Southern Africa by the London Missionary Society (LMS), the Methodist Wesleyan Mission, the Presbyterian Glasgow Missionary Society, the Church of England, the Paris Evangelical Missionary Society and the German Moravian, Rhenish, Berlin and Hermannsburg societies. There was also a scattering of Norwegian, Swedish, Finnish and Swiss missions as well as the American Board of Missions and, eventually, the missions of the Dutch Reformed churches (Davies and Shepherd, 1954).

The church of early modern Europe provided a template for the identification of religion by missionaries and colonial settlers as well as the emerging social sciences (Masuzawa, 2005). For them religion was recognisable when it was monotheistic, revelatory, transcendent, institutionalised and accompanied by theologians and sacraments. The first response of colonials and missionaries to societies that had no written sacred texts or full-time institutionalised religious specialists they could discern was to say that they had no religion. Africans were described as Godless heathens whose culture was insufficiently developed to be religious. In early accounts this reported 'lack of religion' was often coupled with a lack of other defining human characteristics: language, law, marriage, political organisation. It was a fundamentally dehumanising ascription (Chidester, 1996).

From the first systematic contact between Boeretrekkers and Xhosa-speaking peoples, which took place in about 1702, the term 'Kaffir' – derived from the Arabic word for infidel – was used as a European designation for the Xhosa (Davies and Shepherd, 1954:16). It remains a racial slur today.

Johannes van der Kemp, the first LMS missionary to the Xhosa, who arrived in 1799 (Ndletyana, 2008), claimed that the Xhosa had magic and superstition, charms, oaths and curses in abundance, but no religion.

Without priests, the missionary found himself at a loss for interlocutors (Chidester, 1996). Perhaps the best ethnographic account of a South African colonial frontier is the Comaroffs' *Of Revelation and Revolution* (1991), which includes a reconstruction of some elements of a Tswana precolonial polity, the Thlaping, who lived between the Vaal and Molopo rivers. It gives a detailed account of their encounter with European non-conformist missionaries who also found them to be without religion (Wilson, 1971). Robert Moffat is quoted by Comaroff and Comaroff (1991:202) as saying in 1842:

> The situation of the missionary among the Bechuanas is peculiar, differing ... from any other among any nation on the face of the earth ... He seeks in vain to find a temple, an altar, or a single emblem of heathen worship ... Thus the missionary could make no appeals to legends, or to altars, or to an unknown God, or to ideas kindred to those he wishes to impart.

David Chidester (1996:3) reports that '[t]he discovery of local religious systems in Southern Africa can be precisely correlated with the establishment of control over Africans'. He found that across all the early frontiers of what was to become South Africa, the 'discovery' by various Europeans of local or indigenous religion correlated precisely with the establishment of political control over African polities and their territories. Once these polities were broken by disease, warfare and territorial appropriation, groups that were subsequently called Khoisan, Xhosa, Zulu and Sotho-Tswana were credited with religion.

But the religion that was ascribed to various inhabitants of Southern Africa was not understood by missionaries or settlers to be equivalent to Christianity. On the contrary, it was called false religion, primitive religion; undeveloped and regressive. This ascription was part of a broader movement of what Chidester (1996:3) calls 'Imperial comparative religion', practised in the European metropole from the 1850s. It was characterised by the organisation of fragmented and decontextualised colonial traveller accounts and 'ethnographies' into a vast hierarchical system of religious and civilisational progress, the pinnacle of which was said to be Protestantism. This thin comparison reduced complex and multifaceted traditions to a variety of racial or national 'mentalities'. The publication of Charles Darwin's *The Origin of Species* in 1859 gave impetus to this form of ranking and ordering.

In Southern Africa the content and form of religion was said to be 'primitive' and 'communal' and repeated attempts were made to identify its 'lost' or 'weak' ideas of a monotheistic deity. Otherwise the 'primitive religion' of the inhabitants of Southern Africa was said to comprise ancestors and 'ancestor worship'; divination; witchcraft; curses and spells; rain-making; the protection of warriors by occult means; 'witchdoctors', who controlled lightning; and divination by throwing bones. These were viewed with contempt but also some fascination by missionaries and travellers.

In opposition to this 'false religion', the missionaries sought, by their own accounts, to bring, as a gift, the 'true religion' of Christianity to black Africans. But missionaries did not only aim for 'spiritual' salvation; they had a broader related object: through conversion and enculturation into modern economic forms, the 'savage' could be made 'civilised'. Missionaries were interested in the souls of indigenes, but at the expense of almost everything else about them.

Conversion to Christianity was not just about the acceptance of a doctrine or a matter of individual spiritual salvation. It was about enculturation into an alternative 'civilised' and European economy, sovereignty, law and mode of being. Barnabas Shaw, a Methodist missionary, wrote the following in 1840:

> Some have thought that missionaries should take no concern in the temporal affairs of the people among whom they labour, but that they would be exclusively employed in promoting their spiritual welfare. This is correct as it regards nations already in a state of civilisation, but will not apply to the commencement of a mission among savages. (Quoted in Davies and Shepherd, 1954:170)

For a wide range of reasons, early Christian converts left the physical structures of what remained of the land's traditional polities and moved onto mission stations, differentiating themselves by modes of dress and gender roles. Mcebisi Ndletyana (2008:4), writing about what was to become the Eastern Cape, states:

> By 1848 ... the colonial administration had issued 70 000 acres of land to mission stations, while another 155 000 acres was held by virtue of tickets of occupation. Individuals could lease mission land and generate income for themselves and had to pay rent and taxes.

These mission stations were the first zones of British sovereignty over black subjects. They were also the sites of a Christian community of whites and blacks, albeit with a disenfranchising and paternalistic ranking. Conversion and assimilation promised, as Comaroff and Comaroff

(1997:33) put it, 'personal salvation in membership of a world-wide congregation of believers; thus did they become citizens of, and enter into principled relationships with, a universal moral community'.

Missionaries and many imperial ideologues presumed that these zones of British sovereignty and altered African subjectivity would expand in scope. And in the Cape Colony black inhabitants, freed slaves and labourers came to be included under a common law as British subjects. The height of this non-exclusive polity of Cape liberalism was its non-racial franchise. This franchise nonetheless required that black subjects be Christian, 'civilised' by their religion, landownership and de facto autonomy from chiefs. Conversion and 'civilisation' was a way of overcoming the independence of African polities. But the civilising mission always undermined its own project by educating African elites who became increasingly critical of the limits and hypocrisies of colonial racism. The biographies of many second-generation converts and intellectuals, such as Tiyo Soga, attest to the painful contradictions such men inherited (Ndletyana, 2008).

In these dynamics we can see the identification of religion *as such* in the context of Southern Africa and we can also see the introduction of a universal and comparative concept of religion. First there was no religion, then there was false religion and, in contrast, there was the 'true' religion of Christianity. Heathenism and false religion were identified with African polities. Conversion and assimilation were the means to destroy 'primitive' African religion and replace it with 'true' religion.

In the process, a differentiation was also introduced within the religion and politics of African polities. The political aspect came to be understood by missionaries and administrators as personified by the chiefs. Referring to the LMS mission amongst the Thlaping, Comaroff and Comaroff (1991:11) note that

> [i]n order to facilitate their work, the non-conformists attempted to drive a wedge between the realm of the spirit and the temporal affairs of government, both indigenous and imperial. The object was to lay the ground for a new moral economy based on the clear separation of church and state, of sacred authority and secular power – to establish, in short, a state of colonialism in anticipation of the colonial state.

As mentioned above, this distinction between religion and politics was not part of any Southern African people's emic categorisation. On the contrary, a wide range of sources characterise the indivisibility of the economic, social, spiritual and cosmological aspects of these orders, and chieftainship was central in all these aspects. As Edwin Ritchken

(1995:48) asserts, the precolonial order of what was to become the Northern Transvaal (now Limpopo) shared a common ontology in which the will of the ancestors represented 'the social order in its purest form'. Authority was derived from proximity to the ancestral order through age and linkage with the most powerful lineage, that of the royal house. And 'the will of the ancestors, expressed through the chief, secured the reproduction of the chiefdom and the fertility of the natural world' (Ritchken, 1995:40).

John Mackenzie, writing about the Bechuana community in 1871, said, 'in talking about the chief, Tswana accentuated his role in sustaining order – in its economic, spiritual, social and cosmological aspects, since these were indivisible' (Quoted in Comaroff and Comaroff, 1991:128). According to the Comaroffs (1991:148),

> the bogosi (chiefdom) was the hub of everyday life, the axis around which rotated the cycles of production and ritual performance that yielded human, material and spiritual value. Its suzerainty in turn was mandated by the royal dead, whose potency emanated from their communal grave in the cattle-byre alongside the royal court.

In the Comaroffs' account, the first part of the process of secularisation was the introduction of a distinction between the domain of the spirit and the 'temporal' and material domain of power. 'Marking off the religious domain from the political, therefore, was the first step in isolating the battleground on which Satan was to be defeated' (Comaroff and Comaroff, 1991:259). The missionaries contested practices and relationships between the visible and non-visible that they identified as religious or that they viewed as immoral: rain-making, circumcision, polygamous marriage, witchcraft, sacrifice and ancestors.

Although their arguments were often met with ridicule by would-be converts – through their moral and political economies and their technologies – missionaries, traders and British military and magistrates 'unleashed forces that would pick away at the seams of the indigenous politico-ritual order' (Comaroff and Comaroff, 1991:257), unravelling the fabric of black sovereignty. Missionaries undermined the metaphysical sources of the legitimacy of the chiefs at the same time as settlers, military interventions and the appropriation of land undermined their physical and material bases of power.

Many elements of African practice designated 'customary' rather than 'religious' were considered by British codifiers and their moralising missionary interlocutors to be 'repugnant' to human or universal values. They sought to use a process of codification of 'customary law' to eliminate or transform these customs and the social practices to which they refer. This involved a process of secularisation.

Witchcraft, for example, was treated in this altered law as an imaginary or illusory crime. The techniques of combating witchcraft rather than witchcraft itself became the object of disciplinary intervention (Ashforth, 2005; Geschiere, 2006).

It is important for what follows to note that the 'religious' elements of things African that were partially separated from political ones were never institutionalised as religion. No religious specialists or institutions or texts came to authorise the practices, beliefs and ontology identified as religious. There is a significant silence when it comes to a discussion of the relationships between state and religious institutions in South Africa because, until after 1994, there were no self-identified indigenous religious institutions. This is not to say that these practices, beliefs and ontology disappeared. On the contrary, they have played an important part in various forms of Christianity in Southern Africa, most strongly through the African Independent Churches (AICs), but also in their influence on the mainline or 'English-speaking' and Catholic churches and, later on, black theology. Practices have also continued outside of and sometimes opposed to Christianity in relation to ancestors and rural and urban households (Masondo, 2011:33).

The story of chieftainship and customary law is one of repeated periods of urbanisation and competition and coexistence between black and white, followed by policies of 'retribalisation' that sought to assert traditional leadership in zones of separation, indirect rule and then homeland 'autonomy'. It was often the codification of customary law that provided administrative routes to indirect rule.

POLITICAL THEOLOGIES AND THE METAPHYSICS OF RACE

It is impossible to write about the political history of South Africa without placing race at the centre of the analysis. Political theologies and civil religions in South Africa have historically either asserted or contested the metaphysics of racial difference and white supremacy. It was both logically and politically necessary for white rule to develop justifications for the political right of a white government to rule over black people. These justifications, of course, became the target of theologies of liberation that declared them heretical.

There are three main examples of such political theologies in South Africa. British civilisational and apartheid Kuyperian Calvinist political theologies sanctified a difference between black and white, aimed to legitimise white superiority and sought to provide a rationale for white rule. Liberation theology contested the ontology of racial difference and founded a theology of equality and solidarity.

Imperialism was relatively secularised in its political culture. It certainly drew on Christianity as some kind of a mark of superiority and as a British cultural possession and inheritance, but it was not necessarily or only articulated by religious specialists and it did not draw heavily on scriptural resources. In addition, Christianity was only one element of the cultural possession that was held to grant superiority. Others included secularism itself, rationality, bureaucratic rule, models of law and superior technology. This form of racism located difference in culture, making it at least theoretically possible to assimilate difference through enculturation. It was only when assimilationist policies had moulded subjects who contested racial differentiation and inequality on Enlightenment terms that new forms of racism emerged that identified difference as more fixed, biological or inherent (Magubane, 1996).

Afrikaner civil religion, on the other hand, was far more elaborate and more explicitly theological in its orientation. Probably the most researched aspect of the place of religion in pre-1994 South Africa, it had a number of interlocking elements.

The first was the sacralisation of a bond between Afrikaners in opposition to British imperialism. The second was a political theology of race that was closely tied to biological racism. This located difference in biological matter: essentials, forms, phenotypes, bodies and the very being of people (Costa, 2000). It was a theory of innate difference (Costa, 2000; Martens, 2006). This underpinned the idea that races are fixed and that culture and race are historically and ontologically coterminous, and therefore provide no grounds for meeting or mutual assimilation or influence.

We can see this form of racism in Jan Smuts's 'Native Policy in Africa' speech, given at Oxford in 1929.[2] He argued that Africans were mentally and culturally different from Europeans. Europeans should not, therefore, engage in policy that would result in a de-Africanisation of Africans (Welsh, 1972). Under apartheid, biological racism was linked with a Kuyperian version of political theology. Dutch theologian Abraham Kuyper 'argued that Calvinism had resolved the medieval dualism between the church and world by placing both equally under the sovereignty of God' (Moodie, 1975:54). It was a particularly conservative strand of Christianity. This form of Calvinist Protestantism maintained John Calvin's original position that very few souls would be saved, and Kuyper's version of it added a racial or ethnic dimension, limiting the potentially saved to a chosen racial few. This was certainly no foundation for an assimilationist policy. Kuyper suggested that nations, rather than individuals, were the creation of God, making of apartheid a form of obedience to the will of God in its recognition of national or ethnic differences.

The third was a covenant that identified a manifest destiny in Afrikaner rule (Van der Westhuizen, 2007). The 1838 victory of the Boers over the Zulu at the Battle of Blood River and their 'covenant' with God became the prime symbol of Afrikaner civil religion (Moodie, 1975). Afrikaners were, according to this covenant, the chosen people of God, with a special and burdensome mission to rule over 'the descendants of Ham' (Van der Westhuizen, 2007:56). Prime Minister Daniel F. Malan expressed it this way: 'Our history is the greatest masterpiece of the centuries. We hold this nationhood as our due for it was given to us by the Architect of the universe ... Afrikanerdom is not the work of men but the creation of God' (Quoted in Moodie, 1975:2).

It is possible to see these elements of racialised political theology in apartheid's founding documents. The 1961 Republic of South Africa Constitution Act (No. 32 of 1961) began as follows:

> In humble submission to Almighty God, Who controls the destinies of nations and the history of peoples;
>> Who gathered our forebears together from many lands and gave them this their own;
>> Who has guided them from generation to generation;
>> Who has wondrously delivered them from the dangers that beset them;
>
> We, who are in Parliament assembled, declare that whereas we
>> Are Conscious of our responsibility towards God and man.
>> Are convinced of the necessity to stand united;
>> To safeguard the integrity and freedom of our country;
>> To secure the maintenance of law and order;
>> To further the contentment and spiritual and material welfare of all in our midst.

The Constitution also stated in Part I that '[t]he people of the Republic of South Africa acknowledge the sovereignty and guidance of Almighty God'. Like the South Africa Act of 1909, the 1961 Constitution failed to give any consideration to the political rights or representation of black South Africans 'in our midst', referring only to a patrimonial responsibility for black subjects.

The Republic of South Africa Constitution Act (No. 110 of 1983), which established the tricameral parliament, amended this theology some-what. In bringing Indian and coloured representatives into Parliament it sought to reflect some sort of religious or customary cohabitation. Its preamble reflects the ambivalence of this attempt. It kept much the same wording as the 1961 Constitution but also included the following:

> We declare that we are conscious of our responsibility towards God and man;
> Are convinced of the necessity of standing united and of pursuing the following national goals:
> To uphold Christian values and civilized norms, with recognition and protection of freedom of faith and worship; ...
> To respect, to further and to protect the self-determination of population groups and peoples; ...
> Are desirous of giving the Republic of South Africa a Constitution which provides for elected and responsible forms of government and which is best suited to the traditions, history and circumstances of our land.

In opposition to these racialised theologies, various strands of secular African nationalism, a direct response to the Union and its political exclusion of black people, asserted the equality of people across races. The South African Native National Congress (SANNC), formed in 1912 to contest the Union, was initially a middle-class organisation that included both prominent rural chiefs and missionary-educated intellectuals (Lodge, 1983). It sought to prevent what was to become the 1913 Land Act, then in Bill form, from being passed. At first it dispatched requests and polite complaints to the British Parliament, but it quickly grew to support striking mineworkers and anti-pass campaigns. From the 1920s the emergence of trade unions and worker movements, particularly the Industrial and Commercial Workers Union and the South African Communist Party (SACP), somewhat radicalised the African congress movement. In 1923 the SANNC changed its name to the African National Congress (ANC).

In twentieth-century South Africa it was not the state but these African nationalist movements that sponsored universal Enlightenment values and their political imaginary of freedom and self-government. In the 1940s and 1950s the movement was both radicalised and brutally repressed. The urban locations or townships, which the National Party (NP) presented as a threat to white interests, were increasingly the locus of a black politics of equality. When the ANC and the SACP mobilised against the pass laws and the migrant labour system, the NP responded by smashing the unions, banning the ANC and the SACP and using the Suppression of Communism Act (No. 44 of 1950) against a wide range of political opponents (Van der Westhuizen, 2007).

These black political organisations not only opposed government policy, but in the development of the Freedom Charter, finalised in 1955, they sought to articulate the rights and responsibilities of an economic distribution that was not based on race. According to academic Stephen Clingman:

> If the intent of the apartheid government was to prove some misguided point about God-given hierarchies and distinctions, then the anti-apartheid movement would show through its most intimate gestures as much as its wider institutional structures that not only were racial cooperation and harmony possible, but that the only kind of superiority there could be was moral. (Quoted in Van der Westhuizen, 2007:72)

As white South Africa entrenched itself in apartheid, and as the repression of black people increased, black politics was radicalised and the 'liberation' parties, the ANC, the SACP and the Pan Africanist Congress of Azania (PAC, which had broken away from the ANC), were harassed and exiled. It was during this period that church and other religious leaders began to play a greater role in the struggle against apartheid. Some mainline church leaders used their relative freedom of speech and organisation to contribute to anti-apartheid activities. Others became linked with ANC structures in exile and were able to liaise with people within the country who were banned or jailed.

There was also an important theological element to their actions. Drawing on the emergence of Catholic liberation theology and on the writings of German theologians and their reflection on the Nazi regime, a Protestant liberation theology developed. Nurtured particularly in conversation with the Black Consciousness Movement and the Protestant ecumenical Federal Theological Seminary, it contested racialised political theologies on biblical and theological terms. It also articulated a political theology of equality on the basis that everyone was made equal in God's image. Desmond Tutu, then general secretary of the South African Council of Churches and later to become archbishop of Cape Town, was the most prominent of many liberation theologians who became increasingly active in the 1980s at the height of the states of emergency and the inauguration of the anti-apartheid United Democratic Front (UDF).

The visibility of this liberation theology was an important counter to the apartheid ideology that linked the ANC, the SACP and the threat that together they would introduce a 'heathen' government or one that would seek to repress religion.

Black politics of equality in both its secular and theological forms can also be contrasted with the political imaginary of tradition, customary authority and chieftainship. The apartheid state made considerable investments in policies that asserted a fundamental difference between black and white culture and being. The NP ideology of 'separate development' was about 'reinvigorating, refashioning and rewarding "traditional" African notions of authority and political culture' (Posel, 2011:25). A prime architect of this approach was Werner M. Eiselen, who, in the 1920s, was an anthropological 'expert' on 'indigenous African religion' and became apartheid founder Hendrik Verwoerd's right-hand man in the 'Bantu Affairs' administration in the 1950s (Chidester, 1996). The ideological discourse around homelands and ethnic nationalism was threaded through with mention of the divine right of traditional leaders, the authority of traditional leaders according to custom and the legitimacy that derives from the historical legacy of their rule.

Govan Mbeki, one of the staunchest opponents of traditional leadership in the ANC, wrote:

> Verwoerd drew a picture of chieftainship restored to its ancient glory before the arrival of the white man, and assured putative chiefs that the government would empower them with the authority that was theirs by divine right to rule over their people. To show how serious the government was, it immediately appointed a large number of recognised chiefs, and raised their stipends to levels undreamt before. (Quoted in Goodenough, 2002:11)

This discourse and the resources the apartheid state brought to it provided an alternative political imaginary of autonomy, self-determination, freedom and also autochthony. It provided the imaginary for some traditional and then homeland leaders of a world without whites, and without the economic and social degradation they brought with them.

CHURCH AND STATE UNDER WHITE RULE

Anthony Gill and Arang Keshavarzian (1999) have suggested that the most important determinants in a relationship between states and religious institutions are their relative powers in periods of state formation and consolidation, and the ideological ambition of modern states to appropriate or subdue the powers of religion.

Each of the four formations of political secularism outlined in the previous chapter, and the relationships between religious and government institutions they took to be the ideal, involves a coherent normative account of the place that religion, officially or legislatively, should occupy in the nation-state and a set of tools to argue for and discipline these relationships. This aspect of political secularism was impossible under the Union and apartheid governments.

Institutional relationships were not based on a normative account of religion per se or politics per se; they were always subject to the furtherance of white rule. They could not be stated in principle because they depended on the relationship of the religious institutions with racial ideology and practice.

Relationships between government and religious institutions depended on the particular version of racialised ideology in operation, the power of the government and the forms, ambitions and race theologies of the religious groups with which they interacted.

MISSIONARIES

Before Union there was no South African state or nation. There were localised and subnational forms of rule. It is not strictly accurate to speak of the possibility of political secularism before the advent of either nation or state, but in the case of colonialism, missionaries and administrators often shared objectives and presented two faces of European rule. They also often shared the objective of 'civilisation' and the inclusion of black subjects under British sovereignty. But in South Africa and Kenya, both of which had relatively large white settler populations, missionaries and colonial administrators were also sometimes in conflict.

To give just one example, the missionary Johannes T. van der Kemp, head of a missionary station in Bethelsdorp, concerned about genocidal and exploitative settler treatment of the Khoi peoples, sought to create a place in which the Khoi could be on equal footing with colonists. This was very much against the wishes of the Cape authorities (Giliomee, 1988). Van der Kemp put pressure on the colonial administration to publicise in the British press cases of abuse of Khoi by farm owners. Under pressure from British humanists, the Cape government established a Black Circuit Court in 1812 to investigate these charges of cruelty, but there was a backlash from settlers.

A decision by Governor H.C.D. Maynier to allow Khoi to worship in churches shared by whites caused great dissatisfaction among the settlers. As a magistrate in the district of Uitenhage said at the time,

> It is difficult and often impossible to get the colonists to understand that the Hottentots [sic] ought to be protected by the laws no less than themselves, and that the judge may make no distinction between them and the Hottentots. According to the unfortunate notion prevalent here, a heathen ... can in no wise be believed, and only by violent measures can he be brought to do good and shun evil. (Quoted in Moodie, 1975:29)

40

In this instance, the colonial government acted in favour of the settlers rather than on the complaints of the missionaries on behalf of the Khoi.

On the other hand, the British administration provided financial and other support to missionary efforts. Education and health services were provided by missions and later by the mainline Protestant churches that were their heirs. From 1854 the colonial state subsidised missionary institutions 'that would undertake to train Bantu youth in industrial occupation and to fit them to act as interpreters, evangelists and school masters among their own people' (Ndletyana, 2008:3). By 1887 there were nearly 50 000 African children studying in church schools. Horton Davies and Robert Shepherd (1954:xix) suggest that because 'civilisation' had been the goal of black education until this point, governments granted religious bodies 'considerable liberty in their control of the work'.

The close relationship between the colonial administration and mission churches was transferred at the time of Union to what came to be known as the mainline churches. South Africa under the Union government remained a part of Britain's constitutional monarchy and the Church of England. Locally, the Church of the Province had very close relationships with British imperialism. Because the formal locus of South Africa's sovereignty was the British Parliament, it was not necessary to write this establishment into a Union constitution. And while some missionaries regarded indirect rule as a postponement of civilisational policy, the English-speaking church as a whole was supportive of white minority rule (Cochrane, 1987).

THE PROTESTANT MAINLINE CHURCHES

At the time of Union these churches, sometimes called the 'English-speaking' churches, emerged from earlier missions. Like the Union government, the churches took control of their internal affairs on a national level and gained a degree of autonomy from European offices. In line with national policy, most initiated segregationist policies within their churches. Some sought to 'Africanise Christianity', as they put it, by introducing a complete separation of African and European parishes and church hierarchies. The Dutch Reformed Church (DRC) was segregated as early as the 1850s. In 1923 the Bantu Presbyterian Church was established by the Presbyterian synod. Many other mainline churches were to follow (Cochrane, 1987). Only Anglicans and Roman Catholics refused to introduce racial segregation. In other words, the first process of state formation subordinated the churches to national policy with respect to race.

The Union government continued to fund educational institutions run by churches, but almost as soon as the NP came to power in 1948 it launched a policy and budget assault on church schooling and the educated black elite it was producing. Such people were the very antithesis of the apartheid political project.

In 1949 the government appointed a commission under Eiselen to formulate education policy for Africans (Moodie, 1975). Its report based its recommendations on 'the premise that educational practice had to deal with African children trained and conditioned in an African culture, speaking African languages and imbued with values, interest and behaviour patterns "learned at the knee of a Bantu mother"' (Welsh, 1972:49). The commission claimed that such an education would not 'alienate' pupils from 'their culture'. To this end, it proposed what became the 1953 Bantu Education Act, which centralised all black African education under the Native Affairs Department (Moodie, 1975).

The NP replaced Christian control of education with state-controlled Christian National Education that furthered apartheid racial theology – a good example of secularising in the context of a consolidating state. Many churches tried to retain ownership of and control over black education and continued to provide schooling for as long as they could, but without government subsidies one after the other closed or was turned over to government administration and the Bantu Education curriculum. The introduction of Christian National Education was anathema to other religious groups too – private and variously funded Jewish and Muslim schools were established in opposition to the education on offer at government schools.

For many reasons the mainline churches, which had a majority black membership, were mobilised from the 1960s to the 1980s to oppose the practices and policies of apartheid. Until the early 1980s religious groups enjoyed a form of indemnity from violence and political harassment by the apartheid state, which, taking religion and religious authority seriously, was loath to suppress them or subject them to the same violence perpetrated on other groups. But as black and white ministers began to contest the Christian foundations of Afrikaner nationalist ideology the relationship became increasingly oppositional and, on the part of the state, repressive.

A new generation of black leaders aligned to the ANC and the PAC was elected to positions of authority in these churches from the early 1980s. The Methodist Conference, for example, was headed by Stanley Mogoba and then Mvume Dandala. More famously, Tutu became the Anglican archbishop. In the mid-1980s these church leaders became very visible in the activities of the UDF. Churches themselves became sites of both theological and political struggle (Walshe, 1997). The state took its gloves off with respect to Christian ministers and many religious leaders were arrested and tortured for their political activities.

AFRICAN INDEPENDENT CHURCHES

In contrast, an African separatist church movement developed between 1890 and 1910 in the context of the urbanisation brought about by the discovery of diamonds and gold (Sundkler, 1948). During this period black preachers and catechists drawn from the rural areas to work in the mines of the Witwatersrand were influenced by the charismatic African Methodist Episcopal Church. Like the African Methodist Episcopal, many international missions supported the indigenisation of clergy across the globe. But local missionaries sought to maintain paternalistic white or European control over religious activities (Sundkler, 1948).

In this context, Mengena Mokone and other lay preachers founded the Ethiopian Church in Pretoria, the first Christian church independent of missionary or white control. This started a movement that grew rapidly. At first, the independent churches were politically active, their leaders involved, for instance, in the Bambatha rebellion against British rule and taxation in Natal from 1906 to 1908. The British South African government, which was looking for ways to unite the four colonies, responded to their independence and political activism with violence and intense administrative intervention.

Missionaries, politicians and some black Christians expressed concern about what they termed the growing 'Ethiopian problem'.

> It was ... feared that the Ethiopian movement was an African political underground movement aiming at ousting the White man from South Africa, or, at least, that it might establish a Pan-African National Church which would cause harm by hampering the evangelisation of the Bantu peoples. (Sundkler, 1948:13)

In 1903, J.H. Scott, a chief magistrate in the Cape Colony, claimed that the Ethiopian movement was 'a political and social movement, not a religious movement at all' (Sundkler, 1948:66).

The Natal colony tried to repress independent churches in order to negate their possible political influence. The Natal Native Affairs Commission of 1906/07 made the threat to the Ethiopian movement that opened this chapter. The first form of punishment was the withdrawal of state support for ministers of religion and a restriction on their ability to preach and mobilise in public. Natal passed regulations to the effect that:

> No Native Minister of a Church, independent and free from direct and effective European control, shall be registered as a Marriage officer. No official recognition in any form by grants-in-aid schools, or

otherwise, shall be given to Native Churches independent of, and free from, European control or to any religious movement amongst Natives embodying race cleavage as a principle ... That it be unlawful for any Native Minister or member of a religious movement and not under European control and not recognised, whether exempted or otherwise, to address meetings or assemblies of Natives. (Sundkler, 1948:70)

Part of the mandate of the Native Affairs Commission was to resolve the problem of the different ways in which the four colonies treated independent churches. The Transvaal had already recognised its first Ethiopian Church in 1893 but, after the turn of the century, both it and the Orange Free State largely concurred with Natal. In the Cape Colony separatist churches were treated the same way as mission churches in terms of law and the Native Affairs Commission leaned towards the Cape position.

Not wanting to be seen as repressing religious freedom, the Commission declared that 'any measure capable of being represented as religious persecution should be avoided'. It eventually recommended that 'such Native Churches as are possessed of sufficiently stable organisation to control their pastors and enforce discipline where necessary and to ensure the appointment to the ministry of reliable and worthy men only' be recognised (Sundkler, 1948:67). Over time increasing numbers of independent churches sought recognition that brought with it the right of their ministers to become marriage officers, possible access to land for churches and schools and access to a travel rebate for ministers using the South African Railways.

The massacre at Bulhoek in the Eastern Cape put an end to this policy. In 1921 Enoch Mgijima led a group of some 3 000 Christians calling themselves the Israelites. As they had on a number of occasions at Easter, they formed a temporary village at Ntabelanga. That year Mgijima prophesied that if his followers stayed there, white people would be crushed. The Israelites stayed in pursuit of this prophecy, earning the ire of many in the surrounding area, black and white, for overgrazing and not paying hut taxes. The situation escalated until 800 police surrounded the area and attacked the sword- and knobkerrie-wielding Israelites with live ammunition. Nearly 180 Israelites died and many more were injured.[3]

In response to the massacre the government initiated a Native Churches Commission, which laid down some general rules for separatist churches (Sundkler, 1948). The Commission included a member of the DRC and a 'native education expert', but, of course, no members of any of the independent churches. It decided that 'so long as the movement is not mischievous it should be tolerated and where it springs from a worthy motive and is working in harmony with the Government it should be encouraged' (Sundkler, 1948:73). Some administrative regulation of these churches was built into the conditions for such toleration.

In their formative years the independent churches had been politically active. AIC leaders participated in the formation and early workings of SANNC, the precursor to the ANC. But after the radicalisation of the ANC and the violence that befell the Bambatha rebels and Mgijima's Israelites, they became noticeably quieter.

Reflection on these churches brings us back to the question of the grounds for differentiation between religion and politics. Many who write about these church formations struggle with the ways in which they defy the categories of liberal political theory. Amongst contemporary scholars, Liz Gunner (2004), for example, writes of the Shembe Church, the second biggest AIC, as 'outside of, yet constantly overlapping with the overtly political discourse of the region'. Robin Peterson argues that to assess the political role of the AICs means that it is necessary to 'stretch ... the semantics of the political' (Quoted in Gunner, 2004:6). Like the earlier black millenarian prophets, they do not contest political power in any conventional political sense, which is perhaps their greatest independence.

The disposition of these churches against engagement in the explicitly political domain and their disavowal of politics as such meant that the AICs became almost invisible to national political life. Their very independence removed them from contesting the ideological or institutional foundations of white power, even as they grew to include the biggest number of black South Africans.

DUTCH REFORMED CHURCH

The DRC (in Afrikaans, the Nederduits Gereformeerde Kerk, or NGK) was never officially established in law as the state church of the apartheid government. A differentiation between church and party was consistently maintained even as a great number of people moved between these spheres. But while religion and politics were differentiated, there was very little separation between them. The DRC and the Hervormde and Gereformeerde (reformed) churches were 'civil society extension(s) of Afrikaner nationalism' (Van der Westhuizen, 2007:50).

From 1948 to 1960 the NP drew heavily on the NGK to help secure the Afrikaner alliance. In this relationship the church gained a great deal of power and influence and secured Calvinist social conservatism. This was legislated in publication control or censorship and statutes against entertainment and trading on Sundays. There was also a common law offence of blasphemy (Van der Vyver, 1999:1). Afrikaner churches were active in their support of racialising 'immorality' legislation, seeing themselves as the moral guardians of poor white women, in particular.

The first open contestation between the religious and nationalist elements of the NGK took place over what was called the church clause, which marked the strengthening of the NP and its increasing capacity to discipline the Afrikaner churches. Enacted in 1957, the clause sought to give the minister of constitutional co-operation and development the power to prohibit black attendance at services and functions in areas other than those designated for black people under the Group Areas Act (No. 41 of 1950).

There was a huge outcry from almost all the English-speaking churches, which saw this as an affront to mission and pastoral activities. Some prominent leaders in the NGK synod also spoke out against the clause, but they were convinced by Verwoerd to withdraw their opposition. In so doing, the NGK allowed the government to erode its evangelical mission. But given the need to continue bringing English-speaking voters into the nationalist fold, the NP could not afford to alienate them and, as a result, the church clause was never implemented (Van der Vyver, 1999:2).

The brutality of the Sharpeville massacre on 21 March 1960, in which police opened fire on a group of demonstrators, killing 69 people, and the decision to become a republic galvanised increasing opposition from the 'English-speaking' churches against the apartheid state. The majority of the members of these ex-mission churches, both mainline Protestant and Catholic, were black.

In 1960 the World Council of Churches called a meeting about the 'social and racial situation' in South Africa in response to what it called the 'disturbances' of March 1960. The meeting, which became known as the Cottesloe Consultation, was historic in bringing together black and white church leaders for the first time, even though there was no representation from the independent churches. All but two delegations were multiracial and about a quarter of the participants were black. Many of the discussions remained racially patronising, referring to 'Bantu members' of the Consultation, for example, and affirming that 'apartheid with consultation is not un-Christian' (World Council of Churches, 1960).

Despite its shortcomings, the Consultation represented the beginnings of the ecumenical movement in South Africa – a coalition of Christian groups which, despite their theological differences, represented Christianity to the state in some way. At least initially, Afrikaans churches were invited to join this ecumenical movement. In its official statement Cottesloe took positions that were new in South African church–state relations. The Consultation came out against racial exclusion in church worship, was concerned about what it called 'the revival of heathen customs' within

Christianity and could find no scriptural grounds for the prohibition of mixed marriages, 'even though they may be inadvisable'.[4] It also called attention to the debilitating effects of migrant labour, supported the direct representation of so-called coloured people in Parliament and urged the release of enquiries into the police action in Sharpeville and during similar demonstrations in Langa township in Cape Town.

While the Afrikaans churches participated in Cottesloe, at the end the Nederduits Hervormde Kerk noted that it could not subscribe to the Cottesloe declaration and wished to place on record 'our gratefulness to the Government for all the positive steps it has taken to solve the [native] problem, and to promote the welfare of different groups'. Not surprisingly, the Nederduits Hervormde Kerk was represented by an all-white delegation. The NGK, on the other hand, supported the resolutions. But its delegation still considered them compatible with a policy of race differentiation which, they suggested, could be defended from a Christian point of view.

After Cottesloe, Verwoerd called the members of that NGK delegation to a meeting. As Christi van der Westhuizen (2007:51) notes, the 'synod buckled under pressure from Verwoerd, aided by the Broederbond, and renounced their own representatives, who had adopted the World Council of Churches' Cottesloe Declaration in 1960'. But Cottesloe also marked the start of anti-apartheid sentiment among a small band of Afrikaner theologians. In 1961 a group of them published 'Delayed Action', which refuted the biblical and moral bases for apartheid (Moodie, 1975:290).

This was the beginning, T. Dunbar Moodie writes, of a 'comprehensive theological reconsideration' (1975:291). But this reconsideration by Afrikaners of race political theology was harshly punished. In 1966 far-right-wing politician Andries Treurnicht, who was still in the NP at the time, conspired to have Afrikaner cleric Beyers Naudé excommunicated from the DRC and prominent Afrikaner theologian A.S. Geyser was charged with heresy for his condemnation of the churches' racial exclusion (Van der Westhuizen, 2007:52).

The South African government's treatment of all these churches – Afrikaans, mission, mainline Protestant and African independent – can be explained by its theologies and practices of race. Where churches supported white rule and black subordination, they were given institutional support by the state and rewarded with administrative recognition, state subsidies, access to participation in state-sponsored schools and military chaplaincies, and access to Christian public broadcasting. But where they questioned the theological legitimacy of apartheid or race rule, and where they provided institutional support or leadership to anti-apartheid activities, they were treated with increasing levels of violence. This was first evidenced in the appropriation of schooling from Christian bodies to the state, and the state's articulation of a Christian National Education that was not under the control of religious authorities or theologians. Later, when mainline churches began actively to oppose apartheid and articulate liberation and black theology, the state responded with violence towards individual religious leaders.

The mechanisms of statecraft with respect to political secularism, including co-option, appropriation, critique and violence, were all applied to churches from 1910 to 1994. But there could be no culture of political secularism, no normative or vernacularised account of what place religion 'ought' to play in the state and the nation. This is because relationships between the state and religious institutions were subordinated to the politics of racial rule.

MOVING TOWARDS NEGOTIATIONS

By the middle of the 1980s some Afrikaner intellectuals and NP members were realising that apartheid was not sustainable. Even the synod of the DRC, under the leadership of Revd Johan Heyns, started distancing itself from apartheid in 1986. Increasing numbers of Afrikaner leaders, both progressive and conservative, travelled to Lusaka or London, where they were charmed by urbane ANC exiles who disproved their racial stereotypes.

Within the country, major shifts were taking place and, on 2 February 1990, President Frederik W. de Klerk made a dramatic and unexpected speech unbanning the ANC, PAC and SACP and committing the NP government to negotiations to end white rule. Nelson Mandela and many other senior ANC leaders were released from prison within days of the announcement and negotiations began between the ANC and the NP about talks to reform South Africa's politics, though neither side brought all their supporters with them.

Attempts to start the talks were regularly interrupted by violence. The ANC, for instance, called off negotiations when 16 activists were killed by police who opened fire on unarmed demonstrators (Ebrahim, 1998). But in May 1990, three days of meetings between the ANC and the NP led to the adoption of the Groote Schuur Minute. With more than 400 journalists watching, the NP government agreed to lift the state of emergency and the ANC agreed to reconsider the armed struggle. There were discussions about the release of political prisoners and conditions for the return of nearly 40 000 exiles (Waldmeir, 1997:162). A few months down a rocky road the two parties signed the secret D.F. Malan Accord and, later in August, the Pretoria Minute, in which the ANC renounced the use of violence as it formally suspended its armed struggle (Spitz and Chaskalson, 2000).

In September 1991 a National Peace Accord was signed, laying the foundations for multiparty talks.

South Africa was not secular before 1994. Its various governments articulated a political theology and a civil religion to legitimate white rule and appropriated imaginaries of African independence, chieftainship and a customary social order to exclude black people from national wealth and membership of the political community. They appropriated church resources, drew on some churches for moral and theological legitimation and unleashed violence upon some religious groups and leaders. Aspects of modern statecraft were turned towards the antidemocratic politics of white rule.

This is the morality tale of South African race rule. There was no moral community (Fields, 1982) between rulers and ruled, between the social and the political communities. Religion and tradition were deeply entangled in white rule. In this, aspects of modern statecraft usually associated with secularism were turned towards non-secular ends. On the other hand, religion was mobilised towards liberation and also towards secular political values of equality. Religion and tradition became the grounds on which politics was contested.

3

NEGOTIATED CONSENSUS AND RELIGIOUS RIGHTS

*Strip South Africa of its multitude of religions
and it is no longer South Africa.*
Albie Sachs (1990)

*A very important argument for a Bill of Rights is that it is
subscribed to by almost every religious persuasion
or group represented in our country.*
South African Law Commission (1989)

There are three requirements for religious–state relationships to be secular. The first is a clear, well-understood and administratively mobilised *differentiation* between the religious and the political. The second is a *separation* of 'church and state', as it is referred to in Christian terms. More inclusively, this refers to a separation of religious and political institutions. Separation immediately implies their relationship. The third requirement is *exclusion from contestation for political power*. Political secularism does not, therefore, denote an absence of religious institutions in public life. Instead, it is best understood as a form of unequal relationship between religion and politics in the political public and the institutions of the state.

All three elements of secular institutional relations were decisively instituted during the period of state formation in South Africa in the late 1980s to mid-1990s, at least with respect to 'world religions', and secular institutional relations were entrenched in South Africa's postapartheid Constitution. Religious institutions became subordinated to political authority during the negotiations through the co-optive mechanisms of human rights and constitutionalism.

NEGOTIATING THE TRANSITION

Political negotiations led South Africa out of apartheid and into a regime that, for the first time in the nation's history, was not based on race. The negotiations were conducted in three phases. In the first, the African National Congress (ANC) and the National Party (NP) engaged in 'talks about talks' in which they felt their way towards a negotiated settlement of the increasingly intractable conflict. During the second phase the Convention for a Democratic South Africa (Codesa) and then the Multiparty Negotiation Process (MPNP) secured a framework for a settlement, the form of a future government and an interim constitution. The democratic elections of 1994 and the inauguration of Nelson Mandela as president ushered in the last phase of negotiations, one in which the final Constitution was written by a democratic Parliament acting as a Constitutional Assembly (CA). This final democratic Constitution came into effect in 1996.

PHASE ONE: TALKS ABOUT TALKS – HUMAN RIGHTS AND CONSTITUTIONALISM

NP and ANC leaders held tentative and then increasingly formal meetings from 1985 to 1991. These contacts and the agreements they reached prepared the way for negotiations (Ebrahim, 1998). Under pressure from the international community as well as internal debate, both parties were persuaded to pursue negotiations through a framework of human rights and constitutionalism.

New political imaginaries of freedom and power took hold in the mid-1980s as the ANC's internal workings became increasingly subject to international scrutiny. The mutiny at the Quatro Camp in Angola and an internal investigation into torture used by ANC security personnel in exile resulted in an ANC conference in Zambia in 1985 that called for a code of conduct, and a process to deal with those accused of spying or criminal activities (Klug, 2000; Sachs, 2009). To this end, Zola Skweyiya, holder of a German law PhD, was appointed to head a new law department within the ANC (Klug, 2000:78). When formal contact with the apartheid government began in 1986, a constitutional committee was formed from that department.

The Commonwealth Mission and the UN both put pressure on the ANC to begin to formulate a vision of future governance in South Africa and its position on negotiations. By October 1987 the ANC had produced a 'Statement on Negotiations' that outlined its preconditions for talks and accepted the necessity of a Bill of Rights. In 1988 it published its proposed Constitutional Principles (Klug, 2000:78) and then held a series of international law conferences to interact with South African lawyers and sitting South African judges, who met the organisation in defiance of the apartheid minister of justice.

The fate of the Soviet Union was central to these shifts in the format of political claims and also to the willingness of the South African government to negotiate. According to Hugh Corder (Pers. comm., 2008), professor of Public Law at the University of Cape Town, the ANC showed that it wasn't a proxy for the Soviet Union by seeking Western support for sanctions in the latter half of the 1980s. 'How do you do that?' he asked: '[B]y saying that we'll have a written constitution, including a Bill of Rights, and statement of rights, basic protective rights. And this is also a sop to the white minority.'

By the early 1990s the ANC leadership had dropped much of the socialist rhetoric popular among the unions and United Democratic Front (UDF) affiliates, at least in the talks about talks. The language of democracy, black advancement and human rights was more strongly emphasised (Beinart, 2001). This shift to a human rights discourse must also be seen against the background of the rise of constitutionalism as global political norm (Ackerman, 1997). South Africa's transition took place amid an avalanche of new constitutions. 'Over fifty-six percent of the 188 states of the United Nations organisation made major amendments to their constitutions in the decade between 1989 and 1999' (Klug, 2000:12). This wave of constitutionalism was marked by the introduction of Bills of Rights in each new democratic regime and a great deal of faith in the rule of law.

The move towards constitutionalism in South Africa was remarkably rapid. The ANC was not the only party that turned to constitutional rights as a platform for increased international credibility and support. The NP was trying to find a way out of negative scrutiny. In 1986 then Justice Minister Kobie Coetzee asked the South African Law Commission (SALC), headed by Stellenbosch Law professor, Pierre Olivier, to 'investigate and make recommendations regarding the definition and protection of group rights ... and the possible extension of the existing protection of individual rights' (Klug, 2000:84). The NP hoped that it could translate apartheid into a more respectable language of group rights.

The request to the SALC was a response to international pressure on the NP and a strategy to avoid sanctions. But the SALC came to the unexpected conclusion that it would be 'juridically unsound to adopt the standpoint that there are statutorily definable groups with statutorily definable "rights" in this country' (Klug, 2000:84). At some point Olivier was persuaded against the group rights perspective, arguing that the group is best protected through the individual. Apartheid is impossible on that basis.

In its 1991 publication, 'Manifesto for the New South Africa',[1] the NP argued for the first time for a constitutionally guaranteed and justiciable Bill of Rights. By the end of that year it was commonly agreed amongst all political parties that South Africa should have a Bill of Rights. For the next two years almost all political parties and some legal non-governmental organisations developed drafts, of which three were seriously considered in the negotiations: those of the ANC, the NP and the Democratic Party (DP) (Spitz and Chaskalson, 2000:252). While political organisations were preparing their drafts, non-governmental organisations, university-based policy research units and individuals in the judiciary and media gave thought to the content of these bills of rights.

PHASE TWO: MULTIPARTY NEGOTIATIONS

Multiparty negotiations took place intermittently and precariously from December 1991 until the April 1994 democratic elections, amid a rising tide of political violence. Contrary to the received wisdom about a non-violent transition and the miracle of negotiations, the processes that ended white rule were contested, violent and uncertain.

Until the very cusp of the historic elections there was little guarantee that invidious and widespread violence would not spiral beyond the control of all the negotiating parties. While political organisations played their hands during the generally polite negotiations, assassinations, revenge killings, secret police campaigns, illicit funding and mass mobilisation were used to strengthen their positions. Talks were held at gunpoint. But with many near misses, Codesa, and then the MPNP, agreed to a process of political transition and drew up an interim constitution. It established a Transitional Executive Council and an Independent Electoral Commission to organise the first democratic elections, set the framework for a government of national unity (GNU) and created the nine current provinces and three tiers of government.

Codesa

In 1991 Mandela and Frederik W. de Klerk publicly committed to starting substantive negotiations. In late November of that year a multiparty Codesa steering committee agreed by trade-offs and compromise on who, in principle, could participate in the Codesa negotiations. The participants would be political parties, political organisations, the South African government and the administrations of the so-called independent homelands – Transkei, Bophuthatswana, Venda and Ciskei (the TBVC states).

The first Codesa plenary took place on 20 and 21 December 1991. Despite the tentative agreements already reached, the main negotiating parties brought very different agendas to the negotiating table (Du Plessis, 1994). The ANC wanted only the most basic legal structures in place to open up democratic politics. A free political climate, the reincorporation of the TBVC states, an interim government and agreements on constitutional drafting mechanisms were its immediate objectives. The ANC thought it would take 18 months at most before a national election could be held (Friedman, 1993:16). The NP, on the other hand, had in mind a time frame of ten to fifteen years, during which a power-sharing government would rule (Friedman, 1993:26).

The place of homeland leaders was particularly contested. The NP, arguing that the TBVC states were independent and not part of South Africa, wanted to exclude them from the negotiations (Muriaas, 2002:84). They bolstered this argument on the basis of 1986 legislation that restored the South African citizenship of homeland nationals living permanently in South Africa, distinguishing between homeland residents and those to whom homeland citizenship had previously been ascribed (Klaaren, 2000:9). But the ANC insisted that all homeland citizens be part of the negotiations. As a compromise, the governments of the TBVC states were included on the grounds that they would have to negotiate their return to a unified South Africa. Since the remaining self-governing homelands were under the sovereignty of the South African government they did not require representation, but, to balance things out, leaders of the ruling political parties in the self-governing territories were invited to participate.

A similar balancing act took place when political parties from the Indian and coloured houses of the Tricameral Parliament were included, balanced by the ANC-aligned Transvaal and Natal Indian congresses, both of which had refused to participate in Tricameral politics. The other political parties included were the DP, then the official opposition, the South African Communist Party (SACP) and Inkatha Freedom Party (IFP), both of which claimed national reach (COD NA61 Volume 1). The Pan Africanist Congress of Azania (PAC) withdrew from the first planning meeting and did not return until after the democratic elections. The Conservative Party (CP), Herstigte Nasionale Party (Reconstituted National Party), Afrikaner Weerstandsbeweging (AWB; Afrikaner Resistance Movement) and the Azanian People's Organisation, all of which were invited, declined to participate in negotiations they believed had no standing (COD NA61).

Others were welcomed to Codesa's plenary sessions as dignitaries or observers from important 'interest groups' but were not allowed to participate as negotiators. They included the Congress of South African Trade Unions (Cosatu), which was not recognised as a political entity for the purposes of the negotiations at the preliminary meetings, international and civil society organisations and religious groups. Traditional leaders were considered an interest group by all participants except the IFP and some were invited to attend Codesa events as observers. In addition, many individual traditional leaders were present within delegations from the TBVC states or homeland parties.

Codesa did not start well. The first day was held in plenary and, aside from the many and rousing speeches, its centrepiece was to be the signing of a Declaration of Intent for negotiations. But at the last minute Ciskei, the IFP and Bophuthatswana publicly refused to sign, although the Ciskei did sign the following day and the IFP eventually signed an amended version. The day ended with a dramatic public argument between Mandela and De Klerk (Ebrahim, 1998:104). When De Klerk raised the issue of the armed struggle, going against the agreements reached during the D.F. Malan Accord, Mandela responded by assassinating De Klerk's character and chastising him for his lack of judgement and his discredited rule.

As Patti Waldmeir (1997:191) writes, 'never had South Africa heard a black man speak to a white man that way' in public. Suspicion of the South African government was widespread. While the NP had hoped to present itself to the world's media as an enlightened interlocutor, delegates from the Inyandza National Movement, the Natal and Transvaal Indian congresses, the SACP and the Transkei pointedly and publicly warned it against using state security apparatus to undermine negotiations (COD NA61).

Codesa was organised into a number of working groups designed to attend to different elements of the transition and report and make recommendations to plenary. But even the most basic issues of decision-making were contested. Senior ANC and NP officials together introduced the notion of 'sufficient consensus' the night before negotiations began. As Steven Friedman (1993:25) writes: 'Publicly this rule was never explained in understandable terms, but no one was in doubt about its real meaning: "sufficient consensus" was achieved whenever the ANC and the NP agreed.'

By any substantive reckoning Codesa failed. Friedman (1993:29) notes that '[a]t township meetings, a person who talked at length without apparent purpose was dubbed a "Codesa"'. Violence escalated. Because of public discontent and the need to show some progress, a second plenary was held before negotiators had reached vital decisions. Codesa collapsed at this premature second plenary on 15 May 1992. It opened late and immediately adjourned for five hours in the hope that a deadlock in the crucial Working Group 2 could be broken. When it finally reconvened at 4pm, it descended into a verbal brawl in which all the underlying mistrust was brought to the surface (Ebrahim, 1998).

Attempts to continue the negotiations became tangled in allegations that the South African government had tapped ANC and SACP telephones. In the meantime, ANC supporters and more radical leaders, frustrated by the lack of progress, turned to mass action to flex their muscles. At the end of May 1992 an ANC policy conference sanctioned a mass action campaign to begin on 16 June, the famous date of the 1976 Soweto uprisings.

The next day shack-dwellers in the ANC-aligned informal settlement of Boipatong were attacked by 'IFP-supporting hostel residents' (Friedman, 1993:145). In four hours, 38 people were hacked, stabbed or shot to death (Sparks, 1994). On 22 June the ANC formally suspended talks. Mandela publicly held De Klerk accountable for the violence. A war of memoranda began. At this point, what became known as 'the channel' was set up between the ANC and the NP in the persons of leading trade unionist Cyril Ramaphosa and NP politician Roelf Meyer.

Three events brought this troubled and unpromising phase to a close. Cosatu, at the height of its strength and effectively leading the ANC's mass action campaign, began talks with the South African Employers' Consultative Committee on Labour Affairs, a negotiating wing of big business. In Friedman's words, this brought the two bodies 'within a hair's breadth of an embryonic social contract' (1993:148). In the second development the two most militant ANC regions of Border and the Midlands turned their sights on the 'independent' homelands. ANC and SACP strategists were confident that they could form an alliance among Ciskei soldiers, public servants and 'comrades' that would collapse the homeland administration.

As part of their strategy the ANC marched on Ciskei's capital, Bisho, and the Ciskei defence force opened fire, killing 28 marchers. With the ANC troubled by what became known as the Bisho massacre, the NP was at pains to return to negotiations. International criticism of the NP after Boipatong, as well as revelations of its secret funding of the IFP, had seriously damaged its cherished international reputation. On 15 July the UN Security Council invited all Codesa participants to a debate in New York, at which a resolution was adopted expressing concern about the breakdown of talks.

On 26 September 1992 the ANC and the South African government met face to face to sign what came to be called the 'Record of Understanding', the fruit of the behind-the-scenes negotiations between Ramaphosa and Meyer. As a result, some 400 political prisoners were released, 24 IFP-aligned hostels were fenced and patrolled by police and a prohibition against carrying 'traditional' weapons in public was to be enforced within two weeks.

Just a few days later the SACP's Joe Slovo opened the way for concessions by outlining possible sunset clauses. These included entrenched power-sharing for a fixed period, guarantees on regional government, amnesty for security police and the honouring of contracts for civil servants (Friedman, 1993). Heinz Klug (2000:104) calls these clauses the 'very epitome of an elite pact'. Over the following six months the ANC and the NP went on to reach agreement on the form of a transitional executive authority and a five-year GNU under an interim constitution. The ANC and the NP together 'formulated a joint negotiating position to guide their participation as a block in a future multilateral forum' (Barnes and De Klerk, 2002:3).

Agreements between the ANC and the NP infuriated the IFP and, at a Shaka Day rally, IFP leader Mangosuthu Buthelezi announced the first of the party's many withdrawals from the negotiations.[2] In bilateral talks between the IFP and the ANC, and the IFP and the NP, the IFP demanded that the ANC's armed wing, uMkhonto weSizwe, be disbanded. It also formed what must be one of the strangest alliances of the negotiations, the Concerned South Africans Group (COSAG). By October 1992 the IFP was in partnership with the CP and the governments of Brigadier 'Oupa' Gqozo of the Ciskei and Lucas Mangope of Bophuthatswana in a front for federalism. In December 1992 the IFP launched a 'federal' constitution for KwaZulu-Natal (KZN) that was very close to a secessionist document. After some initial enthusiasm, organised business in Natal warned that it had no chance of independent economic survival and withdrew its support (Friedman, 1993).

The Multiparty Negotiations Process

On this shaky ground talks resumed in April 1993 in the form of the MPNP, which was immediately very nearly derailed. On Easter Saturday the popular SACP and uMkhonto weSizwe leader, Chris Hani, was assassinated by right-wing immigrant Janusz Waluś, in collusion with Clive Derby Lewis, a senior official of the CP (Waldmeir, 1997). Mandela appealed for calm and within hours of the murder the ANC announced that it would not call off negotiations.

At the next meeting of the MPNP, Slovo proposed the date 27 April 1994 for the elections. This was drafted as a declaration of intent, promising that setting a date would 'send a ray of hope and optimism throughout the country' (NA NEG 1/4/2/8). The IFP was outraged by this bilateral move, contending that violence should be stopped before negotiations could continue. The CP walked out of the negotiations at the announcement of the election date, never to return.

Violence would continue to dog the negotiations, particularly from groups and organisations that had refused to participate and were outside the emerging consensus. But this time it spurred the ANC and the NP to greater decisiveness and unity. In June the far-right-wing AWB attacked the World Trade Centre where the negotiations were being held. In July the Azanian People's Liberation Army, the armed wing of the PAC, opened fire on more than 1 000 worshippers at St James Church in Kenilworth, Cape Town, killing 12 and injuring 56. American student Amy Biehl was killed by PAC youth in Cape Town's Gugulethu township. The South African government shot dead five children in what it said was a South African Defence Force attack on the PAC in Umtata (Sparks, 1994). Violence between ANC and IFP supporters in rural KZN escalated. But, as violence between the ANC and the NP petered out and their agreements strengthened, the centre of negotiations held.

In addition to the 208-member Negotiating Council, the planning committee of the MPNP introduced technical committees composed largely of lawyers to draft documents for political deliberation (Spitz and Chaskalson, 2000:65). Political parties were required to produce written submissions, which the technical committees used to draft compromise texts towards an interim constitution. The Consultative Business Movement, a Christian business association, provided administrative services under the leadership of its chief executive officer, Theuns Eloff (Cassidy, 1995). This ensured a much smoother and more bureaucratic operation.

Behind closed doors the technical committees drafted an interim constitution that was almost entirely congruent with the preceding agreements between the ANC and the NP. Late on the night of 17 November 1993 De Klerk and the NP finally accepted the reality of majority rule when they gave up on veto powers in the transitional executive that was to rule until the 1994 elections (Waldmeir, 1997). The next morning the NP Cabinet met to discuss the deal. According to Waldmeir, Tertius Delport, the NP's chief negotiator, screamed at De Klerk for 'giving South Africa away' (1997:231). But at midnight on 18 November the interim constitution was passed at the World Trade Centre.

This failed to put an end to the violence. Instead, the bloodshed increased in those territories and constituencies that were left out of the compromises of the MPNP. In March 1994 Mangope announced that he would not bring Bophuthatswana into the elections. Civil servants and military staff immediately went on strike. Mangope appealed to his *volksfront* COSAG allies for assistance, imploring Constand Viljoen to keep the AWB out of the fray. But the AWB's Eugene Terre'Blanche sent his men in anyway and they shot at black passersby at random, causing the Bophuthatswana forces to mutiny. During the fray a Bophuthatswana police officer was caught on live television fatally shooting two wounded and pleading AWB members, ending 'heroic' visions of Afrikaner independence militancy. When a strike was called in the Ciskei, Mangope's equivalent, Brigadier Gqozo, resigned and handed over his administration to the Transitional Executive Council. Venda and the Transkei, which were aligned to the ANC, put up no opposition to their reincorporation into South Africa (Beinart, 2001).

But that left KwaZulu in the then Natal province. Natal was the murder centre of South Africa. In that province alone 10 651 people died violently in 1994 and 1995, bringing the toll to more than 14 000 people lost to political violence since the mid-1980s (Gloppen, 1997). In early 1994 a state of emergency was declared in Natal and South African troops were sent in on the recommendation of the Independent Electoral Commission. It looked as though a military intervention would be needed to bring territorial unity to the country. It would no doubt have been a violent and costly intervention. But in a show of support by the national security establishment, the South African police broke the back of a series of military camps established by the IFP and the KZN police. Then, in defiance of the upcoming elections, the IFP led a march in the Johannesburg city centre on 28 March. Thousands made their way towards the ANC's headquarters, Shell House, where ANC security guards killed eight people and police another 45 (Waldmeir, 1997).

High-profile international mediators were initially unsuccessful in persuading Buthelezi to participate in the elections but, at the last minute, he changed his mind (Waldmeir, 1997). The ANC and the NP were forced to make a number of concessions in order to bring the IFP and white right-wing groups into the formal political process (Elazar, 1994). These included constitutional amendments 'securing the powers of the provinces', the possibility of establishing a separatist Afrikaner homeland (*volkstaat*) and a constitutional role for the Zulu monarch (Gloppen, 1997:201). These deals brought retired General Viljoen's Freedom Front (FF) into electoral politics (Klug, 2000). In a dramatic and not at all inevitable conclusion to the negotiations, violence came to a near standstill on 27 April 1994, the day of South Africa's first democratic elections.

PHASE THREE: THE CONSTITUTIONAL ASSEMBLY

The final phase of the transition took place in the CA. The elections put the ANC into power in a coalition GNU. The CA had 490 members, with seats divided according to the proportional representation results of the 1994 elections. The interim constitution gave this democratically elected body just two years to finalise the text of a new constitution. To do this it formed a constitutional committee, a management committee and six theme committees made up of legal drafters. Again the IFP decided to withdraw early in the proceedings, despite its continued involvement in Parliament and the Cabinet of the GNU (Gloppen, 1997).

While the ANC ensured that justiciable socioeconomic rights were included in the Bill of Rights, other issues deadlocked, among them minority influence on the executive, the role of the provinces and their national council and the balance of power between Parliament and the executive. The last bones of contention were the property clause, language and education and rights of strike and lockout (Gloppen, 1997).

Unlike the situation with the multiparty talks, the CA went out of its way to secure public participation. It set up a 'talk line' and received more than two million written submissions and petitions. *Constitutional Talk*, a magazine publicising deliberations at the CA, was widely distributed. Most impressive perhaps were the four million copies of the text of the draft constitution in all 11 official languages, which were circulated to the public in late 1995 for final comment. Radio and television programmes supplemented community meetings and more than 1 000 public hearings and local briefings were held, reaching some 95 000 people. While public input made little impact on the text of the final Constitution, the process of consultation gave it a great deal of legitimacy.

The new Constitution was passed by eighty-five per cent of the CA (Ebrahim, 1998) and was sent to the Constitutional Court for certification. It was certified on 11 October and President Mandela signed it into law on 10 December 1996; significantly, in Sharpeville (Gloppen, 1997).

POLITICAL PERSPECTIVES ON RELIGION

Aside from occasional ceremonial appearances, religious bodies were not directly involved in the negotiations. They supported the political process, most of them believing that to do so would be in the best interest of religion in the future. In terms of the first condition of political secularism, this clear differentiation and separation between religious and political bodies is relevant and was acknowledged by both religious and political institutions. It is therefore important to understand the aspirations and ideas about religion that the political parties brought to the table.

AFRICAN NATIONAL CONGRESS

Within the ANC the most developed thinking about the future public and legal place of religion was presented by Albie Sachs in his book *Protecting Human Rights in a New South Africa*. Published in 1990, it argues for human rights and their progressive political possibilities. Its third chapter deals specifically with religion's place in a future democracy.

Sachs acknowledges the importance of religion and the spiritual life. Conscience, he adds, is the most fundamental human right of all, one that is deeply personal but that also has social, cultural and even national dimensions. Religious communities, he asserts, should have autonomy and be 'free to worship as they please'. We should be allowed 'to organise our own religious communities, to consecrate our own holy places, and to acknowledge our own holy texts, to appoint our own religious leaders and follow our own rituals and dietary practices' (Sachs, 1990:44). In other words, there are certain areas in which religions have legitimate authority and other rights should not be affected by a person's religious commitments. The state, writes Sachs (1990:45), should be neither theocratic nor atheist, 'but secular, tolerant and accepting of the deep importance [of] religion'.

To be secular, in Sachs's formulation, 'does not mean [to be] antireligious, but rather that there is no official religion, no favouring of any particular denomination, and no persecution of or discrimination against non-believers' (1990:45). The difficulty, he suggests, is to find a coherent constitutional format for what he sees as an ideal relationship between religion and the state. He outlines five possible forms of religious participation: theocracy, where religious organisations hold public power and religious law is the law of the state; a 'partly secular partly religious state' in which there is legal power-sharing; a secular state with 'an active interaction between state and religious organisations', each with autonomy; a secular state in which religious organisations have a tolerated private sphere of activity but no collaboration with the state; and a secular state that 'represses religious organisations' (Sachs, 1990:45–46). Reflecting on the second option, Rashid Omar (2002:3) refers to it as a situation where 'the religious interpretations and moral standpoints of one particular religious denomination dominate', as was the case under apartheid. Sachs strongly advocates the third option – a secular state with active interaction between an autonomous state and religious organisations.

This articulation is by far the most coherent and sustained input about political secularism by any party to the negotiations and although it was never presented as a submission, members of the technical drafting team that dealt with religion were aware of its existence and it informed the more piecemeal ANC inputs throughout the negotiations. Importantly, the SACP supported the ANC in this stance, calling for religious, linguistic and cultural rights for all individuals (see, for example, COD NA61). The SACP did not advocate a Soviet-style antireligious secularism, nor did it reference Karl Marx's critique of religion.

This position on religion and the secularity of a future state was generally consistent with the perspective and makeup of the ANC leaders involved in the negotiations, especially those who had returned from exile and were highly cosmopolitan. They included Protestants, Catholics, Muslims, secular Jews and atheists, whose religious positions did not undermine their political solidarity. Leaders of the UDF and the unions were more likely to be practising Christians and Muslims, but their religion was ecumenical and increasingly interfaith. The ANC's position was also a strategic response to NP and Afrikaner fears about the future of Afrikanerdom. Strong support for the right to religion would go a long way to settling white Christian fears that the ANC's alliance with the SACP would result in a state that repressed religion.

NATIONAL PARTY

De Klerk's NP, even with its many Nederduits Gereformeerde Kerk (NGK) members, appears to have been less tied to the NGK as an institution than any of its earlier incarnations. Nowhere in the negotiations did it advocate that Christianity be recognised as an official religion. As with many other issues, most notably race, the party was strangely silent on the principles it had so vehemently asserted throughout the apartheid era.

The negotiating position of the NP and representatives of the old South African government can be reconstructed from their internal documents and submissions. Having been persuaded to a human rights framework and a Bill of Rights, it actively supported the individual right to religion. In one submission, for example, the party calls for the right 'of individuals to hold (and not to hold) any religious or secular convictions and the right to express, profess, practise and propagate them publicly and in association with others' (NA CA 2/3/1/41). The objective of this right, it said, was to 'prevent the state from interfering in people's personal beliefs and from favouring certain beliefs over others' (NA CA 2/3/1/41).

The NP made two other religion-related demands. The first concerned the relationship between religious groups and the state. The apartheid government had supported the presence and practice of Calvinist Christianity in the state and state-sponsored bodies such as schools and public broadcasting. Not only did the state appropriate Christian theology, it also employed religious personnel in their religious capacity. The public broadcaster hosted and funded Christian programming; police, military and prisons employed Christian chaplains on state funds; schools were run on the broad educational philosophy of Christian National Education and also had religious instruction during class. The party envisaged a continuation of these arrangements, albeit on less exclusive terms.

The NP also sought to avoid an 'absolute separation' between the church and the state and criticised American-style political secularism with its disestablishment or strict Jeffersonian wall of separation. In its 1995 submission to the CA it stated, 'an absolute separation would prevent the state from any action whatsoever, including fulfilling its duty to create the opportunity and space for different religions to exist, practise and flourish', a situation which would lead 'to rather absurd results not always concomitant with public opinion'. In this it was referring to what is known as the neutrality dilemma, where 'the individual is protected against instruction favouring religious convictions, but not against instruction offending religious convictions' (NA CA 2/3/1/41:1–2). The party favoured Germany's constitutional provisions, according to which freedom of religion is coupled with a duty of the state 'to promote religious observances in state institutions such as schools' (NA CA 2/3/1/41). In order to prevent any imposition on the freedom of religion or non-religion, such observances are required to be voluntary and inclusive. Throughout the negotiations the NP advocated this German formulation.

The party's second claim was part of a broader desire to retain some degree of Afrikaner cultural independence and autonomy. It distinguished itself from Afrikaner groups to its right by participating in negotiations towards a unitary state and therefore by seeking 'cultural' autonomy through the recognition of group and collective rights to culture, language and religion in the Bill of Rights. Groups to the right, on the other hand, asserted that territorial and political sovereignty was the only possible guarantee of autonomy. Many NP documents include proposals for the protection of the rights of 'cultural, religious and linguistic communities', a phrase taken from Article 27 of the International Covenant on Civil and Political Rights, or 'minority rights'. But this phrase never referred to the establishment, recognition or entitlement of Christian communities per se. Instead, the NP suggested that Christianity (or a particular version of it), a language group or a set of cultural practices could define a community in need of minority protection. The phrase 'cultural, religious and linguistic communities' was a proxy for race or ethnicity.

The most comprehensive rendition of this perspective is to be found in a submission to the CA at the beginning of its deliberations in 1995. In 'Our Future Together' (NA CA F3 1/11/12) the NP proposed the establishment of statutory cultural councils that could represent the religious, cultural or linguistic interests of minorities. Another iteration of this proposed minority protection was to be found in the demand that single language, cultural or religious medium schools, public and private, should receive state support.

MINORITY PARTIES

During the MPNP's drafting of the interim constitution the IFP, some other homeland leaders and the Afrikaner right wing disagreed with the emerging political consensus. The IFP sought a federal regime in which the standard protections for civil and political rights, including the right to religion, were entrenched.

Somewhat surprisingly, the FF the 'moderate' right-wing Afrikaner party, also proved to be within the consensus on matters of religion. Its submission on the right to religion reads: 'The nature of the duty imposed on the state is to give full rein to human conduct based on the diversity of religious convictions in South African society, thus fostering mutual tolerance between different religious groups' (NA CA 2/3/1/41).

Two political formations, however, contested the future place of religion in a democratic South Africa. The CP, unable to imagine the possibility of a racially or religiously integrated country in which 'differences' could be accommodated or transcended, regularly invoked the spectres of religious conflict in Northern Ireland, Yugoslavia and India. In a submission at the beginning of the CA's deliberations, the CP wrote:

> Boer Afrikaners are aggrieved at having to live in a heathen country and under a heathen government ... The recognition of other 'religions' and the view that Christianity is simply another 'religion' mean that citizens are enjoined to think and live in accordance with aChristian [sic], or faithless heathen viewpoint. For the faithful Boer Afrikaner there is only one living God, while the gods of the other religions are human idols or fanciful inventions which do not truly exist. (NA CA 2/4/1/6/14:4)

The CP used a religious argument to support its demands for territorial secession for what it called the Boer Afrikaner. 'Boer Afrikaners,' the party wrote, 'are devout Christians and Churchgoers and would therefore prefer to live and work in their own republic under their own government.' The submission sought to distinguish these Boer Afrikaners from other Christians, continuing, 'our people are the only people on Earth that do not have a heathen past. Our unique people came into being and grew into nationhood in the light of the Protestant Christian Faith. This historical experience infused his [sic] tradition and culture and requires that he has a Christian state' (NA CA 2/4/1/6/14).

The CP withdrew from the MPNP, did not contest the elections and was not, therefore, represented in the first democratic Parliament. Its submission to the CA was the result of an invitation intended to take its view into account and bring it into the new dispensation.

The second dissenting party was the African Christian Democratic Party (ACDP). Founded on the eve of the 1994 elections, the ACDP had an explicitly religious agenda. Despite its strong stance against the philosophical foundations of secularism, the party supported 'a separation of religious and state institutions, and high levels of church autonomy' (NA CA 1/18/3). It did not criticise the political consensus on institutional relations or offer an alternative formulation. A second religious party that stood for election in 1994, the Africa Muslim Party headed by Gulam Sabdia, suggested that 'the prevailing political, economic and social systems should be replaced by alternative indigenous systems' (Tayob, 2008:583). It did not win enough votes to get a seat in Parliament and therefore had no influence on the CA.

MOBILISING RELIGION TO SECURE RIGHTS

The forms of political secularism that are negotiated at times of political transition have a lot to do with the strength and kind of religion in the country at the time. Protestantism, for example, is fissiparous, invariably leading to many independent and voluntary denominations that are unlikely to present a collective threat to the state. Historically at least it also tends towards individual piety and a more easily privatised religiosity (Sullivan, 2005). As a result, accommodating formations of political secularism tend to be found where there is significant religious diversity and where no one religion or denomination can monopolise. Where that happens, religions other than Christianity have increasingly taken on the institutional characteristics of Protestantism (Masuzawa, 2005).

In such circumstances the emerging state does not have to discipline religious groups but it does need to prevent interreligious dissent and violence through some form of neutrality towards religious differences. It is therefore important to understand the religious demographics of the period in which the postapartheid state took form. It is also helpful to understand how religious groups were able to communicate and work with each other to present their needs and demands to the political process.

'SOUTH AFRICA IS A RELIGIOUS COUNTRY'

The census has provided the most useful data on religious affiliation in South Africa. The 1996 census, the first in which 'everyone counted', resulted in a reasonably accurate account of the demographics of black South Africans, including those living in the growing informal settlements. A second postapartheid census was conducted in 2001. It is possible to compare affiliation across these surveys, since, for the first time, the religion categories were similar in the census instruments.[3] It would have been ideal to have subsequent census data to understand the religious trends over the period of transition, but no such inclusive national data exist. The 2011 census unfortunately scrapped questions about religion, leaving no national data sources on religious affiliation beyond the turn of the century.

Christianity is by far the largest religion in the country, claiming the adherence of about seventy-four per cent of the country's inhabitants. It includes a wide range of denominations that can be aggregated under mainline Protestant Christianity, Reformed churches, Roman Catholicism, African Independent and Pentecostal-Charismatic churches. David Goodhew (2000) has suggested that mainline Protestantism experienced a serious decline between 1960 and 1990. But mainline membership remained more or less in equilibrium between 1996 and 2001, showing as a slight decline in the population proportion. Methodists dropped from 6.9% to 6.7% of the total population, Anglicans from 3.9% to 3.8%, Lutherans from 2.6% to 2.5% and Presbyterians increased slightly from 1.8% to 1.9%. But Reformed churches were certainly in decline. The NGK had about 3.5 million adherents in 1996, or 8.6% of the population. Half a million were lost to other churches by 2001 (Hyslop, 1995). Other Reformed churches, which include both the mission black Reformed churches as well as the conservative breakaway Afrikaanse Protestante Kerk (Afrikaans Protestant Church), also lost membership. The Roman Catholic Church, which also had approximately 3.5 million adherents in 1996, saw a slight decline in membership.

Much more dramatic changes are seen in the numbers for African Independent churches (AICs). Between the Zion Christian Church (ZCC), Ibandla lamaNazaretha and what are classified as Zionist- and Ethiopian-type churches, membership decreased from about thirty-four per cent of the population in 1996 to just under twenty per cent in 2001. If the census data are to be believed, the AIC aggregation masks the fact that the ZCC grew its membership by around one million (to nearly five million) in the five years, consolidating its dominance amongst AICs.

The other significant change to Christian demographics was the rapid rise of Pentecostal-Charismatic religiosity during the transition. In 1996 the category made up 5.4% of the population, with 2.2 million adherents, probably already significantly higher than it would have been five years previously. By 2001 the numbers had grown by 1.5 million to make up 8.2% of the population. This growth does not adequately capture the increasing Pentecostalisation of Christianity in South Africa.

The census figures also reveal a fragmentation of Christian denominations as people moved away from big established churches to smaller

Apostolic and Charismatic groups. If the census is accurate, the membership of the Apostolic Faith Mission Church, for example, which was 2.2 million in 1996, declined in those five years to just 250 000. A catch-all category of 'other Apostolic', on the other hand, grew from 3.5 million in 1996 to 5.6 million in 2001, and the even less definite 'other Christian churches' category more than doubled, from 1.3 million to nearly three million.

Most of these smaller 'other' churches are likely to be Pentecostal, which points to a net increase of about four million. In 1986 the editor of the *South African Christian Handbook* noted a move towards charismatic churches 'which are growing at a rate of a new church every 2.1 days' (Froise, 1986:vii). Ten years later she reported that the Baptist Union had 'planted no less than 110 churches in the past five years'. She noted a major shift from large denominations to 'small, mainly charismatic churches, many of which are autonomous' (Froise, 1996:21). This increase was accompanied by a rise in the number of international missions to South Africa, particularly from the USA, and an explosion of South African missions to other African countries.

The 1996 census figures include two other interesting categories. Nearly 11.5% of the population (4.6 million people) said that they had 'no religion'. Another nine per cent (3.75 million) declined to answer the religion question. This is a considerable proportion of respondents. By the time of the 2001 census there were far fewer refusals (1.4%), but the number of people who said they had no religion increased to 6.7 million (15%). It appears that people are more comfortable declaring their atheism or agnosticism in a more secular public space.

Christianity is by far the dominant religious affiliation in South Africa and people with 'no religion' are the second-biggest demographic. The remainder vary in their religious affiliation. Each of the other religions is relatively small. According to the 2001 census, Muslims made up just less than 1.5% of South Africans (about 650 000 people). There were 550 000 Hindus and a little more than 75 000 Jews (about 0.2%). A catch-all category of 'other faiths', which include 'Buddhists, Taoists, Confucians, New Agers, Jehovah's Witnesses and Baha'is', grew from nearly 200 000 in 1996 to nearly 300 000 by 2001.

The 1996 census for the first time included 'African Traditional Belief' as an option. That year, just 17 097 people identified with this category. In 2001, however, the number had increased to nearly 126 000. All the figures for the 'minority religious' listed above should be treated with considerable caution since sampling errors are likely to be greatest where the population proportion is low and there is no way of independently verifying these figures.

Important as the demographics are, it is also necessary to understand the mobilisation of religious groups to represent their interests, needs and claims on state and society. Although religious institutions did not participate as negotiators, some certainly made sure their views were represented by lobbying and partnering with political parties and making collective and denominational submissions to the MPNP and the CA. They also petitioned for changes to various constitutional formulations.

THE WORLD CONFERENCE ON RELIGION AND PEACE

The greatest religious influence on the negotiations came from an interfaith group, the World Conference on Religion and Peace (WCRP), whose affiliates included progressive and moderate members from all the major world religions. The South African chapter of the WCRP was founded in 1984 by the ubiquitous Archbishop Desmond Tutu.[4]

The first South African interfaith meeting under the auspices of the WCRP, which had been active internationally since 1984, took place a year before the opening of Codesa. From 2 to 4 December 1990 more than 350 delegates met in Johannesburg and debated Sachs's five models of state relations to religion (Omar, 2002). A relatively high degree of consensus was reached at the gathering and the WCRP executive drafted statements and held single-faith gatherings to confirm their support for a joint declaration. In correspondence with Codesa, the organisation said it was considering questions that would need to be addressed in the transition. These included whether South Africa should be a secular state and what should be done about religious schools and state subsidy, religion and the public media, personal religious law and a possible missionary code of conduct (COD NA61 Folder 27). In November 1992 another WCRP interfaith conference, described by Moosa (2000a:160) as 'the most inclusive religious gathering of its kind in South Africa', was held to ratify a final declaration.

The declaration (COD NA61 Folder 27) sought to guide relations between religions and the state, and also between religious groups. The technical committees of the MPNP and the CA relied heavily on its view (see, for example, Corder in Spitz and Chaskalson, 2000:333).

The declaration set out the terms of a social pact between religious groups and the state-to-be. It made a series of demands and, in turn, offered support from the 'religious community' in the process of reconstruction and development. It called on the state to recognise and affirm religious diversity and guarantee the autonomy of religious communities. To this end, it asserted that 'people shall enjoy freedom of conscience' and that 'religious communities shall be equal before the law' and, by implication, the state should not favour or identify with any one religious community.

The declaration also stated that 'people have the right to religious education', or, more specifically, that parents, guardians and religious communities are primarily responsible for the religious education of children. Local communities should be in a position to decide on matters of religious education in their schools – whether it should be single or interfaith, theological or comparative. It also declared that 'people in state institutions shall enjoy religious rights', by which was meant the continued existence of chaplaincy services.

The declaration advocated state recognition of 'systems of family and customary' law, particularly in relation to marriages and their dissolution, the accreditation of marriage officers and civil registration. Religious holidays, it suggested, should be respected by 'authorities' and employers, but it stopped short of anticipating national holidays based on religious holy days. The remainder of the declaration dealt with religious communities' ownership of property, tax regimes and exemptions and access to municipal land for burials, cremations and religious buildings according to community needs. Under apartheid all these rights and privileges had been awarded preferentially to Christian groups.

The WCRP also suggested a formulation for the right to religion in a new Bill of Rights:

> All persons are entitled to (1) freedom of conscience, (2) profess, practice and propagate any religion or no religion, (3) to change their religious allegiance. 2. Every religious community and/or member thereof shall enjoy the right (1) to establish, maintain and manage religious institutions; (2) to have their particular system of family law recognised by the state, and (3) to criticise and challenge all social and political structures and policies in terms of the teachings of their religion. (In COD NA61 Folder 27)

Religions saw a role for themselves in the creation of a democratic country. The WCRP declared religions willing to be self-critical and to eliminate discrimination on the basis of race and gender in their own ranks; a willingness that points to the influence of progressive feminist Muslims and Christians. They asserted the 'moral responsibility' of religious communities to the new society to produce good citizens through education in moral values, service and the direction of land resources to 'the landless'. Dealing with the sometimes difficult question of interreligious relations, the declaration asserted the right of all religions to propagate their teachings 'with respect for people of other religious communities' and without taking unfair advantage of age, weakness or economic or other vulnerability for conversion.

There were a number of elements in this proposed compact that the political parties had not yet taken into consideration. The most important of these was the demand for recognition for religious personal law in general, and specifically for the recognition of Muslim and Hindu marriages. Religious groups also brought to the fore the administrative and institutional powers religious bodies need in order to function, the right to propagate a message, ownership of places of worship, tax exemption and access to public media.

The WCRP was influential in the negotiations for a number of reasons. It presented a broad front and its consensus document was translated into terms that could easily be drafted in law and was presented in substantively secular language. Even more important was its close ties with the ANC, a factor that was evident in the numbers of its personnel who either had worked or would work for the organisation.

Close relationships between the ANC and the WCRP had been forged throughout the late 1980s. In 1987 the WCRP hosted a consultation with the ANC in exile in Lusaka, titled 'Religion and the South African Crisis'. The WCRP team was headed by Tutu. The ANC took the meeting seriously, its delegation including no fewer than five members of its National Executive Committee. A pithy recounting of this meeting announces that 'common understanding' was reached. Apartheid, it was agreed, was a heresy and 'a falsification of Christianity, a denial of true religion and of religious pluralism'.[5]

The WCRP and the ANC agreed on the importance of interfaith cooperation as a platform for critique of the apartheid state. 'True religion', they said, would flourish where there was no established religion and where every individual had religious freedom. The meeting also 'recognised the centrality of the ANC to any solution in the South African conflict'.[6] The WCRP was later party to the conference, chaired by Tutu, at which the 1989 Harare Declaration, which set out the ANC's conditions for starting negotiations with the NP and included the need for a Bill of Rights, was adopted.[7]

Two things stand out when one puts South Africa's religious demographics and the influence of the WCRP together. The first is that the size of a denomination had very little to do with its political clout. Through the personality and commitments of then Archbishop Tutu and the strong ecumenism of Anglicanism, that denomination, despite the fact that its adherents constitute less than four per cent of the total population, has all but dominated the South African Council of Churches (SACC) and the ecumenical and interfaith movements, along with a handful of Muslims, Methodists, Congregationalists and Catholics. The second is the converse of this observation. The majority of people in South Africa are followers of Pentecostal-Charismatic churches or AICs, neither of which was much involved in the WCRP declaration. Although two bodies representing AICs were members of the WCRP, neither represented the biggest AICs such as the ZCC or the Shembe church Ibandla lamaNazaretha. A few individual Pentecostal liberationists did participate in the WCRP (Balcomb, 2004) but on the whole they were not part of the WCRP process, consensus or declaration.

RELIGIOUS RATIONALE FOR SECULAR INSTITUTIONAL RELATIONS

Religious individuals and groups sought to influence the political process in a wide range of areas, not only to secure religious rights. Ecumenical groups were involved in peace initiatives large and small. The National Peace Accord and the Ecumenical Monitoring Programme, for example, were both interfaith projects that invited the involvement of other civil society bodies.[8] Many of these initiatives mobilised the Christianity that political opponents shared and this role for religion continued in the theologies and practices of the Truth and Reconciliation Commission. The SACC and others also contributed to a number of more general provisions in the draft constitution as it was being written. The SACC, for instance, supported the inclusion of sexual orientation in the equality provisions, a position that earned it the ire of its more conservative members, but the backing of Archbishop Tutu. It also argued for socioeconomic rights and for a Constitutional Court.

Most of the workings of the Kempton Park negotiations were invisible to members of the general public and there was little correspondence between the public and negotiators. The majority of submissions to the MPNP were requested by political parties or technical committees, or were offered via individual political parties. Most of the communication from religious groups to the MPNP in particular came through the WCRP. Exceptions include a host of submissions from *ulama* groups,[9] bodies of traditional Islamic legal authorities that advocated the recognition of Shari'a or Muslim Personal Law (MPL). Much of the remaining religious correspondence to the MPNP was from exceptionally angry Afrikaners.

The CA was a more open book, actively encouraging public participation. It received hundreds of thousands of submissions and petitions and also hosted a Religion Public Hearing on 25 and 26 May 1995 (NA CA F4 1/12/6). Although the public hearing included some Pentecostal groups and an African Traditional Religion representative, it was still dominated by the WCRP.

Letters, submissions, petitions and the verbatim transcription of the public hearing all suggest that most religious people actively supported the establishment of a religiously neutral state and a separation between religious and public institutions. A wide range of religious arguments was made for secularism, the separation of institutions and support for the role of the state as guardian and guarantor of religious freedom, generally suggesting that religious freedom and state neutrality provide the proper conditions for religion to flourish.

One of the most pained and hesitant renditions of this argument came from the Dutch Reformed Church at the CA public hearing. Professor D. de Villiers, who presented the position of the NGK, contended that most Christians wanted a Christian state, but this was simply not possible. 'We live in a plural society,' he said, and a Christian state would garner 'fierce opposition' from other religions as well as from proponents of political liberalism. But beyond such pragmatism he also conceded that a Christian state is 'ethically undesirable'. It is 'unfair' because especially recognised religion leads almost inevitably to intolerance and repression (NA CA F4 1/12/6). For religion to maintain its integrity it needed to be free from the state.

The strongest arguments for a secularism that could guarantee religious freedom and equality came from members of minority traditions that had experienced Christian privilege and dominance under apartheid. Widespread and open criticism of Christianity and its collusions with apartheid were voiced at the public hearing. This history of 'Christianity used as a political weapon', as Swami Jivananda put it in a letter dated 31 May 1995 (NA CA 2/4/1/5/35), was an argument for the separation of state and religious institutions. Only separation could guarantee equality and non-discrimination. Moulana Ihsaan Hendricks of the Muslim Judicial Council called the Bill of Rights 'a contract which we sign with non-Muslims' (NA CA F4 1/12/6).

The negotiators heard about a wide range of religious needs from representatives of the smaller religions. The Institute of Islamic Shari'a Studies, perhaps in anticipation of conflicts over the veil, were concerned that nobody should ban or punish Muslim dress in the workplace. Muslim prisoners should be able to worship on Fridays, have access to the Qur'an and receive halaal food (NA CA F4 1/12/6). A similar request came from politician Amichand Rajbansi, who sought adequate nutrition for vegetarian Hindu prisoners. Hindu leader Moushami Joshi raised the problem of the proximity of Diwali to the matriculation exams (NA CA F4 1/12/6).

Both Hindu and Muslim participants sought the recognition of religious marriages and their clergy as marriage officers. They also sought some sort of accommodation and recognition for their religious holy days. The Rastafarian Burning Spear movement and the Helenvale Dagga Forum pressed for the legalisation of marijuana as a religious right. The Christian

Science Committee argued that healing prayer should be recognised as a medical practice and sought exemption from regulations governing medical practice and nursing (NA CA F4 1/12/6). One Hindu group sought recognition of healing modalities from African and Indian subcontinents, particularly Ayurvedic medicine and acupuncture (CA 2/44/4/1/7/49), and Chief Rabbi Cyril Harris submitted his concerns about hate speech and ways to prevent it (NA CA F4 1/12/6).

Christian groups, on the other hand, were more concerned about their theological, ecclesiastical and institutional autonomy, contending that religious groups could only remain critical and uncorrupted by state power if they had autonomy. Many of the larger evangelical charismatic churches also supported the secularity of an institutionally non-partisan state for reasons that were more conspicuously theological. The Evangelical Fellowship 'endorsed' the separation of church and state because of the 'distinct spheres of responsibility given by God. [T]he Church must submit to the state even as it is its conscience', they said (COD NA61 Volume 37). His People wrote that '[t]he church as an institution should remain structurally separate from the state', but the state, they argued, should 'recognise and submit to the rule of Almighty God' (NA CA 1/19/2).

Some Christians were unable to accord recognition and equality to other religious groups. Most of the submissions to this effect were angry and fearful about both Islam and communism. The Baptist Union declared itself 'disturbed by the attitude of the Muslim community and the persecution of converts' (COD NA61 Folder 38) and the Christian Education Foundation supported religious freedom but not religious equality. In its view, religions were simply not equal (NA CA 2/4/4/1/7/53). More unguarded statements appear in individual letters. A man from Somerset West wrote: 'It's all very nice sounding to give room to others, the non-Christians, but Jesus commanded us to go into the whole world and make disciples of all people. He also said that the gates of Hell cannot stand against Him.' Another, writing to Codesa from Machadodorp when interfaith prayers were introduced, wrote: 'Many people will cry out that there must be freedom of religion.' But, he wrote, it is important not to recognise these other so-called religions. 'It is not to persecute those who follow false gods but to lead them into the truth. The leaders must return to God and teach the people to follow' (NA CA 2/4/1/5/34). Other submissions were concerned about differentiating between acceptable and unacceptable religions and practices. The Christian Voice, for example, declared itself against Satanism, occultism, animism, witchcraft, spiritualism and similar practices, which, it said, should not be accepted as religion and therefore protected.

These types of submissions were a very small minority and went against the mood of the times and the ethos of the negotiations. Apart from the fact that they were meticulously catalogued, filed and stored, they were generally ignored by the negotiators.

NEGOTIATING THE RIGHT TO RELIGION IN A NEW SOUTH AFRICA

For the Kempton Park negotiators, caught as they were in the whirlwind of escalating violence and insecurity, religion was not of immediate political concern. It was common sense that South Africans should have the right to practise religion. Chief Justice Michael Corbett's opening speech at Codesa specifically acknowledged the importance of this right and the ANC submitted that general constitutional principles should include 'universally accepted human rights, freedoms and civil liberties including the freedom of religion, speech, assembly' (COD NA61 Volume 47/27) and similar.

THE MULTIPARTY NEGOTIATING PROCESS

The legal framing of religion in South Africa's postapartheid law was done at the MPNP. In just nine months a bevy of technical experts drafted an interim constitution and South Africa's first ever Bill of Rights, written by the Technical Committee on Fundamental Rights during the Transition (TC4). It is here that religious rights are to be found.

The TC4 committee had five members: Lourens du Plessis and Hugh Corder were law professors; Zac Yacoob was an experienced advocate and UDF activist, later to become a Constitutional Court judge; Gerrit Grové was deputy state law advisor; and Sibongile Nene, the only woman, the only African and the only non-lawyer, was a sociologist with an interest in gender. For most of TC4's life she was almost silent and it was the four lawyers who developed a Bill of Rights with religion, cultural and language provisions that were retained, almost word for word, in the final Constitution.

All the technical committees at the MPNP worked in a similar way. They first defined their ambit and then received submissions from political parties on their various elements. Taking the wording of these submissions as a basis they formulated draft legal provisions to go into the proposed interim constitution. These, with explanatory notes or memoranda, were then delivered as progress reports to the plenary MPNP Negotiating Council, where political parties debated the draft formulations. If there was 'sufficient consensus' the subject became almost impossible to reopen. If there was no agreement further submissions would be made. In a few cases it was impossible to resolve decisions in this way and parties traded concession in bilateral negotiations. Alternatively, an ad hoc committee comprised of senior political party representatives met with the TC4 committee to hammer things out.

With regard to the Bill of Rights, the ANC wanted a minimal document so that a final Bill of Rights could be developed by a democratically elected assembly, while the NP wanted a substantive document that could shape the postapartheid Constitution and include significant minority protections. The NP won this key battle and, as a result, had an enduring influence on the postapartheid Constitution. But whatever their disagreement about the extent of rights in the transition, all parties agreed that religion formed part of a basic set of first-generation rights that were, in the words of the technical committee, 'minimal or essential rights and freedoms' (NA NEG 1/3/3/2/1).

In early June 1993 the Negotiating Council received the following draft text for inclusion in the Bill of Rights: 'Every person shall have the right to freedom of conscience, religion, thought, belief and opinion, provided that nothing shall preclude the practice of religion in State or State aided institutions on a free, voluntary and equitable basis' (NA NEG 1/3/3/2/4). The first part is the positive assertion of the right to religion. The second derives from the NP position that South Africa should not replicate the USA's law – a disestablishment clause that would erect a strict wall of separation.

The government submission, endorsed by the NP, argued that the right to religion should not 'preclude ministration to the forces, the public services and other state institutions, religious instruction or exercise in schools, and religious broadcasts by an entity instituted by or under any law' (Corder Collection).

The ANC did not make a specific submission on religion at this point, but the technical committee referred to the ANC's 1990 'A Bill of Rights for a New South Africa' document (Corder Collection) for content. The TC4 lawyers considered three elements from the ANC, the first being 'freedom of worship and tolerance of all religions' and 'no state or official religion shall be established'. The second was '[t]he institutions of religion shall be separate from the state, but nothing in this constitution shall prevent them from co-operating with the state with a view to furthering the objectives of this constitution nor from bearing witness and commenting on the actions of the state'. The last clause sought to ensure respect for places of worship and prevent racism that might bar anyone from entering such places (Corder Collection). Nothing in this ANC formulation suggested a contradiction with the first draft text.

The Negotiating Council agreed to the June draft and TC4 cleaned up the text as the overall Bill of Rights took shape, separating the religion clause into two parts. It became clause 8, the first part of which grants that 'every person shall have the right to freedom of conscience, religion, thought, belief and opinion' and the second, which became extremely lawyerly, reads: 'Without derogating from the generality of subsection (1), religious observances may be conducted at state or state-aided institutions under rules established by the appropriate authority for that purpose, provided that such observances are conducted on an equitable basis and attendance thereat is free and voluntary.' Responding to the fourth progress report, Sachs wrote, 'the clause is balanced, ensures the state doesn't favour one religion over another' and provides a 'sense of security', presumably to the NP's constituency (Corder Collection). This version of the Bill of Rights was included in the first complete draft of the interim constitution presented to the Negotiating Council on 21 July 1993 (NA NEG 1/3/2/2/1).

The ANC's response to the complete draft constitution was explosive. A 'private and confidential' submission written by SACP lawyer Halton Cheadle attempted to delay the constitution's release. It slammed the size and complexity of the Bill of Rights and proposed a radically altered formulation which was just two paragraphs long. The first would guarantee that 'all fundamental civil liberties necessary for free political campaigning, debates, criticism and opposition shall be respected' and the second would include a handful of special guarantees to ease fears in the transitional period. These could include a right to language and culture and some education provisions.

Religion, complained the ANC submission, was one of the clauses that had become too complicated. The first part of the religion right was essential for the transition but the second 'pre-empts the constitution-making authority deciding whether or not there should be state-sponsored religions or whether there should be an anti-establishment clause in the constitution ... The proviso should be eliminated' (Corder Collection). The Negotiating Council met on 21 July to go over the draft interim constitution. When it reached the section on religion and belief, the ANC again proposed that the second half of the clause be dropped. No one else present agreed.

Two weeks later the ANC suggested written amendments to the draft Bill of Rights. In this document it stated that,

> it is our view that the freedom of conscience and religion is in no way inconsistent with school prayers. The USA constitution has a special formulation which forbids religious observances at state schools. It is not even necessary to raise the problem here; doing so introduces unnecessary prescriptiveness. (Corder Collection, Folder D1)

The ANC garnered the support of both the General Council of the Bar and the Law Reform Project of Lawyers for Human Rights for their position.

In its submission the General Council agreed that nobody wanted a situation like that in the USA but that without a disestablishment clause the second part of the religion right was unnecessary. If it was to be included it should at least be written as a 'permissive formulation' rather than a 'provided that' formulation (Corder Collection). The Lawyers for Human Rights submission suggested that 8(2) should be dropped because 'it is vague and phrased as an exception – which is confusing and inaccurate' (Corder Collection).

But on the same day that this submission was written the religion clause was once again brought before the Negotiating Council as part of a TC4 report. This time the full two-clause version was approved and accepted. No comments were noted and the ANC backed down.

Despite its protestations, the ANC had no ideological problem with the specific content of the clause and by August it had lost the battle for a short transitional Bill of Rights. Without agreement between the ANC and the NP it would have been impossible to reach sufficient consensus on a shortened Bill of Rights, and in view of the fact that the negotiations were increasingly fragile as violence and insecurity escalated it was simply not worth threatening them over this point.

The religion clause remained almost as it was but was moved from clause 8 to 14. 'Academic freedom in institutions of higher learning' was added to the list of conscience, religion, thought, belief and opinion, but the CA later removed it. The second clause, now 14(2), was made slightly less lawyerly, reading: 'religious observances may be conducted at State or State-aided institutions under rules established by an appropriate authority for that purpose, provided that such observances are conducted on an equitable basis and attendance at them is free and voluntary' (NA NEG 1/3/3/2/10). This wording introduced a new concept, possibly even a new institution, into the mix. Who was the 'appropriate authority' for the purposes of establishing rules for religious observances at state and state-aided institutions? This question remained unanswered during the MPNP. In the meantime, on 7 October the Negotiating Council confirmed the clause as agreed (NA NEG 1/3/3/2/10).

It appeared that their work was done on the right to religion, but this was not to be. In the middle of that month Muslim groups made a series of submissions to the technical committee that opened up the issue of MPL and its recognition in the new Constitution (Tayob, 2008). A TC4 report noted: 'At a late stage of the negotiation process representatives of the Muslim community made submissions ... to the effect that the religious laws observed by certain communities ... should also be recognised constitutionally in explicit terms' (NA NEG 1/3/3/2/4). Four weeks of intense consultation followed.

There were two broad perspectives within the Muslim community. Some traditional *ulama* authorities who initiated these representations argued for the recognition of Shari'a law and particularly its family law elements. They also wanted state-funded or -administered religious courts to be established to apply this law. They argued that recognition would provide redress for the second-class status of Islam in South Africa and would sanction the marriages, divorces, laws of succession and custody arrangements practised by most Muslims. It would also legitimise the work of the *ulama* by recognising them and giving them access to non-voluntary modes of redress for the contravention of their rulings through fines or imprisonment. In the view of these *ulama*, Islamic law is divinely sanctioned and should remain immune to the intervention of secular or civil law. And according to Ebrahim Moosa (2001:128), they 'postured themselves as the sole authorities on MPL to the exclusion of other sectors of the Muslim Community'.

A second Islamic perspective came from a broad alliance of progressive Muslims that also included some *ulama* authorities, particularly from the Muslim Judicial Council, whose suggestions were more in line with the WCRP position. Sheila Camerer, who represented the old South African government and was a member of the TC4 ad hoc committee, recalls an important submission by Moulana Ebrahim Moosa, a professor of Religious Studies at the University of Cape Town, and endorsed by a number of Muslim groups. According to Camerer, this submission, sent on 2 November 1993, tipped the balance in the decisions of the Negotiating Council.

Moosa's submission acknowledged the widespread de facto practice of MPL in South Africa, informally administered by various Muslim jurists. 'It is known,' he wrote, 'that most Muslims would prefer to follow the dictates of their religion in matters of personal law, rather than secular law' (Corder Collection). And given the fact that MPL did in fact guide many Muslims' family relations, its non-recognition was problematic. His main concern was that MPL was administered in ways that disadvantaged women. Practices he listed as problematic on the grounds of their gender inequality include divorce by repudiation (*talaq*) and limited maintenance provisions.

Unlike the *ulama* submissions, those of progressive Muslims highlighted the diversity of schools of Islamic interpretation and Muslim cultural practice in South Africa. For this reason it was impossible, they said, to simply recognise any one self-appointed authority on Islamic law. This was a matter that required wide debate within the Muslim community and this debate should always include women. This is, itself, a contentious proposition according to more conservative interpretations of Islamic law. Moosa suggested that the outcome of these discussions should be the codification of MPL, which would also give the Muslim community a chance to reform its practices and bring them into line with human rights norms, particularly in relation to gender. 'It is accepted,' he wrote, 'that a human rights dispensation is in full accord with Islamic law' (Corder Collection).

On 12 November 1993 the ANC proposed a third clause for the right to religion and 'requested consideration' of the inclusion of the following:

> (i) members of religious faiths shall be free to regulate relationships within the family, on a voluntary basis, in accordance with the principles and laws of their faith, provided that they do not violate the rights of others; (ii) legislation may provide for the recognition of religious personal family law within the framework of the Chapter on Fundamental Rights and appropriate legislation by parliament; (iii) legislation shall provide for the equal status of marriages performed by recognised religious officers to be acknowledged. (NA NEG 1/3/3/2/11)

Some of the conservative *ulama*'s demands had been removed from this formulation. The submission about courts was not taken seriously. The TC4 held that it was too specific for a transitional constitution. The issue of courts was also beyond its remit, although, interestingly, the committee suggested that if the issue of religious courts was to be taken up at all, it should be dealt with in the chapter on traditional authorities.

The ANC's suggestion made it clear that the recognition of personal family law should take place 'within the framework of the Chapter on Fundamental Rights'. It would, in other words, only recognise such law where it guaranteed gender equality. Even though the ANC proposed the addition, many within its ranks were concerned about it.

The technical committee worked furiously to produce an addendum to its 12th report on 16 November 1993, just two days before the Negotiating Council was to vote on the interim constitution. It drafted a new section, 'family law under religion', to be included as 14(3) 'in order to address the concern which has been raised about religious law'. It reads: 'Nothing in this section shall preclude legislation recognising (a) a system of personal and family law under religion, and (b) the validity of marriages conducted under religious law subject to specified procedures' (NA NEG 1/3/3/2/13). Like 14(2), about religion and the state, this clause does not actually grant rights. It is an enabling provision that promises the possibility of a future Parliament passing legislation. It also does not explicitly state that such legislation would need to be subject to the equality provisions of the Bill of Rights, an oversight that would be remedied in the final Constitution.

THE CONSTITUTIONAL ASSEMBLY

There is almost no difference between the right to religion as it is formulated in the interim (1993) and final (1996) versions of the Constitution. When elected representatives met at the beginning of the CA, their first task was to review what was already in place in the interim constitution and to make recommendations for the new. But all the parties agreed that the right to religion was more or less as it should be.

The religious public and the WCRP, however, had some concerns. The first of these related to the question of an appropriate authority to guide religious observance at state or state-aided institutions. The NP wanted government institutions, or at least institutions established by law, to be that appropriate authority. Judging by their comments on the matter, they were most concerned about religious observance in schools. The ANC made no submission on this matter.

The Public Hearing on Religion, held on 25 and 26 May 1995, gave religious groups a chance to elaborate on this aspect of religion–state interaction. The overwhelming consensus was that religious bodies should retain autonomy over religious observances, even when they are held in state institutions. Religious bodies envisaged an interlocutory interfaith body, controlled by them, which could advise government on matters religious. J.N.J. Kritzinger, a University of South Africa professor and WCRP leader, called for an 'independent national advisory commission on Religious Affairs', one 'not funded by the state' (NA CA F4 1/12/6). He thought the idea of an 'appropriate authority' was vague and therefore dangerous. If such a body were state sponsored, he said, it would either be used by confessional groups or by government seeking 'divine legitimation' (NA CA F4 1/12/6). Martin Prozeski, a WCRP member and Religion professor at the then University of Natal, was against a 'ministry of religion' under state control (NA CA F4 1/12/6), as were the religious group African Enterprise and the ACDP.

These groups, however, had no leverage over the decision on an appropriate authority when it was finally made. In April 1996, at the very end of negotiations, the ANC and the NP met for a long weekend in Arniston on the coast of the Western Cape. There, in what came to be called the Waenhuiskrans Negotiations, the last deadlocked issues were decided. The NP wanted to make sure that, in schools particularly, the appropriate authority would be the governing body (NA CA 2/4/4/1/7/13). On the party's insistence, the phrasing of the religion clause was altered to read 'the appropriate public authorities'. This inclusion of the word 'public' secured the subordination of religious to non-religious authorities when it came to religion's participation in state and state-aided spaces.

The second change in wording sought to make it unambiguously clear that all rights to religion and culture were subject to the equality provision of the Bill of Rights. To the religion clause, number 14 in the interim constitution and number 15 in the final, was added the following section: '15(3)(b) Recognition in terms of paragraph (a) must be consistent with this section and the other provisions of the Constitution.' Paragraph (a) is the enabling provision about religious personal law. Similarly, the interim constitutional right to 'language and culture' (ss 31 and 30 respectively) stated 'every person shall have the right to use the language and to participate in the cultural life of his or her choice'. In the final Constitution this clause continued, 'but no one exercising these rights may do so in a manner inconsistent with any provision of the Bill of Rights'.

The NP and Afrikaner political organisations to its right all wanted some sort of minority protection under the rubric of cultural and language rights. Although religion per se was not at issue, it was usually listed as part of a triumvirate, with culture and language, to define a minority. This minority protection, or at least this double representation over and above the structures of electoral politics, was at issue in the last-minute Waenhuiskrans Negotiations, where the NP finally succeeded in winning some version of collective rather than individual rights through two new provisions.

The first was the right of 'cultural, religious and linguistic communities' to 'enjoy their culture, practise their religion and use their language', to be included in a new Section 31 of the Bill of Rights. The clause also allowed them to 'form, join and maintain cultural, religious and linguistic associations' and civil society bodies. The language of this new right is exactly the same as that in the International Covenant on Civil and Political Rights (Henrard, 2001). Despite the NP's symbolic victory in this matter, Section 31 does not really grant any entitlements in addition to those already in the religion and culture and language rights section and it, too, requires the exercise of these rights to be in line with the remainder of the Bill of Rights, including the right to gender and race equality.

The second NP victory was the institution of a new 'Chapter nine' commission – the Commission for the Promotion and Protection of the Rights of Cultural, Religious and Linguistic Communities. The most important aspect of the Commission for both the NP and the FF was that it was given the power to suggest the establishment of advisory cultural councils. As at 2017 it had yet to do so.

The result is that South Africa's formation of political secularism is well within a liberal democratic norm, with all religions and individuals in their religious capacity recognised by the Constitution as equal before the law. There is no state religion or officially recognised or favoured religious denomination.

Institutional relations subordinate institutions of religious authority to political authority in the state and state-sponsored public, but it is a very mild form of subordination and was based on the consensus that the arrangement is also in the best interests of religion.

In contemporary South Africa, as in most constitutional democracies, it is the state that promises to guarantee religious freedom and autonomy. The state does not 'do' religion. It creates and legislates the space in which religion operates with some autonomy. The state, through law, grants rights to religious individuals and institutions and also enables and sets conditions for their exercise. Law also limits the right to religion, establishes a framework for its interpretation and subordinates religious rights to general legal and administrative principles.

The relative ease with which religious rights and institutional relations were negotiated into the Constitution is in stark contrast to the heated arguments about the theological and philosophical foundations of the new regime and the place that traditional authorities and customary law should take.

4

RE-ESTABLISHING TRADITIONAL AUTHORITY

The King does not meet the criteria ... But, in general one would be inclined to say that if any organisation has the capacity to render nugatory any decisions taken at Codesa with which they may disagree, it would be advisable to have them present ...
N.J.J. Olivier, Democratic Party Representative, 18 March 1992
(COD NA61 Volume 103)

They [the ANC] want to take power away from traditional leaders. It's natural for political parties not to want any institutional structure to have power that it wants for itself, [power] that it could use.
Patekile Holomisa, ANC Member of Parliament and chair of
Contralesa, 16 October 1996 (O'Malley, 1996)

The negotiations of the 1990s promised a long-delayed liberation from all apartheid had stood for, for black South Africans and, indeed, for all South Africans. The writing of a new Constitution was an opportunity to finally establish the grounds for an inclusive 'moral community between rulers and ruled' (Fields, 1982). Why, then, did the negotiators come to recognise the institution of chieftainship within their vision of a postapartheid society and an otherwise liberal Constitution? Why, in other words, was this element of indirect rule maintained over the threshold of apartheid? And what does this mean in terms of South Africa's secularism?

The situation of the apartheid homelands is critical to an explanation of the recognition of traditional leadership. It was in these homelands that chieftainship endured and where a political imaginary of customary leadership was kept alive by subjects and chiefs as much as by apartheid administrators.

THE VIOLENCE OF THE HOMELANDS

Barbara Oomen (2005) estimates that by 1990 about forty-four per cent of the population, nearly 17 million people, lived in a meagre fourteen per cent of South Africa in areas called homelands or bantustans. These territories were an apartheid intensification of earlier colonial and Union segregationist policies. Reserve lands were set aside for occupation by black people from the early 1900s and from 1951 the ambitious new apartheid government grouped them into territories that became objects of contradictory interventions. They were 'developed' through modernising 'betterment schemes' to improve their carrying capacity as reserves for 'surplus people', that is, people surplus to the requirements of South Africa's white economy. Mechanisms for the exclusion of black people from South African citizenship (Klaaren, 2000), they were also part of an ideological apparatus of ethnic nationalism and were administered by chiefs through tribal authorities (Vail, 1991).

SOUTH AFRICAN HOMELANDS IN 1986

Most homelands were made up of fragmented territories separated by white-owned farms and industrial areas. Bophuthatswana, for example, comprised 19 areas, some of them hundreds of kilometres apart. KwaZulu had 29 major and 41 minor fragments (Muriaas, 2002). Despite this geographic spread and the fact that they were economically unviable, these territories were granted 'self-governing' status by South Africa from 1963 onwards (Muriaas, 2002). In 1970 the Bantu Homeland Citizenship Act passed by the South African Parliament granted black South Africans an 'additional citizenship' in a 'designated homeland' on the basis of 'language, culture or race' (Klaaren, 2000:5).

From 1973 onwards homelands were increasingly subject to a politics of ethnic nationalism. According to apartheid's separate development ideology, each homeland was a nation-state for a tribe or ethnicity. The reality never matched this ideology, but from the late 1970s and in the context of African independence movements, some of these 'self-governing'

Source: Perry-Cantañeda Library Map Collection, courtesy of the University of Texas Libraries, the University of Texas at Austin. Redrawn by Rizelle Hartmeier Stander.

territories took the 'independence' offered by the apartheid state. The leaders of four homelands – the Transkei (in 1976), Bophuthatswana (1977), Venda (1979) and Ciskei (1981) – elected to accept independence. The four, collectively known as the TBVC states, were never recognised internationally, but, somewhat farcically, relations between them and the South African state fell under the government's Foreign Affairs Department (Van der Westhuizen, 2007). With so-called independence, homeland citizens of the TBVC states, including those, like migrant labourers, who didn't actually live in the homelands, lost their South African citizenship.

Chieftainship was the cornerstone of rule in both kinds of homelands – self-governing territories and the TBVC states (Ritchken, 1995). As Oomen (2005:41) put it: 'Traditional leaders formed the majority in all the "national parliaments" and sat in the gargantuan buildings that – like national flags, stamps and other emblems – served to legitimise the existence of polities that only the South African state would recognise.' Approximately 800 traditional leaders were remunerated by the South African government, either directly or through the TBVC states, and were given financial, legal, military and administrative support.

It is in the context of the homelands that the story of chieftainship and its claims on a postapartheid future unfolded. The 1980s was a decisive decade in the fortunes of traditional leadership. Many events undermined homeland leadership and unsettled the social and economic relations of homeland subjects in that decade: a sharp rise in unemployment, an influx into the homelands, a drought from 1983 that undermined what little remained of agricultural subsistence production, increased pressure for land and the dropping of influx control legislation. As significant was the wave of youth mobilisation after the 1976 Soweto uprising and the establishment of the United Democratic Front (UDF) in 1983, both of which returned African National Congress (ANC)-aligned politics to townships and then to rural areas after a long absence. Homeland leaders responded in a variety of ways to these pressures (Marks, 1986). Events in Bushbuckridge in the Northern Transvaal (now Limpopo), Transkei and KwaZulu illustrate the fates of chiefs in the decade preceding negotiations.

BUSHBUCKRIDGE

In 1972 the apartheid state declared two 'self-governing' homelands, Lebowa and Gazankulu, for erstwhile Shangaan and Sotho polities. The populations of the two trebled in the 20 years after their establishment and by the 1980s they were no longer effective agricultural areas (Ritchken, 1995). But an agrarian economy and a stable hierarchical social order that included ancestors formed the basis for idealised chiefly authority over gendered and material relations.

By the 1980s chiefs could not rule in ways set down in customary law. Many of the economic and social relations that would have made sense of that law no longer existed. The many and varied bases of chiefs' authority shifted with circumstances and, over time, came to include an ability to extract local resources, control over the allocation of increasingly small plots of land, jurisdiction over chiefly courts, relations with homeland government officials and police, official recognition by the Native Affairs Department and consequent state salaries and other accoutrements of power.

All these bases of power and legitimacy were fragile and increasingly contested. Peter Delius (1996) reports that there were growing complaints in the 1980s about chiefly extraction of taxes and fines, the abuse of community funds, particularly money for the building of schools, the cost of the annual 'traditional levy' and chiefly demands on their increasingly impoverished subjects for financial support for their cars, bride wealth (*bogadi*) and houses, portions of beer and labour on chiefs' land.

Economic pressures severed connections between youth and patrimonial chieftainship in a number of ways. Initiation schools, for example, became increasingly commodified over the decades preceding the 1980s and no longer initiated their students into a specific chiefdom. The families of initiates rather than chiefs bore the costs of initiation (Ritchken, 1995). This undermined traditional structures of discipline. Added to this was the growing number of young unemployed men and returning migrants unable to raise sufficient bride wealth to marry and establish their own households. From the late 1970s there was an increase in crime, violence, drug use and drunkenness (Delius, 1996).

Chiefs, like apartheid ideologues, mobilised ethnicity as a way of reclaiming and consolidating power. As Leroy Vail (1991) has argued, within a state that divides subordinate groups along ethnic lines, a rural petit bourgeoisie manipulated ethnic sentiments into ethnic nationalist programmes to achieve their own ends. This was certainly the case in Bushbuckridge. In 1984 the chief minister of Gazankulu formed a 'cultural' organisation, modelled on Mangosuthu Buthelezi's Inkatha movement, which bound chiefs and other members of the bureaucracy and local elite under a single umbrella. The mobilisation of ethnic nationalism was sufficiently effective to result in conflicts on the border between Gazankulu and Lebowa during that year.

But this kind of ethnic mobilisation was not able to sap a wave of youth mobilisation allied to the liberation movement. Bushbuckridge, like many other rural areas, became home to youth from urban township schools who had been radicalised by the 1976 Soweto uprising. Many urban parents sent their children to live with rural kin to attend homeland schools, hoping they could continue their schooling despite the pervasive urban school boycotts (Delius, 1996). This infusion of politicised post-1976 youth changed the politics of rural schooling. The Congress of South African Students became a force in homeland schools, as did the UDF when it was launched in 1983 (Delius, 1996). The ANC, encouraging this politicisation, declared 1985 the Year of the Youth and named them the vanguard of the struggle for national liberation.

In Bushbuckridge politically active schoolgoers were joined by young unemployed men. The Shatale Youth Congress (SYC), for example, was founded in the mid-1980s, declaring as its first objective to 'draw up a good guidance for a future community system in a democratic South

Africa' and to maintain law and order (Ritchken, 1995:309). Its first campaign was to institute proper accounting for community funds overseen by chiefs, a demand supported by parents. In response, some chiefs called for assistance from the army and police and together they attacked the SYC. Quite rapidly, skirmishes between youth groups and the homeland police escalated. Schools were closed, a consumer boycott of white and 'collaborator' shops began and a cycle of violence gained momentum as the youth declared war on the Lebowa government (Delius, 1996).

What set these developments apart from those in other homelands was witchcraft. Scholars argue that violence against accused witches was closely related to chiefs' loss of control over the sanctioning of social relations in the area. From the introduction of the administrative structures of Traditional Authorities in the 1960s, magistrates had more consistently prevented witchcraft accusations from coming before chiefs' courts, effectively driving witchcraft underground.

As Delius (1996:164) explains: 'The confidence of communities in the capacity of a system of chieftainship, which had been co-opted and partly discredited, to fulfil its duty in organising their defences against supernatural hazards had ... been further undermined.' Ritchken (1995:335) describes a situation in which witchcraft accusations were never resolved, but were instead left to simmer as rumour and conflict. When the youth sought to save communities from the degradations of homeland rule and impoverishment, they turned against accused witches as embodiments of social distress and suffering. In April and May 1986 youth groups in Lebowa identified 150 people as witches and many of them were burnt alive. The average age of the killers was 19.

It was only when a coalition of chiefs, shop owners and school principals, united under the banner of the Sofasonke Civil Union, called on the Lebowa military that the killings came to an end. Hundreds of youths were arrested, a permanent police presence introduced in the area and schools were reopened. Some chiefs who had fled during the witch-hunts returned to the area under army protection (Delius, 1996). Sofasonke attacked youth leaders, burning houses and beating prominent members of the SYC. It took an intervention by the South African Council of Churches's Frank Chikane to pressure Nelson Ramodike, then chief minister of Lebowa, to disarm Sofasonke and de-escalate the intergenerational conflict and community violence (Ritchken, 1995).

The progressive youth politics of the 1980s introduced the possibility of the removal not only of individual chiefs but of the institution of chieftainship itself. This was a radical change in South African rural politics. Earlier uprisings, such as that in Sekhukhuneland in 1958, had sought to defend the idea of chieftainship against apartheid's pressures, temptations and manipulations of specific chiefs, but, in the 1980s, the youth demanded that the institution of traditional leadership be replaced by democratic forms of local government (Delius, 1996). The youth mobilised to replace chiefly structures of authority and invert the age hierarchies of social control. They also sought to replace chieftainship as a form of local government, introducing 'people's courts' in opposition to chiefly courts and seeking to introduce democratic structures in all areas of social control, including schools and institutions for dealing with accusations of witchcraft.

It is important to understand the relationship between these youth organisations and the structures of the national liberation movements to which they looked. Youth mobilisation was not officially organised by the ANC, which was only unbanned in 1990. Even the UDF did not have much presence in most homeland areas and distanced itself from the killing spree of the young comrades in Lebowa (Ntsebeza, 2006).

The irony was that in Bushbuckridge and elsewhere it was the chiefs and other homeland elites, not the youth movements, that were able to make public alliances with the ANC after its unbanning. Both popular and pariah chiefs in Lebowa and Gazankulu rushed to join the ANC-aligned Congress of Traditional Leaders of South Africa (Contralesa), which had been formed in 1987 by a group of KwaNdebele traditional leaders opposed to independence in their homeland. Chiefs who had supported armed action against the young comrades 'now proclaimed themselves as supporters of the ANC and denounced attempts by the youth and migrants to raise issues of corruption and maladministration in the villages as "uncomradely behaviour", appealing to the ANC leadership for support' (Delius, 1996:207). In 1990 even Ramodike joined the ANC. However, despite his promises to deliver homeland votes to the movement, he prevented the formation of civic organisations and the establishment of ANC branches in areas under his control.

TRANSKEI

Under the leadership of Chief Kaiser Matanzima from the early 1960s onwards, in 1976 the Transkei became the first homeland to take 'independence'. This timing is important since it marks a stark distinction between the liberation politics of the student uprisings in Soweto and the state-authorised 'independence' of the homeland. Matanzima ruled the Transkei until a coup d'état by ANC-aligned Major General Bantu Holomisa toppled him in 1987.

Matanzima's rule illustrates three characteristics of homeland government: political repression, the manipulation and betrayal of customary claims to chieftainship and elite clientelist corruption. The ANC and

Pan Africanist Congress of Azania were banned from 1963, for example, and Proclamation 400 gave Matanzima the power to institute a permanent state of emergency. This allowed him to exclude, arrest or deport all opposition in preparation for the 'elections' for independence in 1976, elections in which he won all but four seats, giving the Transkei government a veneer of democratic respectability (Streek and Wicksteed, 1981:13).

Matanzima continued to harass the opposition after independence. In 1979 he banned 34 organisations, including the Methodist Church, in which he was a lay preacher. He nationalised the church and established the United Methodist Church of Southern Africa, which immediately appropriated Methodist property and deported non-consenting ministers (Streek and Wicksteed, 1981). He also expelled the Federal Theological Seminary from the Transkei, accusing it of engaging in Black Consciousness mobilisation.

Like its self-governing predecessor, the 'independent' Transkeian Parliament comprised a majority of chiefs and a minority of elected officials, many of whom were also chiefs. The authority of chieftainship was protected by Transkei law. The chief minister's official powers included '[t]he division of existing black tribes, the amalgamation of black tribes, the constitution of new black tribes, and the recognition, appointment, conditions of service, discipline, retrenchment, deposition, dismissal and pensioning of paramount chiefs, chiefs and headmen' (Ritchken, 1995:155). Chieftainship was therefore an important currency of homeland legitimacy and, paradoxically, the civil arm of homeland administration had tremendous powers over the appointment and treatment of local chiefs. In the process, hereditary or customary assertions of chieftainship were alternately undermined and supported by bureaucratic-political controls.

Matanzima's own chiefly standing was seriously inflated by the apartheid government. The son of a minor chief of the amaHala tribe in Emigrant Thembuland, he took up his chieftainship after completing his studies. Two years later he was appointed to the pre-homeland Bunga or black council by the South African authorities, who recognised his ambition. With their support Matanzima secured recognition for increasingly powerful 'traditional' positions against the opposition of his more senior family members, the Thembu paramount, Sabata Dalindyebo, and Nelson Mandela (Streek and Wicksteed, 1981:112). First he was appointed as a regional chief. In 1966 he was made paramount, putting him on a par with Dalindyebo despite there being no precedent in customary law for such an elevation. He was then appointed chief minister and, upon independence, state president of the Transkei. He employed as prime minister his brother George, who had been struck off the attorneys roll in 1963 for misappropriating funds and making false statements under oath.

The Transkeian Constitution gave Matanzima the tools to harass and demote his customary senior, Dalindyebo. In 1976 Dalindyebo's allowance was withdrawn on an administrative pretext after he argued against independence. Soon afterwards he was offered the position of state president, in what Barry Streek and Richard Wicksteed (1981:322) called 'an effort to neutralise his power by placing him in an apolitical office that was easy to monitor'. Dalindyebo refused and from then on was subject to administrative and political harassment. In 1978 the Great Place of the paramountcy was raided by military police. In 1979 he was charged on a number of counts and, despite massive popular support, was convicted of the treasonable offence of speaking against the independence of the Transkei. He was stripped of his parliamentary seat and his chieftainship. In 1980 he went into exile with the ANC (Sachs, 2009).

Matanzima had almost complete control over the Transkeian government until he was deposed by force. Most local chiefs recognised their dependence on him and fell into line. The civil service was massively inflated by clientelist appointments and, by 1978, some 64 000 people were employed by the Transkeian state. As Streek and Wicksteed (1981) note, this was twice as many civil servants as there were in Botswana at the same time. This growth was funded by the South African fiscus, which contributed nearly R1 billion in the first four years of Transkei's 'independence'.

Massive South African investment in homeland military power backfired when Holomisa, a general in the Transkei military, staged his coup d'état in 1987. Holomisa, a member of the Transkeian elite and the son of a minor chief, was not eligible for chieftainship. He ruled the territory until 1994, when it was reincorporated into South Africa. Aligned with the ANC in exile, he allowed it to establish bases from which it organised excursions into South African territory.

The exiled ANC's engagement in homeland politics in the 1980s also bore fruit in the Transkei in the person of Patekile Holomisa, heir to the amaHegebe chieftainship and married to Matanzima's daughter. By the time he was called home to assume his chieftainship after graduating with degrees in law and politics from the universities of Transkei and Natal in 1985, he had been radicalised by his involvement in student politics. Unsure about what to do, he went to visit the ANC in exile to ask for advice (O'Malley, 1996). The ANC counselled him to take up his chieftainship and participate as an inside agent in the Transkei legislature. He did this while setting up a law practice in the capital, Mthatha. Like many other liberation-oriented chiefs he joined Contralesa soon after its establishment in 1987. Two years later he took over its leadership and remained at its helm until 2013. A relatively senior member of the ANC, he became a leading figure in negotiating a future for traditional leadership.

KWAZULU, MANGOSUTHU BUTHELEZI AND INKATHA

Like Matanzima, Buthelezi, chief minister of KwaZulu, was an ambitious and relatively junior member of a royal household, in this case the Zulu one. But he was also, at least in his earlier career, both charismatic and publicly aligned with the ANC, whose Youth League he joined in 1975. With ANC president Oliver Tambo's blessing, he launched a 'cultural movement' called Inkatha. It was to be the ANC's Trojan horse – a vehicle to mobilise support for the ANC within the KwaZulu homeland.

While Matanzima was working to undermine Dalindyebo's chieftain-ship, Buthelezi was trying to rein in a figure with much greater historical stature – his uncle, Zulu King Goodwill Zwelithini. In 1979 Zwelithini formed an organisation to rival Inkatha, calling it Inala. Buthelezi, with the powers of Parliament behind him, castigated the king publicly in the National Assembly and threatened to cut off his stipend. He also threat-ened to amend the homeland and Inkatha constitutions to prevent the king from taking part in politics (Sparks, 1994). From that time onwards Buthelezi referred to himself as the traditional prime minister to the king. Drawing on an enduring trope around traditional authority, Buthelezi said the king was 'above politics' and had therefore to be represented by his prime minister. This effectively deprived the king of the claim to represent himself or the interests of the Zulu nation.

Buthelezi proved to be exceptionally skilled in his use of Zulu ethnic nationalism and the mobilisation of the imaginary of Zulu monarchy from Shaka to the present. Assertions of ethnic nationalism were rooted in an idealised Chief Shaka and a precolonial polity that was never as belit-tled or reduced as its southern and eastern neighbours. But this ethnic nationalism would have been impotent without Inkatha's control over the resources of the army and police, South African government funding and clientelist relationships in the homeland.

While the ANC disapproved of this ethnic nationalism, Buthelezi aligned with the movement and its vision of national liberation in many respects. From the 1970s onwards the National Party (NP) repeatedly tried, to no avail, to get Buthelezi to accept independence for KwaZulu. In the mid-1980s they approached him to be a black representative on the interracial council they sought to establish as an extension of the Tricameral system. Buthelezi refused again (Friedman, 1993).

In other homelands the mobilisation of the youth and the involvement of the UDF led to what could be called local skirmishes and intergenerational conflict. In KwaZulu the result was more explosive and exceptionally violent. Seeking support and thanks from the ANC for his resistance to some aspects of homeland policy, Buthelezi instead encountered increasing criticism from the UDF 'comrades' of the ways in which Inkatha colluded with the South African state. The enmity between the two grew rapidly. Soon after its formation in 1983 the UDF began mobilising actively in the Natal Midlands, hoping to 'neutralise' Buthelezi.

Clashes between UDF-aligned 'comrades' and Inkatha claimed 3 000 lives even before Mandela was released from prison (Waldmeir, 1997) and the violence escalated after the ANC was unbanned (Gloppen, 1997). This conflict, like that in Bushbuckridge, was not only about political affiliation; it was also about age, social mobility, rural–urban divides and patriarchal authority (Adam and Moodley, 1993). In response to the growing politicisation of the youth and their escape from rural bonds of traditional affiliation, Inkatha went on a recruitment drive that forced 'virtually every teacher, nurse, policeman and public servant in KwaZulu to join the movement or withhold employment if they did not' (Waldmeir, 1997:174).

Unlike those of other homeland leaders, Buthelezi's ambitions extended beyond the leadership of a future KwaZulu-Natal (KZN) province. He also had national political aspirations, which, in the following two decades, produced contradictory claims, one on the basis of Zulu nationalism and the other on the basis of a secular, black, moderate, free-market agenda.

On 4 July 1990, five months after the ANC was unbanned, Buthelezi relaunched Inkatha as the Inkatha Freedom Party (IFP). It was a political party that would seek, he said, to establish a nationwide support base. It was the vehicle for intervention outside of the homelands and opposition to the ANC. Almost immediately, violence between ANC and IFP supporters erupted in the Natal Midlands and on the Witwatersrand, with the South African government providing covert support, arms and funding to the IFP.

The South African security establishment's Civil Cooperation Bureau planted car bombs, assassinated ANC officials, funded and armed urban vigilante groups and gave support to Inkatha to oppose the 'comrades'. Allegations of a 'third force' were substantiated by revelations in August 1991 of police support for IFP violence and government funding for IFP activities. These were subsequently corroborated in both the Truth and Reconciliation Commission (TRC) and Goldstone Commission reports (Adam and Moodley, 1993).

ANC responsibility for the violence has received little attention but there is a great deal of evidence, for example, that Harry Gwala, who commanded the Midlands region, used hit squads (Sparks, 1994). His membership of the South African Communist Party (SACP) was suspended as a result, but only in 1994, when his work was complete. At the opening of the Multiparty Negotiations Process (MPNP) the IFP claimed that of '312 IFP branch chairmen in the Natal Midlands in 1987, only two were still alive in 1991' (NA NEG 1/5/3/5A).

THE ANC, THE HOMELANDS AND THE CHIEFS

The ANC's response to the establishment of the homelands included public condemnation and a successful campaign to prevent them from being recognised internationally. But the ANC had little direct presence in the homelands from the 1950s until the issue was put on the table at the movement's 1985 Consultative Conference in Zambia. With some form of political change increasingly likely, and with the mobilisation of the young comrades and the UDF, the ANC decided to pay more attention to building up its structures and alliances to fight homeland rule.

In the same year Simon Skosana sought 'independence' for the homeland of KwaNdebele. According to William Beinart (2001:266) there was 'clear evidence of security police involvement' as Skosana attacked communities resisting incorporation. A group of traditional leaders opposed to Skosana formed Contralesa as a political platform. Harassed by the security police, they sought the protection of the UDF. By 1989 Contralesa could claim the support of eighty per cent of chiefs in Transkei and fifty per cent in KZN (Hendricks and Ntsebeza, 1999).

The strategic alliance between the ANC and traditional leaders, which gave the ANC a foothold in the rural areas, was formed against the background of an ongoing debate within the ANC about the status of the institution of traditional leadership. Some within the movement contended that the institution was anachronistic as well as contrary to principles of equality and democratic accountability. Perhaps the best-known advocate of this position was Govan Mbeki, father of Thabo Mbeki who would later become South Africa's second democratic president. Govan Mbeki famously wrote:

> If Africans have had Chiefs, it was because all human societies have had them at one stage or another. But when a people have developed to a stage which discards chieftainship, when their social development contradicts the need for such an institution, then to force it on them is not liberation but enslavement. (Quoted in Ntsebeza, 2006:259)

The influence of Marxist thinking on this argument is apparent and SACP elements within the ANC were most likely to be critical of the institution. Many within the UDF leadership also followed this view. Peter Mokaba, a former president of the ANC Youth League, for example, grew up under traditional authority in Lebowa. He was very clear about the future of chiefs under the ANC: 'We intend removing the tribal chiefs as soon as possible,' he said. 'We have called on them to resign. Our ultimate intention is to allow the people to govern themselves' (Van Kessel quoted in Ntsebeza, 2006:26). Despite this stand, Mokaba was also instrumental in setting up Contralesa.

Official ANC policy until the late 1980s was against the institution of chieftainship. The movement declared in its 1988 draft Constitutional Principles that traditional leadership was anachronistic and should be abolished with the advent of democracy (Muriaas, 2002:9). The ANC also stated that 'because of its relationship with the apartheid regime, there would be no place for chieftaincy in a democratic South Africa' (Williams, 2009:194). Despite this official position, the ANC and its allies came to be deeply invested in chiefly politics.

The situation in Lebowa was just one example of how the ANC was perceived to be allied to militant youth groups, although it was aware that their activities had alienated tribal hierarchies, older people and the business elite (Muriaas, 2002:91). As Fred Hendricks and Lungisile Ntsebeza (1999:107) write, 'the youth and civic movements found the rapprochement between the liberation movement and their former enemies particularly repulsive'. Where local activists viewed chiefs as the puppets of apartheid, the returning ANC exiles were 'more concerned with pursuing a more broad-based liberation movement' (Hendricks and Ntsebeza, 1999:107) and, in pursuit of that aim, attempted to form what Ntsebeza (2006:260) calls its 'desperate and naïve collaboration'.

The official tone of the ANC's relationship with chiefs began to change in about 1988, the year in which a Contralesa delegation went to Lusaka. Afterwards, Jacob Zuma wrote an article in the ANC's *Urambulo* magazine criticising Govan Mbeki's position. Zuma proposed 'the continuation of the institution of chieftainship, *but under our control*' (Ntsebeza, 2006:264, emphasis added). The ANC gave Contralesa its formal blessing that year and 'welcomed the chiefs back to the people'. Where they had portrayed chiefs as collaborators in the past, they now started appearing in ANC rhetoric as patriotic victims of apartheid (Muriaas, 2002:89).

The ANC was particularly worried about the mobilisation of Zulu ethnic nationalism in KwaZulu. In the late 1980s the still-jailed Natal leadership of the ANC met to discuss Inkatha's portrayal of the ANC as 'anti-Zulu, Indian-controlled and Xhosa-led'.[1] It settled on a strategy to counter this representation by giving prominence to Zulu members of the ANC, including Chief Albert Luthuli. In a change of strategy, Mandela's stance on traditional leadership was decisive. On his release from prison he went out of his way to mobilise Zulu speakers and, in doing this, drew on the same symbolic resources used by Buthelezi. In 1990, for example, he was a prominent presence at a Sonke Festival to mark the 165th anniversary of the death of Shaka. There, hundreds of *amabutho* or warriors participated, wearing traditional dress, and the 'people's poet', Mzwakhe Mbuli, 'stirred up the crowd' with tales of Zulu military success (Klopper, 1996:54). The ANC also began to contest the allegiance of King Zwelithini (Klopper, 1996).

It was not until the ANC was officially unbanned that it attempted to set up structures in the rural areas. Then, paradoxically, '[e]fforts were made to allay the anxieties of local businessmen and leading figures in the ANC appeared to embrace precisely the chiefs and homeland leaders whom the youths and some migrants regarded as principle foes' (Delius, 1996:207). By the early 1990s the chiefs and homeland governments had, on the whole, held onto a fragile rope of control over the rural areas and 'Bantustan leaders, for their part, realised that they needed to fortify their power bases or risk being sidelined' (Ritchken, 1995:413).

As the negotiations dawned, homeland leaders followed one of two strategies to try to maintain some of their power. In the first they tried to retain the leadership of sovereign or semi-sovereign territories. Buthelezi, Lucas Mangope and 'Oupa' Gqozo took this route (Elazar, 1994). The KwaZulu government sought a system in which a future KZN would be a constitutional monarchy and a strong regional power with a considerable degree of autonomy. Bophuthatswana's Mangope went even further, saying, in a speech at the plenary of the second Convention for a Democratic South Africa (Codesa), that he 'would like to continue as we are; an autonomous and independent country, preferably with extended borders and continued friendly and cordial relations with our neighbours' (COD NA61 Volume 102). The Ciskei presented a vision of a 'federation of states' in which the 'diversity of cultures and regional interests could be reflected' (COD NA61).

In a second strategy, traditional leaders who were members of or affiliated to the ANC actively sought to have the homelands reincorporated into a territorially unified South Africa. Among them were the leaders of the Transkei and Venda, as well as traditional and homeland leaders from many of the self-governing territories (Friedman, 1993) who were willing to concede territorial sovereignty but still sought to retain power through the institution of traditional leadership itself.

A PLACE IN THE NEGOTIATIONS?

Despite the early consensus outlined in the previous chapter about who could participate as political entities, rather unexpectedly the traditional leaders came to assert their right to participate as political negotiators. As a result, they contributed to framing the new Constitution and thus were able to secure constitutional recognition of traditional leadership.

From the first Codesa planning meeting in November 1991 Buthelezi, as leader of the IFP, requested that the Zulu king participate with a full delegation. The KwaZulu government, also under the leadership of Buthelezi, petitioned for representation too. Since KwaZulu was not 'independent', the homeland government was not eligible for participation. Since neither the king nor the KwaZulu government was eligible, the IFP was asked to make a formal submission on the matter (COD NA61).

At a planning meeting just two days before Codesa began the IFP repeated its demand for the king's participation. When the planning meeting failed to reach agreement, it was decided to take the question up again after Codesa I. As a result of this 'slight' to 'the Zulu people', as the IFP termed it, Buthelezi personally boycotted Codesa I, sending Frank Mdlalose, the man who would become the first premier of what was to become KZN, to represent the party. In his opening speech Mdlalose complained that 'the rejection of His Majesty the King of the Zulus by Codesa was … very painful … The Zulu Nation is excluded'. Buthelezi, as 'traditional Prime Minister to His Majesty', had no choice but to stand by him in his exclusion (COD NA61).

Buthelezi, with his influence over the king, the IFP and the KwaZulu government, was a dangerous man to leave out of the negotiations. Given the spiralling violence in Rand townships and the Natal Midlands, the issue of the king's participation could seriously derail negotiations. On 2 February 1992 Codesa's Management Committee established a subcommittee to look into the matter. Its terms of reference were to 'investigate and make recommendations' on the 'participation of the Zulu King and other traditional leaders'. The inclusion of 'other' traditional leaders was the result of an ANC intervention. The subcommittee was mandated to 'ask experts and scholars to present on the matter' and to pay attention to 'pre-colonial states and governmental structures as well as historical, cultural and ethnic considerations and comparable institutions in Africa and elsewhere' (COD NA61).

The subcommittee, chaired by Revd T.J. Mohapi of QwaQwa's Dikwankwetla Party, had three other members: Mdlalose; N.J. Mahlangu, a representative of Intando Yesizwe Party from KwaNdebele; and M.J. Mahlangu of the United People's Front from Lebowa. Thus, homeland representatives were given the task of deciding the future participation of traditional leaders. M.J. Mahlangu, the committee member most sympathetic to the ANC, was not available for the first meeting. The rest of the committee invited IFP affiliate N.M. Melakane to participate in his stead.

On 5 February 1992 the subcommittee met for the first time and sought to resolve the question once and for all. By the time of the meeting, applications for participation had also been received from Ingwenya D.M. Mabhoko, paramount chiefs of QwaQwa, Contralesa, Lebowa College of Magoshi and Transkei kings and chiefs. The meeting briefly discussed the principle of participation at Codesa and the application of the Zulu king and traditional leaders, taking note of 'certain submissions' (COD NA61 Volume 20/2), and came up with a simple recommendation: 'Recognising that participation in Codesa is primarily the prerogative of political parties, administrations and organisations, but in view of the important role played by hereditary leaders in the country's past and present day, it is recommended to the management committee that ... hereditary leaders be allowed to participate fully in Codesa.'

The subcommittee recommended that the Zulu king should have a full delegation and that a senior hereditary leader should lead a full delegation from each self-governing and TBVC homeland state. The make-up of these delegations, it suggested, should be determined by homeland administrations. It also recommended that traditional leaders should become part of the management committee and join the working groups as delegates with advisors. This would have doubled the size of Codesa. Showing its political colours, the subcommittee recommended that Contralesa itself not be represented. Instead, members of Contralesa could be included in regional delegations at the discretion of homeland administrations.

The subcommittee submitted its report to the Management Committee on 10 February. It was not well received (COD NA61 Volume 103). The Management Committee overruled the report and Colin Eglin of the Democratic Party, Pravin Gordhan of the Transvaal-Natal Indian Congress, the government's Gerrit Viljoen, and Z. Titus, Transkei representative and chair of the Planning Committee, were asked to redraft the terms of reference.

The new terms acknowledged that 'it is accepted that all the people of South Africa ought to be accorded the right to contribute to the negotiating process of Codesa on a meaningful basis' and also that 'Codesa is made up of political parties, political organisations and administrations'. A contingent of high-powered delegates, mostly allied to the ANC, was added to the original four-member subcommittee. They included the SACP's Joe Slovo, Eglin, T.T. Matanzima from the Transkei and the ANC's Zuma. The new terms of reference committed the resuscitated subcommittee to report on the following: '2.1.1 Whether (a) the King of the Zulus, and (b) other traditional leaders should be given the opportunity of participating in the negotiating process of Codesa, and 2.1.2 if so, the appropriate form of such participation, including any other options within which they might be accorded an opportunity to participate on a meaningful basis' (COD NA61 Volume 20/3).

At its first meeting, on 24 February, the subcommittee invited submissions from the heads of all delegations and from expert academic lawyers, historians and anthropologists, to address the background, legitimacy and future of the institution of traditional leadership. In addition, both Viljoen and Mandela were invited to give evidence. Rather strategically, Mandela never did so (COD NA61 Volume 20/3). Six traditional leaders from each region and a six-member delegation from Contralesa were invited to present their cases on 18 and 19 March in a closed hearing.

The submissions, expert reports and verbatim transcripts of these two days reveal a concerted effort by Zuma and Slovo to undermine IFP demands and to reformulate the possible recognition of traditional leadership within a ceremonial register. Zuma chaired the hearings and the Zuma–Slovo team put three questions to each delegation. The first was whether traditional leaders are equal in status or whether there is a national hierarchy of chiefs. This produced a fascinating oral history of chieftainship that recounted colonial and apartheid interventions in the structures of traditional authority. The English terminology proved to be problematic – king, paramount chief, chief and headman were all colonial designations.[2] Although most traditional leaders agreed that it probably did not make sense for senior traditional leaders to participate on political terms in the negotiations, they stressed that if the Zulu king were to do so they would insist on participating. The experts, on the other hand, stressed the unique de facto power of the Zulu kingdom in comparison with other traditional formations.

For their second question, Zuma assumed the position of traditional insider seeking to protect the institution of traditional leadership from the denigrations of politics. Were traditional leaders not 'above politics', he asked, a question that was a direct jibe at Buthelezi. The king had been left out of the earlier KwaZulu indaba because, as Buthelezi said at the time, the king should be above politics.

In general, the experts did not agree with Zuma. Most traditional leaders, however, did. Chiefs, they believed, should be 'beyond reproach' and exercise a 'divine responsibility of nation-building'. To do this they needed to be 'mediators and not politicians' (COD NA61 Volume 103/2). Khoshi Mogashoa of the Lebowa delegation believed that 'Khoshi should be above politics. He should not be seen to be siding with any of the political parties ... So we wouldn't like to see magoshis rubbing shoulders with commoners'. Chief Patekile Holomisa, on behalf of Contralesa, suggested that they could represent the kings 'without having to have their Kings or Paramount Chiefs coming by themselves'.

If Zuma was playing good cop in this interrogation, Slovo, the Marxist, was the bad cop, speaking as an outsider to the traditional world in which Zuma was so patently comfortable. His question was absolutely central to modern political principles. Who and what, he asked, do you represent? The most common answer was that traditional leaders represent those who are not politically aligned: the old, the rural, the ignorant, the 'silent rural majority', as the chiefs put it; those who turned to them rather than to the political parties (COD NA61 Volume 103/2). There was an implicit threat to the political parties in many of the answers: we represent people who do not follow your politics. And, they implied, we are in a position to block your campaigning in the areas over which we have control.

These lines of questioning sought to differentiate political and traditional roles. If they had been successful, the differentiation might have founded a separation between traditional and political authority that could have granted the former ceremonial roles that were not in competition with government.

But in the first signs of tension between the ANC-aligned traditional leaders and the ANC principals within the negotiations, the Transkei delegation made it clear that it was they rather than the ANC who were the appropriate representatives of rural people. After pointing out that 'national liberation movements' have acknowledged that 'there is a place for traditional leaders in this country', they warned that 'we have 90% following in rural areas. Political parties in rural areas have insignificant following, they shouldn't deceive themselves' (COD NA61).

Along the way the hearings also revealed the low levels of local power and legitimacy of many of the traditional leaders. Many bemoaned their loss of power and spoke about people in rural areas who no longer acknowledged their authority or respected their role. In his presentation, Chief Samuel Dickenson Nxumalo of the Ximoko Progressive Party from Gazankulu argued that most traditional leaders were just creatures of the state. This complaint was sometimes coupled with the hope that participation in Codesa would lead to the redress and rebuilding of the institution; a way of claiming dignity back from the manipulations of white rule and the disrespect of the youth.

Neither the Zulu king nor the IFP appeared before the committee. Instead, Mdlalose made some 'remarks' in which he recounted repeated NP assurances to Buthelezi that both the king and the KwaZulu government would be able to attend the negotiations. They had been betrayed.

On 30 March 1992 the subcommittee announced some in-principle decisions. The first was that Codesa should be as inclusive as possible and that the principle of participation 'has widespread support'. The second was that the same principle of participation should be applied equally to the Zulu king and other traditional leaders, thus resolving, to the advantage of the ANC, the question of the equality of traditional leaders, no matter what their historical trajectory. The meeting noted that the nature and form of participation was still under discussion (COD NA61 Volume 73/43) and the subcommittee gave itself a further month to report back to the Management Committee.

Conflicts over the relationships between the ANC, traditional leaders and homeland governments were by no means restricted to the issue of the Zulu king and the IFP. They also flared up in relation to the two other homelands that sought to avoid reincorporation into a unified South Africa. The ANC and Contralesa accused Bophuthatswana and the Ciskei of manipulating and excluding legitimate traditional leaders and of fronting others who did not have popular support.

When approached to constitute a delegation of traditional leaders, Bophuthatswana's president, Mangope, sent a personal submission. Rather contentiously, the subcommittee agreed to accept it as 'a reply from a traditional leader as President L M Mangope is himself a traditional leader' (COD NA61). At the end of February Codesa received a letter from Samuel Morwagabusi II Mankuroane, who called himself the 'deposed Paramount Chief of the Batlhaping-Taung', deposed, that is, by Mangope. He launched a scathing attack on Mangope's failure to sign the Declaration of Intent and his 'suicidal' attempt to retain independence. Furthermore, he maintained that if traditional leaders were to be represented at Codesa, he was the legitimate representative (COD NA61 Volume 103/2).

There was a more dangerous tussle between the ANC and the Ciskei over Paramount Chief Sandile. In February 1992 the Ciskei delegation laid a formal complaint against the ANC for trying to undermine the sovereignty and integrity of the Ciskei. They presented to Codesa's Management Committee documents from the ANC's Border region that outlined its strategy to 'weaken [Brigadier] Gqozo's position at Codesa, isolate him politically … bring about an interim administration in Ciskei, and consequently weaken South Africa's position at Codesa' (COD NA61 Volume 3).

The Ciskei sent a delegation to the March subcommittee meeting that excluded Chief Sandile, arguing that the king was 'above politics'. But on 18 March the subcommittee read a letter of complaint sent by Sandile, who arrived at Kempton Park to present his case himself. The subcommittee decided that Codesa was not mandated to solve this problem of representation and the best they could do was listen to and remunerate the travel expenses of both Ciskei delegations. The official Ciskei delegation sought the full participation of traditional leaders at Codesa. Chief Sandile, on the other hand, wanted kings to be observers only. He said that the committee should 'regard the traditional leaders of South Africa as ... part of the broad liberatory and reform movements' (COD NA61 Volume 3/2).

The ANC's involvement in affairs of traditional authority within the Ciskei continued after the hearing. On 6 April it held what it called a People's Assembly in King William's Town, which passed a series of 'laws'. One read:

> The People's Assembly, Noting the current harassment of traditional leaders in the Ciskei, and in particular the disgraceful treatment handed out to the paramount chief by the Ciskei Administration, And believing that the status of legitimate chiefs should not be undermined by the petty politics of an illegitimate Bantustan Administration, Therefore resolves to Censure the Ciskei Administration, And further resolves to reaffirm the status of the paramount chief and accord him all due respects as a traditional leader of the people. (COD NA61 Volume 103/2)

On 30 March the IFP vented its frustrations in a submission to the Management Committee titled 'The Removal of Some Major Obstacles to the Achievement of a Climate Conducive to Peaceful Negotiations'. The threatening document referred to the 'strong feelings' of Zulu people that they were being marginalised in the negotiations. 'Why exclude the Zulu qua Zulu?' it asked. 'Let His Majesty the King of the Zulus and the KwaZulu government take their seats at Codesa ... If the demands for participation are not met without further ado ... the unfathomable repercussions is (sic) not only abhorrent but frightening' (COD NA61 Volume 22/17).

Against the background of the bloodshed in Natal and the East Rand, the IFP threat worked. The Management Committee meeting on 27 April was the scene of trade-offs. Mdlalose announced that the IFP agreed to withdraw the application of the KwaZulu government to participate in the negotiations. On the same day the subcommittee finally made recommendations to the Management Committee. 'Traditional leaders should have participation at Codesa, which should take the form of one delegation from each of the four provinces, consisting of 12 delegates and 5 advisors' each (COD NA61 Volume 22/17). But this was a pyrrhic victory for the IFP. The subcommittee had yet to determine the composition of the delegations and Joe Slovo, attempting to buy time, wanted it recorded that no agreement could be reached before outstanding submissions had been reviewed. These questions were never answered as Codesa came to a fractious end at its second plenary.

At the end of May 1992, at the ANC's first National Conference on South African soil since its unbanning, a decision was made to turn to mass action. In a document entitled 'Ready to Govern: ANC Policy Guidelines for a Democratic South Africa', the ANC conceded that 'the institution of chieftainship has played an important role in the history of our country and chiefs will continue to have an important role to play'.[3] It was the movement's first official recognition of the future of the institution of traditional leadership.

Noting that the powers of the chiefs would be subject to the Constitution, it provides for 'an appropriate structure consisting of traditional leaders to be created by law, in order to advise parliament on matters relevant to customary law and other matters relating to the powers and functions of chiefs'. It also promised that the functions of chiefs would only be changed after consultation with them. The actual functions of traditional leaders were, however, delegated, advisory and ceremonial. The document also listed traditional leaders among members of civil society along with civic associations, trade unions, religious groups and women's groups. To the traditional leaders of Codesa the ANC made it clear that 'the price of this accommodation was that chieftaincy had to be "transformed" so as to make it consistent with the new democratic political order' (Williams, 2009:191).

CHIEFS' PARTICIPATION IN THE MULTIPARTY NEGOTIATIONS PROCESS

As an olive branch to the IFP and in line with new ANC policy, four full provincial delegations of traditional leaders were invited to participate in the MPNP. From this point onwards debates about the future of traditional authority and customary law took place in three areas: at the Technical Committee on Fundamental Rights during the Transition (TC4) on the Bill of Rights, at the Negotiating Council about Constitutional Principles and in the constitutional committee that dealt with plans for provincial and local level government in a postapartheid order.

IRONIES OF PARTICIPATION

The composition of traditional authorities' delegations was problematic from the start. Each of the four provinces included a mix of 'independent' and self-governing homelands, some of which were for and some against reincorporation. Some were allied to the IFP, others to the ANC. The Cape delegation, for example, included both the Transkei and the Ciskei. Traditional leaders from Bophuthatswana and Venda were to share a delegation, though the former refused to send delegates (NA NEG 1/1/1 and 1/2/1/1). Two 'delegation leaders' from the Free State showed up at the first meeting of the Negotiating Council (NA NEG 1/5/2/3), and the Transvaal complained that there were more than six homelands in the area and five representatives could not cover them (NA NEG 1/2/1/1).

Contralesa, furious about the ANC's failure to champion its position, continued to demand independent representation[4] and it wasn't clear whether the Natal delegation represented traditional leaders or 'His Majesty's KwaZulu government'. Because it was not 'independent,' the KwaZulu government had not been invited to participate in the MPNP, but it insisted that it was present in the place of the traditional leader delegation (NA NEG 1/1/5). Bantu Holomisa then wrote to complain that if the KwaZulu administration was represented, all the other self-governing territories should be too (NA NEG 1/2/1/1).

When the 1994 election date was announced on 15 June 1993 the Concerned South Africans Group (COSAG) staged a symbolic walkout. The IFP, the KwaZulu government and the Conservative Party withdrew from negotiations and the Natal delegation left. As a result, Contralesa chiefs gained the upper hand within the remaining delegations. Before long the traditional leaders from the Cape, the Transvaal and the Orange Free State were working together for the extended recognition of traditional leadership and customary law.

The irony is that the IFP had put the issue on the table through its demands for the representation of the Zulu king. But with its withdrawal from the MPNP it was ANC-allied traditional leaders, brought into place to counteract the strength of the IFP, who articulated the needs of the institution of traditional leadership. They made two demands. The first was a right to customary law under the control of traditional leaders, immune from the equality clause. The second was for the inclusion of traditional leaders in the structures and institutions of the state. In both cases they had the support of the NP and the government delegation. Despite their political alliance with the ANC, they made demands to which the ANC was unwilling to concede.

TRADITIONAL COMMUNITIES, CUSTOMARY LAW AND GENDER

On 21 July 1993 the Negotiating Council debated the first full draft of the Bill of Rights. Chief Mwelo Nonkonyana of the Cape delegation asked why it included no mention of indigenous law. The ANC immediately pointed out that this was only a transitional Bill and that his concerns were covered under the rights to language and culture. Nonkonyana then raised a problem with equality, particularly as it related to gender. He pointed out that many traditional leaders had several wives and that under customary law women had different status depending on their order of marriage.

They are 'equal as women, however, in terms of our culture, they are not [equal] ... We don't want a situation,' he said, 'where we can be challenged ... and then the institution [of traditional leadership] will be gone, all our culture would be gone ...' (NA NEG 1/3/2/2/16).

Nonkonyana also commented on other clauses. Under 'detention' he pointed out that 'traditional communities' do not detain people and suggested that provision should be made for customary courts. Under 'property' he raised the issue of communal landownership and tenure. At the suggestion of the chair, the Cape Traditional Leaders made a formal submission on all these matters containing a general argument for the validity of indigenous law and the systems and precedents 'retained in the memories of traditional leaders and their councillors, their sons and their grandsons' (Corder Collection). The submission conceded the need for political rights for women and also that customary law would need to be codified again. But they were adamantly against gender equality in the social life of 'their communities'.

At the next meeting Nonkonyana contended that the equality principle should not apply to customary law at all. Speaking on behalf of the traditional leaders he said: 'We are objecting that only one set of fundamental human rights shall be applicable to all, even ourselves' (NA NEG 1/5/2/23). In response, the Planning Committee set up an ad hoc committee to help TC4 deal with these difficult debates. At the Negotiating Council meeting on 2 August the Cape Traditional Leaders, with the support of the government, suggested a new clause for the Bill of Rights. It read:

> Every traditional community shall have the right to exist as such and to maintain and develop its distinct cultural characteristic and identity and define its culture as a right. Every traditional community shall have the right to have its rules and customs accepted as binding by such communities. Membership of Traditional Communities shall be based on voluntary association provided that the authority of the Traditional Leader there, its own tradition and culture, is not undermined. (NA NEG 1/5/2/33)

The generally liberal technical committee was alarmed by this addition. The Planning Committee agreed to call in a series of experts, who were asked about the impact of the equality clause on customary law. But the expert reports were widely divergent and it seemed impossible to draft a compromise. The discussion was going nowhere until Sibongile Nene, the only black woman in the TC4, pointed out that this was a political rather than a legal question and that rural constituencies, and particularly women living under traditional authority, had yet to be consulted.

If traditional leadership really was as democratic as the chiefs were claiming, they should consult with their constituencies, including women.

She criticised the proposal that customary law should be applied on a voluntary basis or through freedom of association. Women who chose not to comply with customary law were likely to be discriminated against by their families, she said, and it is these women that a Bill of Rights should protect. Given that widespread independent consultation with women in rural communities was impossible in the few remaining months, she proposed a 'sunset clause' for customary law.

To allow this to happen, the Constitution would have been written to provide a limited or conditional exemption from the equality clause for two years. The ad hoc committee proposed a series of conditions for the exemption: If there was an inconsistency, equality would prevail in law. If a rule was in place it would stay in place until replaced by new legislation. Wherever possible, room would be made for 'free choice' in the application of customary law. And when the time of exemption was over the equality provision would apply in full.

News of the clause led to the first significant civil society mobilisation around a right in the draft constitution. Women's groups were extremely critical of the proposal and many women delegates, particularly from the ANC and its allies, began to mobilise civil society. Hundreds of letters began pouring in to the MPNP as women's organisations lobbied political parties.

Clearly the other traditional leaders were also not happy with the proposal. When Chief Gwadiso, the chiefs' representative on the ad hoc committee, came back from his consultations on 14 September 1993, he objected to the wording of the entire clause and particularly its voluntary provision (NA NEG 1/3/3/5/10). If people did not like a chief's authority, he said, they would have to go and live somewhere else. But the ad hoc committee argued him down and a slightly amended proposal was drafted and included in the tenth report of TC4 on 5 October. For the first time, customary law was included as a right in the Bill of Rights.

When the clause came up for ratification at the council, however, an unexpected new proposal was presented by Chief Netshimbupfe, legal advisor to the Transvaal delegation of traditional leaders. They wanted nothing short of full legal pluralism: two ways of life and law, territorially separated, and where neither civil law nor the Constitution would have the right to intervene in customary law. The customary law clause, he said, should be linked to the right to 'language and culture' rather than to 'freedom of association'. In this way, submission to customary law would be involuntary and entirely under the control of chiefs.

Gwadiso was unavailable for the subsequent ad hoc committee on 2 November and in his absence all but one member agreed that the clause did not belong in a Bill of Rights at all and, if it needed to exist, it should go somewhere else in the Constitution. If dropped, a simple addition could be made to the 'access to justice' right that would state that, within the provisions of the Bill of Rights, parties to a dispute could 'agree to the application of a system of customary law' (NA NEG 1/3/3/5/18). This would ensure that customary law was only applied on a voluntary basis and under the authority of the civil courts and not of traditional leaders.

The minutes of the Negotiating Council meeting on 16 November 1993, just one day before the interim constitution was finalised, record that: 'Discussion and debate proceeded around whether Clause 32 [Customary Law] should be included in the Bill of Rights . . . The proposal was put to the meeting after which the chairperson . . . ruled that there was neither consensus nor sufficient consensus and therefore the proposal stood down' (NA NEG 1/5/2/77). The chiefs had overplayed their hand. Having demanded more and more, they eventually failed to secure a right to customary law completely under their control and exempt from general law.

TRADITIONAL LEADERSHIP AND THE CONSTITUTIONAL PRINCIPLES

Early in the negotiations the ANC and the NP agreed that the parties would negotiate principles on the basis of which a final constitution could be drafted. Codesa went some way towards their development before its collapse. The 'Record of Understanding' of 26 September laid the ground for the resumption of multiparty talks and included a recommitment to 'principles of an interim government and an interim constitution', as well as to drafting a constitution 'based on principles agreed in prior multiparty negotiations' (Barnes and De Klerk, 2002:2).

The constitutional committee of the MPNP acknowledged the political importance of the principles in giving 'direction and security to all relevant interests', particularly 'with regard to future opportunities for political participation and other basic concerns' (NA NEG 1/3/2/2/). The MPNP spent three months listing, drafting and refining proposed principles and taking them to the Negotiating Council for decisions. On 2 July 1993, four months before the interim constitution was tabled, the Negotiating Council adopted 34 Constitutional Principles and set the date for the election.

The first ten principles provided for democratic constitutional government, regular elections, universal suffrage, a common voters' role and
proportional representation. They guaranteed basic human rights and
equality before the law and a constitutional basis for affirmative action.
Constitutional Principles 11 onwards are what Gloppen (1997:202) calls
'concessions to consociationalism'. They promised the participation of
minority political parties in the state, special majorities for constitutional
amendments, protection for languages and culture, collective rights of self-
determination and the recognition of traditional leadership and indigenous
and common law. Throughout the negotiations, parties formulated their
claims in the language of these non-negotiable principles.

Two principles deal specifically with traditional leadership and customary law. The first MPNP draft included one principle which 'recognised
traditional leaders ... in an appropriate manner in the constitution' and
made provision for the application of indigenous law 'to the extent it is
compatible with the provisions of the fundamental rights contained in
the constitution' (NA NEG 1/3/2/2/3). The IFP supported it but the ANC
and its allies disagreed, and it was only by 'sufficient consensus' that the
Planning Committee was asked to look at its implementation (NA NEG
1/5/2/12). The suggestion of alternative wording – 'The traditional leaders
will be directly represented in the constitution-making body and at all
levels of government' – was not accepted.

The Technical Committee on Constitutional Issues produced a
Supplementary Report dealing with customary law, its history, rationale
and the effects on it of economic and political change. Where such law is
recognised in international law, it noted, it is usually made consistent with
fundamental human rights. 'Where a society is in fact culturally plural
as in South Africa the recognition of indigenous law gives effect to the
accepted constitutional principle acknowledging cultural diversity' (NA
NEG 1/3/2/2/6). The technical committee envisaged a situation in which a
hybrid of customary and civil law could be developed, mostly at regional
level. It suggested a new formulation for the Constitutional Principle:

> The status of traditional leaders shall be recognised in the constitution.
> The constitution shall provide for the recognition of indigenous law
> and its application by the courts. Indigenous law shall be applied sub-
> ject to the provisions of the fundamental rights contained in the con-
> stitution and perhaps also to legislation dealing specifically therewith.
> (NA NEG 1/3/2/2/6)

This report elicited a lengthy but inconclusive debate on 18 June and again
the following week (NA NEG 1/5/2/15).

In the meantime, the draft 16th principle read: 'At each level of government there shall be democratic representation.' To take the traditional leader clause into account, an addition was suggested: 'with appropriate provisions for Traditional Leaders at each level where applicable' (NA NEG 1/5/2/17). These two matters were resolved in tense bilaterals over lunch on the day before the Constitutional Principles were finalised (NA NEG 1/5/2/23) and two principles were entrenched. Constitutional Principle 2.12 reads:

> The institution, status and role of Traditional Leadership, according to indigenous law, shall be recognised and protected in the Constitution. Indigenous law, like common law, shall be recognised and applied by the courts subject to the provisions of the fundamental rights contained in the constitution and to legislation dealing specifically therewith. (NA NEG 1/5/2/23)

Constitutional Principle 2.17 reads: 'At each level of government there shall be democratic representation. This principle shall not derogate from the provisions of principle 2.12' (NA NEG 1/5/2/23).

A PLACE FOR CHIEFS IN THE POSTAPARTHEID STATE?

With its work on the Constitutional Principles complete the Technical Committee on Constitutional Issues was responsible for drafting the sections on Parliament, the provinces and local government. Its initial report was debated on 28 July 1993. There, in their first coordinated action after the departure of their COSAG members, the traditional leaders noted that there was no provision in the report for traditional leaders in the national legislature, the constitution-making body or provincial or local government.

Although the technical committee was requested to 'consider and address this sensitive issue' (NA NEG 1/5/2/30), there was still no provision for traditional leaders in the next report. The reason, the committee said, was that the Constitutional Principles 'require legislative structures at all levels to be democratic'. Where an exception was provided for, they suggested, this was only relevant to the role of traditional leaders in local government, a section not yet completed (NA NEG 1/3/2/2/15).

The traditional leaders did not agree and on 13 August the MPNP received a 23-page submission titled 'Joint Position Paper Concerning [the] Role of Traditional Leaders' (NA NEG 1/4/2/14–18). It was signed by all three remaining traditional leader delegations at the negotiations: Cape, Orange Free State and Transvaal. They argued that traditional leadership is itself a democratic institution, that each level of government should have democratic representation and that provision had been made for traditional leadership. Therefore, 'provision should be made for effective participation of traditional leaders in every level of government'.

The Joint Position Paper outlined concrete proposals: Traditional leaders should participate in the Transitional Executive Council, which, like traditional leadership, is 'above party politics'. There, a special subcouncil should be established to protect their interests. It should provide for chiefs' 'conditions of service' and monitor measures, legislative or executive, which 'may affect traditional leader's powers during the transition' and, among other things, 'ensure that traditional leaders are not under the control of existing administrations'. An 'effective role' for traditional leaders should be provided for in the interim constitution (NA NEG 1/4/2/14–18).

Locally, their role should be to 'regulate and control relationships and social behaviour within a traditional community' rather than provide services. They suggested the continuity and establishment of further traditional authorities, those apartheid territorial and administrative structures for chiefly rule created in terms of the 1951 Bantu Authorities Act. These should be composed of traditional leaders as well as 'democratically elected traditional councils' to administer the affairs of the people. A long list of tasks was proposed for these traditional authorities, including land administration, the administration of justice, local policing, health services and soil conservation.

Among other suggestions was that traditional leaders who headed traditional authorities should be represented in district councils, which should be responsible for the provision of services. Another was that there should be a King's Council and the king should 'be entitled, in due fulfilment of his functions, to the loyalty, respect, support and obedience of every resident of the area for which he has jurisdiction'. He should maintain law and order in the area and have powers of arrest, search and seizure, secure the safety of travellers, deal with 'any pretend witchcraft or divination', prevent the gathering of men in times of lawlessness and detain and impound livestock.

Regionally, traditional authorities should be responsible for nation-building and be given significant legislative powers. The Joint Position Paper asserted that a new South Africa should be 'a united Kingdom' and traditional leaders of the country should 'oversee the fairly new process of the adoption of democracy'. For this, a national house of traditional leaders should be established. These demands outlined a continuation and also a significant extension of chiefly power on the basis of the consolidation of apartheid structures of rule.

In their report the traditional leaders made a point of indicating the damage they could do if their demands were not met and also implied, for the first time, that they had the IFP's support. In fact, many of the demands listed in the Joint Position Paper were inspired by earlier IFP demands. The document was littered with threats: they could mobilise traditional communities against political parties, they could refuse to allow political parties to canvass in their areas and they could disrupt local government events and services.

They took these proposals to a meeting with the Planning Committee on 5 October 1993. But the committee's members were evidently unfamiliar with the workings of rural governance and could not understand what the traditional leaders were demanding, particularly with respect to traditional authorities. They convened an ad hoc committee which, between 5 and 20 October, worked to break the proposals down into what was and was not constitutionally relevant, and to clarify which demands were for retaining current roles of traditional leadership and which would involve their extension.

In the meantime, the competencies of national and regional government came before the Negotiating Council. Richard Spitz and Matthew Chaskalson (2000) argue that after the customary law clause was dropped from the Bill of Rights, indigenous and customary law were added to the areas of provincial competence. This was, they suggest, 'a deliberate decision by the ANC to induce Inkatha to enter elections' (2000:159).

The following week the ad hoc committee produced a discussion document in which all the demands about non-statutory bodies such as *imbizos* and king's councils were dropped. Traditional authorities already existed in law and 'there is no threat at this stage that bodies similar to these may be disbanded' (NA NEG 1/4/3/17). The committee believed it was too early to discuss district councils. That left the issues of national and regional representation. The latter was particularly difficult: should bodies of traditional leaders have veto rights over legislation and be part of the legislation-making process? Alternatively, should they have a lesser advisory function that could nonetheless delay legislation that pertained to issues of traditional authority?

In a final report, issued on 20 October, it was suggested that traditional councils should be democratically elected, a major concession to the ANC; that traditional leaders be represented at district councils; that regional houses have full legislative powers over matters pertaining to traditional leadership, traditional authorities and customary law; and that a proposed national house of traditional leaders should have the same powers (NA NEG 1/4/7/10). The next day the group demanded that if regional and national houses were unacceptable, traditional leaders should occupy forty per cent of regional legislature seats and an additional thirty per cent of senate or parliamentary seats (NA NEG 1/5/7).

It looked for a while as though traditional leaders might become part of all governance structures, which would have been a massive extension of their powers. The first debate in the Negotiating Council was inconclusive (NA NEG 1/5/2/61) and the next was positively fractious. The minutes of the meeting of 2 November note that 'notwithstanding the apparent agreement' traditional leaders still disagreed with the regional and national powers proposed, as did the parties (NA NEG 1/3/2/2/26). It was agreed that further bilateral meetings were necessary. On 8 November the council made it very clear that traditional authorities should not constitute or be construed to mean local government. The national and regional houses remained contested too (NA NEG 1/4/2/14–18). The council was given until 11 November to come up with a solution.

After a rush of bilaterals the Negotiating Council passed Resolution 34 on 11 November (NA NEG 1/5/6). Under its terms all matters relating to customary law would be dealt with by statute. Traditional authorities would continue to exist and exercise their functions 'in terms of indigenous law'. There would be elected local government with political responsibility for service provision, but hereditary leaders in the area would be ex officio members of local government. The chair of the local government would be elected from the local government council.

A regional house of traditional leaders could be established in those provinces with traditional authorities, to which all legislation pertaining to traditional leaders and indigenous law must be referred for consideration and comment. But its highest power would only be to delay legislation for 30 days. A national Council of Traditional Leaders, consisting of not more than 20 people, could be established from representatives of regional houses. Again, relevant legislation should be passed to them for comment, but they could not delay legislation from being passed by the National Assembly. It would be an advisory body only, from which 'The State President may seek ... advice on matters of National Interest' (NA NEG 1/5/6). A week later, when the interim constitution was finalised, a new 'traditional authorities' chapter was included to reflect this resolution.

Despite the many concessions to provincial government and traditional leadership in the text of the interim constitution, the main parties to violence remained outside the negotiating process and opposed to the elections. The leaders of Bophuthatswana and the Ciskei prepared to defend their independence with the help of the white right, and KZN remained a stumbling block to territorial unification.

In the meantime the Restoration and Extension of South African Citizenship Act (No. 196 of 1993) returned South African citizenship to those who had been denied it by homeland 'independence' and gave citizenship to children born of parents who had had homeland citizenship (Klaaren, 2000:11), thus removing some of the spoiling power of homeland leaders. It also provided an administrative structure for TBVC residents to participate in the April 1994 elections. The changes did not, however, prevent the IFP from hampering the work of the Independent Electoral Commission.

In a further move, the ANC approached the Zulu king, promising him significant concessions that included allowing the Royal House to appoint its own advisors and install all chiefs in KZN (Klopper, 1996). This would have seriously undermined Buthelezi's control over symbols of royalty as well as the clientelist relationships he had established with chiefs in the homeland. The threat probably played an important part in Buthelezi's eventual decision to participate in the elections.

In a dramatic last-minute move, Buthelezi, Mandela and Frederik W. de Klerk signed an agreement on 19 April 1994. It included the following:

> The undersigned parties agree to recognise and protect the institution, status and role of the constitutional position of the King of the Zulus and the Kingdom of KwaZulu, which institutions shall be provided for in the Provincial Constitution of KwaZulu/Natal immediately after the holding of the said elections.

And

> Any outstanding issues in respect of the King of the Zulus and the 1993 Constitution as amended will be addressed by way of international mediation which will commence as soon as possible after the said elections.[5]

A week later, on 27 April 1994, South Africa held its first democratic national elections.

LIMITING THE PLACE OF TRADITIONAL LEADERS UNDER DEMOCRACY?

Only political parties were represented in the post-1994 Constitutional Assembly (CA), which was dominated by the ANC, with its nearly sixty-three per cent majority. The NP had twenty per cent and the IFP just ten per cent. Mandela was inaugurated as South Africa's first black president and, in an act of political inclusiveness, appointed De Klerk and Buthelezi as deputy presidents in a government of national unity. In the newly established province of KZN, the ANC was unable to secure a majority and install Zuma as its premier, as it had hoped. Instead, the IFP won a little over fifty per cent of the provincial vote, with the ANC winning thirty-two per cent (Muriaas, 2002).

With a significant majority in the CA it was to be expected that the ANC would try to reduce the place and entitlements of traditional leaders. It did, but its attempts were not very successful. Peace between the ANC and the IFP was short lived. The KZN government rushed to write a provincial constitution, hoping it would supersede the national one, but the text was 'unceremoniously thrown out' by the brand new Constitutional Court (Spitz and Chaskalson, 2000:162). The Court's main reason was that the draft provincial constitution allowed for 'traditional authorities in some places to substitute for democratically elected local governments' (Goodenough, 2002:29). In frustration, the IFP withdrew from negotiations once again, even as it continued to govern KZN and participate in Parliament. Buthelezi retained his deputy presidency.

There were two reasons why the powers of the chiefs were not curtailed by the democratic government. The ANC could not risk the return of secessionist politics and the first local government elections were due to take place in 1995. The ANC's 'Building a United Nation' document states: 'The ANC insists that local government should be democratically constituted and function in accordance with democratic principles. Traditional leaders may and should participate in local government, subject to the principle of democratic and accountable local government' (NA CA 2/1/2/36). Despite the ANC's political dominance and the fact that for the first time it had executive control over the instruments of the state, traditional leaders were in a position to hold local elections to ransom, which they did – the first local government elections had to be postponed three times. Traditional leaders were concerned that proposed municipal boundaries would cut across the demarcation of traditional authorities, which, the chiefs argued, would cause them to 'lose control over various functions which they had traditionally performed' (Muriaas, 2002:121).

A press release from Contralesa in March 1995 makes the threats explicit. The 'current process of registering voters is only possible if clarity is reached on the role and function in local government', it reads. Signed by Patekile Holomisa, it goes further: 'the constitution must acknowledge and protect the status of Traditional Authorities as fully fledged local government in rural areas' headed by chiefs. Furthermore,

> Provision should ... be made for traditional leaders to become more involved in the current negotiations, the development of a new constitution, participating in the formulation of policy options, especially

regarding the social and economic restructuring of South Africa, and the implementation of RDP [Reconstruction and Development Programme] and other policy measures. (NA CA 2/4/2/1/1/17)

The memorandum made the fears of the traditional leaders clear: 'Theoretically speaking, it is possible in our areas that any political party including those that are opposed in principle to our institution and those who took our land may win the elections and introduce policies designed to destroy our institution' (NA CA 1/5/12).

The ANC won this battle in so far as there is no mention of traditional leaders in the local government chapter of the final Constitution. But by the time the local government elections took place nearly two years later, traditional leaders had secured a more beneficial place for their institution. The ANC also tried, unsuccessfully, to take the administration of traditional leadership away from the provinces, particularly KZN. In 1995 the Payment of Traditional Leaders Bill was brought before Parliament. It 'sought to abolish provincial control over payment' and nationalise it (Goodenough, 2002:19). Buthelezi contested the Bill in the Constitutional Court, which, in 1996, ruled that KZN had the right to pass legislation to the effect that the province would have the sole power to pay traditional leaders (1996 (4) SA 653 (CC); 1996 (7) BCLR 903 (CC)).

The ANC's final attempts to reduce the provincial control of traditional leaders under the Constitution came to nothing when the Constitutional Court also refused to certify the draft final text on a number of grounds, among which was the diminution of regional powers in comparison with the Constitutional Principles. The draft final Constitution had included 'the ability of the National Assembly to override provincial legislation', which was, the Constitutional Court ruled, 'at the expense of Provincial Powers'. Weaker provincial powers with respect to police, local government and traditional leaders meant that the draft final Constitution did not meet Constitutional Principles 17 and 18(2) (NA CA 2/3/1/67).

In the end Contralesa filed 'objections to certification of [the] constitutional text' (NA CA 1/5/12). Patekile Holomisa was brought in front of an ANC disciplinary hearing for 'bringing the ANC into disrepute' with his Contralesa activities. Bantu Holomisa, who was a deputy minister in Mandela's Cabinet, a member of the ANC's National Executive Committee and number 14 on the party's electoral list, was expelled in 1996 after testifying before the TRC. After his departure he formed the United Democratic Movement in part on a platform of mobilising chiefs and rural constituencies. Although he did not become a national player, the United Democratic Movement secured nearly thirteen per cent of votes in the Eastern Cape in the 1999 elections (Muriaas, 2002).

And despite last-minute attempts to get the IFP back into the CA, the party also refused to endorse the final Constitution.

AMBIGUOUS CONSTITUTIONAL ENTITLEMENTS

The final Constitution attempts to frame the place of traditional leadership and customary law in postapartheid South Africa. Appendix 2 in this book includes the relevant sections of the Constitution in full.

Sections affecting traditional leadership and customary law are scattered throughout the Constitution, with the most important contained in Chapter 12, which deals with the recognition and role of traditional leaders. Section 211(1) provides that the 'institution, status and role of traditional leadership, according to customary law, are recognised, subject to the Constitution'. Section 211(2) states that 'a traditional authority that observes a system of customary law may function subject to any applicable legislation and customs' and Section 211(3) states: 'The courts must apply customary law when that law is applicable, subject to the Constitution and any legislation that specifically deals with customary law.'

Clearly it is the Constitution itself that provides the legal foundation for the legitimacy of traditional leadership after apartheid. But paradoxically, the constitutional text asserts that the institution, status and role of traditional leadership are recognised according to customary law. Nowhere are the contours or limits of that recognition specified. The section on the role of traditional leaders is similarly unspecified and open ended. The first provision, 212(1), states that 'National legislation may provide for a role for traditional leadership as an institution at local level on matters affecting local communities'. This is an enabling provision and does not, by itself, confer any entitlement. It is followed by a further enabling provision. Section 212(2) provides that, 'To deal with matters relating to traditional leadership, the role of traditional leaders, customary law and the customs of communities observing a system of customary law', new legislation may be developed. This new legislation may provide for the establishment of provincial houses of traditional leaders (Section 212(2)(a)) and a national council of traditional leaders (Section 212(2)(b)).

Other sections of the Constitution build on or supplement this main chapter and deal with traditional courts, the relationship between traditional leaders and territorial and local administration and customary law and rights. But the agreements of Chapter 12 are not integrated with the remainder of the Constitution's entitlements. Chapter 8 deals with courts and the administration of justice, but makes no direct reference to customary or chiefs' courts. It merely mentions, in Section 166(e), 'any other court established or recognised in terms of an Act of Parliament'. Although the

Constitution does not explicitly recognise traditional courts, at the end of the constitutional text, Schedule 6 provides for transitional arrangements. According to Section 16, 'Every court, including courts of traditional leaders, existing when the new Constitution took effect, continues to function and exercise jurisdiction in terms of the legislation applicable to it, and anyone holding office as a judicial officer continues to hold such office.'

A similar disjuncture is to be found in sections that affect traditional leaders' roles within local governance and administrative structures. In Chapter 6, which concerns itself with provinces and their competencies, provincial legislatures are given the power to pass legislation as set out in various schedules. Schedule 4 includes 'cultural matters' as well as 'indigenous law and customary law subject to Chapter 12' and 'traditional leadership subject to Chapter 12 of the Constitution'. Schedule 5 deals with areas of exclusive provincial legislative competence, which include 'provincial cultural matters'. In addition, there is a provision in Section 143 for provinces to write constitutions which 'must not be inconsistent with' the national Constitution. The section also states that provincial constitutions may provide for 'the institution, role, authority and status of a traditional monarch, where applicable' (143(1)(b)).

The provinces chapter does not, in other words, grant or confer any specific powers to traditional leaders and does not specify anything about provincial roles and governance, except to say that legislation may be developed. The section on the recognition of a traditional monarch is clearly a reference to KZN, but it does not specify any powers or roles for such a monarch.

The local government chapter is even more telling. Traditional leaders and traditional authorities are not mentioned at all. And notwithstanding the 17th Constitutional Principle, the main object of local government is given in Section 152(1)(a) as 'to provide democratic and accountable government for local communities'. This, too, contradicts their potential recognition in Chapter 12 and certainly limits the scope of any future legislation authorised by that chapter.

The last area is that of the relationship between human rights and customary law. Customary law is not a right and chiefs are not in control of the articulation or development of customary law. It is subject to the development of legislation and jurisprudence. Nor do chiefs have any monopoly on its application. The application of customary law is not limited spatially to traditional authorities or other territorial communities that might elect to practise it. Unlike the framework for customary law in the past, this articulation does, however, promise that the powers of the state could be used to implement decisions taken on the basis of customary law. Importantly, customary law, like religious law and common law, was made subject to the Bill of Rights, which includes, of course, the equality provision.

Where customary law and the Bill of Rights overlap most concretely is in the right to religion. This includes the enabling provision, Section 15(3) (a), which 'does not prevent legislation' that would recognise 'marriages concluded under any tradition, or a system of religious, personal or family law', nor does it prevent the legislation of 'systems of personal and family law under any tradition, or adhered to by persons professing a particular religion'. Any such marriage or family law provisions must also be consistent with other elements of the Constitution. This provision opens the possibility for the state's recognition of customary marriages.

The imaginary of the institution of traditional leadership stands in an ambiguous relation to the terms of modern differentiation between religion and politics, civil society and the state, and religion and culture. Its relationship to the institutional differentiations of economics, society, politics, law and the administration of justice, of which political secularism is a part, is equally ambiguous. I am not suggesting that religion and tradition are the same thing. As concepts, practices and institutions, chieftainship and religious authority have different referents, genealogies and histories.

But there are three similarities between the public or institutional forms of world religion and that of traditional authority that are important for an analysis of political secularism in South Africa. The first is that, like religious institutions, the institution of traditional leadership is both a potential obstacle and a potential resource for state formation and consolidation. The second is that traditional authorities, like religious authorities, seek to regulate the conditions of intimacy and social, sexual and cultural reproduction. Practically, this is reflected in various comparable codifications of contract, custom and prescription around marriage, succession and inheritance in Shari'a and Muslim Personal Law and customary law, for example. The third is that both religion and tradition draw on transcendental legitimacies, whether God, Allah or the ancestors. This legitimacy was at stake in an entirely more contested debate about the foundations of a postapartheid South Africa.

5

THE SPIRIT OF A NEW SOUTH AFRICA

And there is a special debt to the religious leaders who have sought with such richness and dignity to infuse a spiritual dimension into an occasion of momentous political and secular significance.
Justice Corbett, opening address to Codesa I Plenary (COD NA61 Folder 18, File 70)

Thus we are in danger of throwing out the baby of Judeo-Christian values and ethics with the bathwater of apartheid.
Michael Cassidy (1995:220)

During the constitutional negotiations some Christian groups mobilised to have God recognised as sovereign authority over the polity, a demand that presupposed God's willed intervention in history and a human obligation to act in ways that could guarantee God's blessing.

This was coupled with a widespread belief that an acknowledgement of God in the preamble to the Constitution would lead to the assertion of 'biblical principles' in social morality and public life. Linked with this was the demand that biblical principles, or at least 'public morality', should be included in the Constitution's interpretation clause, providing a Christian or moral majoritarian interpretation of rights that would preclude the legalisation of termination of pregnancy, gay rights and the availability of pornography.

CHRISTIAN FOUNDATIONS?

The foundational principles of apartheid were explicitly religious in at least two senses. The first was a political theology of race that precluded the possibility of representation as a basis of political power and legitimacy, except where this representation was limited to whites. Political power, therefore, needed a constitutive outside or transcendental authorisation. The political theology of apartheid acknowledged a God that differentiated between the country's inhabitants and sanctioned that difference.

The second foundation was a Calvinist sociosexual morality which, like everything else under apartheid, was shot through with race (Theron, 2008). Closely linked with social panic about the purity of Afrikaner women, apartheid policy was extremely concerned about sexual morality and what it construed as miscegenation (Van der Westhuizen, 2007). In its racial incarnation this led to the Prohibition of Mixed Marriages Act (No. 55 of 1949) and the Immorality Act (No. 21 of 1950), both of which sought to preclude intimacy, love and the creation of families across racial lines.

But it also drew on Christianity as a source and standard of social ethics. It was a narrow Calvinist sociosexual morality that the Kairos document (1986) called a 'Church Theology'. Calvinist social mores were legislated in a wide range of areas. These included publication control or censorship of sexually explicit materials, legislation against the termination of pregnancy, sodomy, liquor trading and entertainment on Sundays and a common-law crime of blasphemy.

While the Christian basis of racialised political exclusion was increasingly called into question within the churches and without, the conservative Christian social morality of apartheid was more widely shared, at least as an ideal. This was the case even as the migrant labour system and widespread forced removals of the 1960s to 1980s did incalculable damage to social relations of marriage and family.

In the end, no Christian group actively sought to retain the racial political theology of apartheid in the constitutional negotiations. The only participants who did were representatives of far-right Afrikaner political parties that placed themselves outside the negotiations. There was, however, a concerted attempt to retain and entrench the social morality of apartheid's theology (Chipkin and Leatt, 2011). Many Pentecostal-Charismatic Christians sought to draw a distinction between the two. As Michael Cassidy (1995:220) framed it in 1995:

> Many are embracing the view that to liberalise on race issues, as was so right and necessary, requires us also to abandon family values and

liberalise on every issue relating to sexual behaviour, pornography, abortion on demand, Sunday Observance, gambling, prostitution, and what is appropriate in the media and entertainment. Thus we are in danger of throwing out the baby of Judeo-Christian values and ethics with the bathwater of apartheid.

The Pentecostal collective that mobilised in relation to the transition was exclusively Christian and avowedly opposed to interfaith cooperation. It included many but not all of the major Pentecostal churches. Anthony Balcomb has written very usefully on the variety of responses by evangelicals to the democratisation of South Africa. He distinguishes between positions he labels 'conservative', 'pragmatist', 'protagonist of the third way', the 'alternative community' and 'liberationist' (Balcomb, 2004, 2008).

For example, the conservative Pentecostal bishop, Frank Retief, founded the St James Church in Kenilworth, Cape Town, for English-speaking whites who broke away from the Anglican Church in the 1970s in opposition to the leadership of Archbishop Desmond Tutu. In July 1993 the armed wing of the Pan Africanist Congress of Azania (PAC) attacked the church. Condemnation of what became known as the St James massacre has generally failed to mention the church's active support for white supremacy.

Pastor Ray McCauley and the Rhema Church, on the other hand, were the most prominent of Balcomb's category of pragmatists, construing themselves as 'apolitical' until mobilised in the late 1980s in terms of racial reconciliation and social services. From then onwards Rhema moved closer to the South African Council of Churches (SACC), where it eventually assumed observer status.

Cassidy was a proponent of what Balcomb termed 'the third way', opposed to both apartheid state violence and violent attempts to overthrow it. Trained by the US tele-evangelist Billy Graham, Cassidy emphasised personal reconciliation across political and racial boundaries and was particularly involved in attempts to reconcile the warring parties in KwaZulu-Natal (KZN) in the 1980s by invoking a common Christian belief. The liberationists were Pentecostals whose political but not theological position quite closely matched that of the Christian Institute and the SACC. The most renowned liberationist was the Reverend Frank Chikane of the Apostolic Faith Mission Church.

The year 1990 was a turning point for many evangelical churches. McCauley was one of the organisers of what came to be called the Rustenburg Conference. There, a variety of church leaders, both mainline and Pentecostal, rejected apartheid as a sin and 'confessed their guilt in relation to it' (Balcomb, 2004:15). In 1992 and 1993 Cassidy called a consultation of Christian leaders, most of them Pentecostal-Charismatic, to deliberate on the future of religion in South Africa. This consultation produced a document of 'affirmations and declarations' to rival the World Conference on Religion and Peace (WCRP) declaration. It was to form the basis of demands in the writing of the final Constitution. McCauley was a member of the steering committee of the National Peace Accord in 1992, along with Chikane and the Reverend Johan Heyns of the Dutch Reformed Church.

There is a Christian narrative of the constitutional negotiation. Although not generally part of the national public discourse, it created an important evangelical public in the late 1980s and the 1990s. Cassidy, in his book *A Witness for Ever*, describes an 'explosion' of prayer between 1991 and 1994, a period that saw significant growth in Pentecostal-Charismatic church membership. Pentecostal activity centred on praying for a safe political transition and racial reconciliation, some of which was taking place within the churches themselves.

Cassidy's African Enterprise acquired the use of a luxury game farm at which mid-ranking members of political parties were invited to attend Christian retreats. In the 'African bush' and in a 'Christian brotherhood' their racial prejudices could be overcome and they could find one another through their personal stories (Cassidy, 1995). The importance of this kind of racial reconciliation should not be underestimated, particularly for its role in demilitarising some Afrikaner conservatives (Hyslop, 1995). Cassidy's weekends away provided some white apartheid politicians with their first personal encounter with black Christians from liberation organisations. These encounters, wrote Cassidy, allowed them to break through the stereotypes of the African National Congress (ANC) and the South African Communist Party as communist atheists.

In the Pentecostal public the most significant moment of political transition took place on the eve of the 1994 elections when, it is recounted, an evangelical Christian, Kenyan Professor Washington Jalang'o Okumu, succeeded in brokering a deal between the Inkatha Freedom Party (IFP), the ANC and the National Party (NP) that led the IFP into the elections. Okumu, who had arranged a meeting with Mangosuthu Buthelezi, whom he knew personally, was delayed by traffic en route to Lanseria Airport in Johannesburg to meet Buthelezi, only to find that the chartered flight had already taken off. An instrument malfunction, however, necessitated a return to the airport, where Buthelezi told the waiting Okumu, 'God has brought me back.' When the pilot, also a 'Bible-believing Christian', checked the dials back on the ground, there appeared to be no problem. It was, according to this story, the moment in which God's hand reached out and changed the course of history. Against a background of fervent prayer Okumu presented his plan and Buthelezi took the opportunity to find a way out of deadlock.

Whether or not one believes that God miraculously intervened through the mechanics of Buthelezi's plane, there is no doubt that during this period many evangelical Christians were motivated to prayer and to the mobilisation of social and political networks through a version of Christian faith that made that faith consequential to the future of South Africa.

The broad alliance of Pentecostal-Charismatic Christians that resulted from the Rustenburg Conference made three main demands of the Constitution, although they varied greatly in the form of their interventions. The first was to see an acknowledgement of the sovereignty of God in the preamble, preferably a recognisably triune Christian God that could not be mistaken for a Muslim or Jewish God. Many believed that the inclusion of a phrase recognising the sovereignty of God over human affairs would secure God's blessing for the country and, as far as possible, assure further intervention towards reconciliation and peace. Secondly, they wanted the Bill of Rights to be interpreted in terms of what they understood to be Christian sexual and social morality. Once sexual orientation was included in the equality clause in the interim constitution, the third demand was that it be removed and that gay people and homosexuality not be protected against unfair discrimination.

The preamble was left until quite late in the Multiparty Negotiations Process (MPNP) in 1993. The Technical Committee on Constitutional Issues, drawing largely on ANC and Democratic Party (DP) submissions, produced a first draft preamble that made no reference at all to God. Cassidy secured a meeting with Nelson Mandela, who asked him to contact Albie Sachs, who liaised with the religious community. Cassidy, along with Ron Steele from the Rhema Church and University of South Africa theologian Gerald Pillay, asked that a reference to God be included in the preamble and also a prayer, perhaps *Nkosi Sikelel' iAfrika*, at its end. He recounts that Sachs was amenable to the proposal and promised to take it to the leadership of the ANC. By 12 November 1993, 'in humble submission to Almighty God' was added to the preamble and was passed into law. Sachs denies that he was responsible for its inclusion (Pers. comm., 2009).

On the basis of this achievement, as well as a massive charismatic revival and God's intervention in South Africa's history on the eve of the 1994 elections, Pentecostal-Charismatic Christians faced the postapartheid future and the finalisation of the Constitution by the democratic Assembly. But they were deeply troubled by the avalanche of sex and sex talk in a South Africa newly liberated from Calvinist constraint. The deregulation of publications control in 1993 allowed for an influx of sexually explicit and pornographic material. To this was added the increased visibility of the gay rights movement and the possibility that termination of pregnancy on demand would be legalised. It is in this context that the other demands were made in the Constitutional Assembly (CA): for the introduction of biblical principles in the interpretation of human rights and for the exclusion of sexual orientation as grounds for non-discrimination in the equality clause.

A confused, drawn out, ill-tempered altercation on the spiritual or philosophical foundations for the new South Africa took place at the CA. The principal advocate of a theological foundation was the African Christian Democratic Party (ACDP). Formed by conservative Pentecostals just before the 1994 elections and closely allied with St James Church, the ACDP won two seats that were taken up by Revd Kenneth Meshoe and Louis Green.

The CA's Theme Committee One (TC1) had the title of 'Character of the Democratic State'. Its mandate was to engage with political abstractions such as democracy, equality and the supremacy of the Constitution as well as 'name and symbols', official languages and the separation of powers. Most of these were already covered by the Constitutional Principles and were drafted into law by other committees. It is a testament to the vagueness of its mandate that none of the bigger parties delegated top negotiators to TC1. While it was dominated by the ANC, the eight-member core group responsible for the day-to-day and technical work comprised only two people from the ANC and one from the PAC. The remaining five were from the NP, the DP, the Freedom Front (FF), the IFP and the ACDP.

The question of secularism was not even on the agenda of the CA. But this technical committee, tasked with compiling a work programme in February 1995, included a seemingly innocuous item, identified as a 'non-contentious' point, that '[t]here shall be a separation between State and Religion' (CA 2/4/1/4/14). Meshoe suggested that it should read 'separation between state and religious institutions' (CA 2/4/1/2/31). All major religious groups, including Pentecostal churches, agreed to an institutional separation. But this debate in TC1 brought into contention the question of secular foundations. In reply to Meshoe, the ANC's Nkenke Kekana asserted that religion as such, and not just its institutions, should be separate from the state. 'We are not talking about an institution versus another institution. We are talking about an institution (the state) and a particular concept called religion' (CA 2/4/1/2/31). But Meshoe held that such a foundational separation is impossible, both in politics and in people. 'Man [sic],' he said, 'is a religious being whether you believe in God or believe that man is the supreme, but everybody is religious' (CA 2/4/1/2/31).

When ANC negotiator Blade Nzimande asked the ACDP if it was petitioning for a Christian state, Meshoe said that it was not. Nzimande then suggested that 'the best way to deal with this is to ... put a sentence like South Africa will be a secular state' under 'contentious issues' (CA 2/4/1/2/31).

The technical committee's next report, on 28 February 1995, elaborated on the point that 'South Africa shall be a secular state', stating that 'there is no disagreement between the parties on the fact that the constitution should provide for a separation of religion (often expressed as "church") and state' (CA 2/4/1/2/31). But, it said, it was not clear what this means in practice.

It sought to outline some of the possible practical consequences: 'Should there be references to deities in the Constitution? ... Would religious office bearers be barred from holding offices of state? ... Should the state allow religious observances in its institutions?' (CA 1/18/6). Much of this was already settled in the right to religion clause, but the report's rather speculative musings were to become a source of great distress to some Christians.

Meshoe, and perhaps some from the NP and the FF, circulated the report among Christian groups, who were quickly convinced that Christianity and the freedom of religion were under threat. Thinking their worst fears about a Soviet-style repression of religion were about to be realised, they started to mobilise. A month later Harvey Ebrahim, the manager of the CA, tabled a Christian leaflet at the Management Committee and reported 'a flood of submissions' against South Africa becoming a secular state. An organisation called Christian Voice was planning a march to Parliament on 30 May to hand over a memorandum, he said (CA 2/3/1/40).

The leaflet read as follows: 'The ANC has proposed that South Africa become a secular state, and that state and religion should be separated.' What this meant, it continued, was that 'anyone who is a Christian leader would not be able to hold any public office in any state institution; No Christian services could be held at any state land or building (including schools, hospitals etc); No Christian prayers would be allowed in any state institution or ones funded fully or partially by the state'. A handwritten sentence read: 'Christian churches will be compelled to perform the marriage ceremony of lesbians and homosexuals.' The ACDP, the pamphlet claimed, was the only party to speak out against this 'travesty' (CA 2/4/1/6/39).

Two white women from Durban, calling themselves the Constitutional Awareness Campaign Coordinators, called on all Christians to write to the ANC's negotiator, Cyril Ramaphosa, in person to protest this ANC submission. If people did not do so, they warned, 'the very words God Almighty will be removed from the new constitution' (CA 2/4/1/6/39). A Christian Voice 'Open Letter to Fellow Christians' followed. The country, it said, was being flooded with filth – pornography, homosexuality, abortion, Satanism and the interfaith movement – profane activities taking cover under a regime of human rights. In bold letters it demanded that 'Christians take a stand' (CA 2/4/1/5/33).

As Ebrahim reported to the Management Committee, these pamphlets inspired a flood of submissions. His People Christian Ministries, the Reform International Churches Association of South Africa, the Baptist Union of South Africa, Christian Digest, United Christian Action, the International Fellowship of Christian Churches, and the African Enterprise Consultation on Human Rights and Religious Freedom, all white-led and mostly white-membership Pentecostal-Charismatic groupings, made submissions. These were followed by thousands of letters from individuals. At first, the correspondents were English- and Afrikaans-speaking whites. But as the petitions, pamphlets and sermons spread, black Christians from Thohoyandou, Guyani, Mabopane, Hillbrow, Orlando and Joubert Park were moved to write in support of the 'Trinity: Father, Son and Holy Spirit' and against a secular state.

The ANC was angry. On 25 May Pravin Gordhan demanded an apology from the ACDP for 'distorting the CA process' and making 'malicious allegations against the ANC'. The next day Ramaphosa petitioned the Constitutional Committee, demanding that the ACDP apologise and refrain from emotive campaigns and that it be disciplined (CA 2/1/2/36). The ACDP had smeared the CA and the ANC, he said, and had 'whipped up the feelings of a large section of the Christian community'.

On 26 May the CA issued a press statement, signed by Ramaphosa, on 'The Relationship between State and Religion'. It noted the 'concerns of the Christian community' and pointed to the interim constitution's Constitutional Principles, which recognised religious freedom as a fundamental right. It stated 'unequivocally that at no stage in any debate of any structure of the Constitutional Assembly' has the pamphlet's interpretation of secularism been suggested by any party or person (CA 2/3/1/41). There was nothing to prevent Christian ministers from holding government jobs or prayers being said in schools. Despite this reassurance, about 20 000 people marched to Parliament four days later to hand over a petition on the issue of the secular state. Ramaphosa was there to receive it, Bible in hand and filmed by national television.

This 'problem of the secular state' continued to rattle around the halls of Parliament as the ACDP raised the issue of sexual orientation and the interpretation of rights at every opportunity. Chris Nissen, an ANC Cabinet minister, wrote to the chair of TC1 and Ramaphosa suggesting that the Western Cape Provincial Council of Churches (WCPCC) and the Ecumenical Foundation of South Africa address TC1 to help them to think through 'the current debate on religiosity in our new South African society' (CA 2/4/1/2/34). 'These two organisations,' he wrote, 'have a history of struggle for political and religious freedom and I value their opinion highly.' Nissen himself was a minister of the Uniting Presbyterian Church and member of the executives of the WCPCC and SACC.

On 1 August 1995 a racially mixed delegation from the WCPCC came to the committee chambers.[1] Minutes of that meeting state that they made an oral submission, followed by a debate that covered biblical principles, gay and lesbian rights, references to race in the Constitution and 'the possible mechanisms the state should use to uplift the poor'. The discussion ended with talk of 'assisting politicians in reassuring those Christians amongst whom there was uncertainty regarding the new constitution' (CA 2/4/1/2/38).

A week later the theme committee received a request from United Christian Action to be allowed to address it (CA 2/4/1/2/39). The request was granted and on 14 August Revd Peter Hammond and a Mr van Wyk made an oral submission to TC1. Notwithstanding the presence of people of other faiths on the committee, Hammond opened by saying, 'We greet each of you in the precious name of the Lord and Saviour Jesus Christ.' He then outlined the demands of what he called 'the more than 75 percent Christian majority'. Speaking particularly, he said, for the 'Bible-believing Protestant or evangelical community', he demanded a 'Christian constitutional republic'. If Muslims could have Islamic states, he said, South African Christians could have a Christian state. He claimed that the Christian faith 'has made more positive changes on earth than any other force or movement in the history of the world'. Christianity gave us hospitals (that is why they are marked with a cross), literacy (most languages were put into writing by Christian missionaries), the elevation of women and the concept of charity. 'A Godless state,' he said, would be 'a hopeless state' (CA 2/4/1/12/17).

Hammond was a deeply unstrategic choice to present to a majority ANC committee of mixed faith. He was a gun lobbyist known to have assisted the opposition *Resistência Nacional Moçambicana* (Mozambican National Resistance (Renamo))[2] in Mozambique, and had been arrested for gun-running, treason and insurrection in Sudan. He later co-wrote an anti-gay book, *The Pink Agenda: Sexual Revolution in South Africa and the Ruin of the Family*.

Even the Pentecostal Christians on the committee felt the need to distance themselves from Hammond. Carl Niehaus, later employed by both the Rhema Church and the ANC, said, 'we must accept that the particular presentation of Christianity that Reverend Hammond and Mr Van Wyk represent here is not representative of all Christians in South Africa' (CA 2/4/1/12/17).

Kekana laid into the aggrandising history of the church presented by Hammond, countering with its contribution to colonialism. Sister Bernard Ncube, a Catholic nun and ANC Member of Parliament, was angered by Hammond's patronising tone. 'It looks,' she said, 'like you are talking to some pagan government that does not know much about what God is all about.' Mr Booi continued in the same vein. The march, he suggested, was all based on rumour and suspicion that the ANC is communist and that there are no Christians in government. 'But there is no truth in this .... no truth at all that we are not Christians' (CA 2/4/1/12/17).

Hammond's intervention definitely put the nail in the coffin of the ACDP's attempts to have the sovereignty of God retained in the preamble and to have a biblical basis for interpretation written into the Bill of Rights. But there were other reasons too. The party, which had entered the political process very late in the transition and acted against the social compact of negotiators who had been locked in both friendship and enmity over the previous five years, had simply failed to win support within the CA or from powerful civil society groupings, and it failed to represent effectively what was in fact majority opinion in South Africa.

The ACDP also failed to garner unequivocal support from other Pentecostals and some of the big churches were extremely critical of its strategies, if not its demands. McCauley was a 'vociferous' opponent and Chikane criticised the party for lacking 'political acumen' and being 'embarrassing', particularly in 'its narrow concerns with the "sins of sex"' (Balcomb, 2004:30). While the ACDP sometimes had in-principle support from the NP, the latter was, on the whole, unwilling to be seen to be standing with it. In the end, the ACDP, like the IFP, voted against the adoption of the final Constitution.

By the time the public debate died down at the end of 1995 nearly 39 000 people had petitioned Parliament against a secular state and against 'secular humanism'. Added to this were 16 400 petitions against tolerance of sexual orientation, 10 250 against abortion and euthanasia and for capital punishment and nearly 18 000 for reference in the preamble to a triune God (CA 1/18/10). In addition, about one-third of the 11 000 written submissions to the CA covered these issues.

Demands for 'democratic representation' for 'the religious majority' were belied by the divisions among Christians on these matters, divisions that were seen in the competing representations to TC1. The powerful WCRP lobby did not support the ACDP or its demands. For one thing, their multifaith constituency would not endorse calls for the recognition of an explicitly Christian God. Nor did they think that a reference to God in the preamble would automatically secure the kinds of interpretation that some claimed. Perhaps most importantly, there was criticism of 'Church theology' and its apolitical moralising. Where the WCRP did mention morality, it identified the big moral issues of the country as racism, unemployment and violence. Tutu also supported the retention of the sexual orientation clause. 'I would strongly urge you to include [it] in the final constitution,' he wrote in a much publicised submission on 2 June 1995 (CA 2/4/4/1/7/85).

While the Christian groups claimed that the proportion of Christians in South Africa could stand as a form of democratic political representation and that majoritarian moral views carried direct political weight, it was clear that these 'moral values' did not determine voting behaviour at the time. The ANC won the majority of the votes in the first democratic election, even as they stood for a range of non-traditional and counter-majoritarian values such as gender equality, support for sexual orientation provisions, abortion and an end to capital punishment (Pillay, Roberts and Rule, 2006).

TRADITIONAL FOUNDATIONS?

Ethnic nationalism was a central part of the apartheid ideology of 'separate development' and its institutional realisation in the homelands. State-sponsored ethnographic folk studies (*volkekunde*) were part of the state's substantial investment in the reification of ethnicity, as were single-language newspapers, forced removals which attempted to separate settlements according to ethnic ascription and local-language community radio (Chidester, 1996; Vail, 1991).

The South African government and some homeland leaders made every effort to ensure that the imagined community was not one of African nationalism or pan-Africanism or even national non-racialism, but one of tribe or ethnicity under the 'immemorial rule' of traditional leaders and customary law. Tribal or ethnic nationalism was an important technique of homeland power, along with South Africa's financing of institutions of state, legislation, taxes, influx control and all the other mechanics of apartheid power (Delius, 1996; Marks, 1986; Ritchken, 1995).

The Zulu ethnicity sponsored by the IFP had all the classic elements of nationalism (Anderson, 1991). It valorised Shaka as the founder of the nation and asserted a correspondence between Zulu speakers, Zulu ethnicity and a Zulu polity under traditional rule. It posited continual lines of hereditary chieftainship, a heroic struggle against British and apartheid rule, a history of martyrs, sacred places of victorious battles, sacred times of historical victory, rituals of collective action, mythologies of power and markers of cultural identity. Together they constituted a cultural and political imaginary of heroic Zulu ethnicity.

The IFP sought to institute something along the lines of establishment secularism in KZN and Buthelezi wanted the institution of the Zulu monarchy to be legitimated in terms of divine and ancestral rule. This would be the public regime of provincial or federal legitimacy. Like establishment secularism in the postrevolutionary period, the symbolic and ceremonial recognition of monarchy would not be a reflection of the monarch's political powers – it would be a way to expand the bases of legitimacy for other political actors. In this, Buthelezi exemplified the multiplicity of legitimacies involved in this procedure. He was head of the IFP, chief minister of KZN and therefore head of its government and head of the KZN military. He also claimed the position of 'traditional Prime Minister to His Majesty the King of the Zulus' (COD NA61).

KZN is also home, to use their apartheid designations, to fairly large white and Indian minority populations. For these Buthelezi also suggested an establishment solution – non-Zulu citizens of the federal state would be able to exercise political and other rights independent of their ethnicity. The IFP did not succeed in the end in winning secession from the rest of South Africa, or a strong version of federalism, but the Zulu king was recognised as a monarch in the agreement that brought the IFP into the 1994 elections. This strategy proved, however, to be a double-edged sword. On the one hand the IFP sought to extend its political role from that of homeland leadership to national political player; on the other, its agenda was so closely tied to Zulu nationalism that its national scope was severely restricted.

The second position through which tradition and chieftainship were presented to the negotiations was that of the Congress of Traditional Leaders of South Africa (Contralesa). Traditional leaders aligned with the ANC scrupulously avoided the use of ethnic signifiers in the negotiations. As Patekile Holomisa said on behalf of Contralesa at the Convention for a Democratic South Africa (Codesa):

> We formed Contralesa in order to forge unity among ourselves and to combat tribalism by inculcating in both ourselves and our people the feeling that we are all South Africans who have common goals, aims and destiny. We are fully aware that the apartheid system has exploited our tribal and language differences to the extent that our people are made to believe that the African section of the South African community were [sic] constituted of ten different nations. (COD NA61)

Contralesa-aligned traditional leaders drew on two regimes of legitimation, both of which sometimes found common ground with IFP-aligned chiefs. The first was an application of Enlightenment values to traditional or customary rule. It was often asserted that chieftainship is a democratic institution (CA 2/3/1/6/11).[3]

The second regime of legitimation was the positing of a non-ethnic pan-black cultural world that was corrupted or dissipated in urban areas but still survived more or less intact in rural areas. It was an argument that drew on the idea of chieftainship as protector of the social good and social fabric, a discourse that was particularly set in opposition to the activities of the ANC-aligned comrades of the 1980s.

Take, for example, the statement by Brigadier 'Oupa' Gqozo at the opening of Codesa. He claimed that forty-two per cent of the population consisted of black youth without proper education who had been indoctrinated with ideas of disobedience. For this reason, he argued, '[m]ajority rule is a simplistic solution ... there can be no liberation when discipline, respect for moral and traditional values is lacking' (COD NA61).

Traditional leaders argued that there were areas in South Africa in which modern political processes were, at best, marginal. In such areas, they claimed, 'African values' and modes of rule and life ought to be recognised and practised by traditional leaders and what they called traditional communities. To support these claims they called upon both divine and historical authorisation for the institution of traditional leadership in terms of God's assertion of their rule, hereditary blood lineage, ancestral lineage and the custodianship of custom and land.

The QwaQwa delegation at the Hearing on the Participation of the Zulu King and Other Traditional Leaders claimed that traditional leaders had the 'divine responsibility of nation-building' and the KaNgwane Council of Chiefs in their presentation to the same subcommittee said:

> Above us is God Almighty and it was He who placed us over our tribes to rule them. Just like we cannot raise ourselves to God, the King of Kings, we do not expect politicians, who are our subjects, to raise themselves to our level. Neither are we prepared to lower ourselves to the level of politicians. (COD NA61)

On the whole, traditional leaders who participated in the negotiations did not claim that such values should have universal or even national scope. In fact, it was exactly as a territorial entity that these foundations were asserted. Chief Mwelo Nonkonyana, Contralesa provincial chairman and Bhala Traditional Council head, for instance, objected during a debate at the MPNP that 'only one set of fundamental human rights' should be applicable to everyone, including traditional leaders. 'It means in our understanding,' he said, 'that the rights of people in Ulundi; the rights of the people in the Eastern Cape; the rights of the people in the Chris Hani Squatter Camp …' should be protected if they are universal in the sense that they exist in all these areas. But, he continued, 'if that right exists only in Ulundi and [is] not existing in the squatter camps then it is not universal' (NA NEG 1/3/3/3) and it should gain special and specific recognition.

A memorandum submitted by *Amakhosi* of the Kingdom of KwaZulu-Natal in May 1995 made a similar point, this time criticising what they called 'the ANC's hostility to the notion of "social and cultural pluralism"'. They also criticised the interim constitution on the grounds that it revealed 'little understanding of African societies and of the importance of traditional communities as a different and specific model of societal organisation' (CA 1/12/3). They did not seek the integration, representation or presence of elements of black South African and social life in the national dispensation; they sought an enclave of rule by traditional leadership and customary law.

Contralesa addressed the issue of the future interpretation of law, particularly the Bill of Rights. Referring to principles of democracy, non-racialism, non-sexism and representative government, it suggested that these principles 'cannot be practised as if in a vacuum; they should be applied in the context of the realities on the ground, and, most importantly, they should be interpreted from an African rather than a European point of view' (CA 2/3/1/6/11).

Although this appeared to be a broader view it was immediately asserted that in South Africa, where 'the natives are in the majority', true liberation should be embodied in a constitution that would result in the 'restoration of all that was unjustly usurped from the indigenous people of our land' (CA 2/3/1/6/11). Contralesa sought the restoration of enclaves of an idealised precolonial past, untouched by modern economic or political processes, and nothing was said about what interpretive principles an African point of view might actually entail.

The dominance of traditional leaders in representing 'things African' at the negotiations all but silenced other possible ways of addressing these issues. And, as women's organisations repeatedly pointed out, there was little input on 'things African' from anyone other than traditional leaders; little comment from rural communities, traditional healers, African Independent churches or any other possible locus of articulation. A CA summary of submissions for the period to February 1996, for example, reported that of the 250 000 submissions only 42 addressed the issue of traditional leadership. And apart from debates over traditional leadership per se there were only a handful of inputs about custom and tradition more broadly. Among these were submissions on witchcraft, the recognition of traditional healers and polygamy, issues which, according to a technical committee lawyer, were impossible to frame in constitutional terms.

On the whole, the monopoly by traditional leaders of 'things African' in the negotiations meant that the many other possible elements of cultural and social life were simply not reflected in the debates or in the final Constitution except via the recognition of traditional leadership and customary law, the content of which was never really debated.

The exception is the scattering of universal claims made in the name of African culture through the concept of *ubuntu*. Johann Broodryk, the white director of the uBuntu School of Philosophy, wrote to suggest that 'uBuntusim can become what liberalism became for America', a philosophy that encompassed values such as 'sharing, love, collectiveness, empathy and understanding' (CA 2/4/1/6/9).

For a brief moment the postamble to the interim constitution brought the concept of *ubuntu* directly into South Africa's postapartheid legal regime. On the night of 17 November 1993, just 24 hours before the final voting on the interim constitution, Ramaphosa and Roelf Meyer presented an extraordinary postamble with the title 'National Unity and Reconciliation'. It is included in full as Appendix 1. The text was never discussed in the MPNP. Unlike all the other provisions of the interim constitution, it did not go through the process of technical committees and drafts debated in the Negotiating Council. It was presented as a complete document and sanctioned by the full Negotiating Council of the MPNP at its first discussion.

The postamble was later incorporated into the Promotion of National Unity and Reconciliation Act (No. 34 of 1995), otherwise known as the TRC Act. The CA decided not to include a postamble in the final Constitution and reference to the TRC Act was excluded from the final Constitution when the Constitutional Court certified the text.[4] *Ubuntu* is not, therefore, included as an explicit value or political principle in the Constitution. It has, however, become part of South African jurisprudence through its sojourn in the interim constitution (1995(3) SA 391 (CC); 1995(6) BCLR 665 (CC)).

SECULAR FOUNDATIONS: POLITICAL AND LEGAL CONCEPTS

How can the secularity of South Africa's postapartheid foundations be characterised positively? One way is from the constitutional text itself and its stated political concepts. These are to be found in its preamble, founding provisions and framework for interpretation, which are saturated with Enlightenment political values.

The preamble of the final Constitution begins by identifying the political community for the Constitution: 'We, the people of South Africa.' It is 'us', 'the people', who authorise the Constitution and, for the first time in South Africa's history, it is not a racialised political community. The preamble then turns to four actions that this 'we' will undertake; actions that 'recognise', 'honour', 'respect' and 'believe'. We recognise past injustice, honour those who have suffered for justice and freedom, respect those who have built and developed the country and believe 'that South Africa belongs to all who live in it, united in our diversity'. Here are the echoes of the Freedom Charter.

The preamble goes on to assert the work that this 'supreme law of the Republic' must do. The Constitution was adopted to 'heal the divisions of the past' and to establish a new society based on 'democratic values, social justice and fundamental human rights'. In this new democratic society, government will be based on 'the will of the people' and every citizen will be 'equally protected by law'. The preamble promises not only the guarantee of political freedom – it also seeks to 'improve the quality of life for all citizens and free the potential of each person'. The role of the Constitution is to help build 'a united and democratic South Africa' which can take its place 'as a sovereign state in a family of nations'. The preamble ends: 'May God protect our people' and then 'God Bless South Africa', in English and the other official languages, beginning with *Nkosi Sikelel' iAfrika*.

The first chapter of the Constitution, titled 'Founding Provisions', proclaims the official languages, national flag, national anthem, citizenship and supremacy of the Constitution. It opens with a general statement that asserts that the Republic of South Africa is one sovereign democratic state founded on the values of human dignity, the achievement of equality and the advancement of human rights and freedoms. 'Non-racialism and non-sexism' are given as foundational values, as are the supremacy of the Constitution and the rule of law. This is followed by a list of political rights written as values: 'universal adult suffrage, a national common voters' roll, regular elections and a multi-party system of democratic government' to ensure 'accountability, responsiveness and openness'.

Interpretation takes us straight to the heart of the declared values of a constitutional dispensation. Human rights themselves constitute a kind of value, but, once established, how are we to interpret their meaning, scope and the grounds on which they can be justifiably limited? Take, for example, the right to life. On its own it is not contentious, but should euthanasia be allowed, or abortion, or capital punishment? The grounds for interpretation are themselves written into law in the interpretation clause of the Bill of Rights.

The wording of the clause, which was largely derived from the Canadian Constitution, was developed early in the negotiations and remained consistent. Petitions by the ACDP and the NP for the addition of biblical principles and public morals failed. The final Constitution states that when a court, tribunal or forum interprets the Bill of Rights, it must 'promote the values that underlie an open and democratic society based on human dignity, equality and freedom'. It also 'must' and 'may' consider international and foreign law, respectively. The interpretation clause ends with the statement that 'every court, tribunal or forum must promote the spirit, purport and objects of the Bill of Rights'.

In the context of a discussion on secularism, two things stand out. First, the political foundations are not religious. They derive from the tradition of Enlightenment political thought and exclude any explicit reference to God as authority or to scriptures as a basis for legislation or arbitration. Second, neither the Constitution nor the South African state is identified within the text as secular. Nowhere does the Constitution declare that South Africa is a secular state; nowhere does it name secularism as a value in itself. The CA's experience warned of the multivalence and ambiguity of the term and the ways in which it could be used to mobilise some Christians against an otherwise widely supported dispensation.

SACRED CONSTITUTION, SACRED NATION

Accepting that the conceptual and legal foundations of the Constitution are secular, it is necessary to turn to the ways in which the law, the nation and the people were sacralised in the process of forming the state. What was the political culture of the negotiations relative to religion and tradition? And how was this 'new South Africa' represented to the public and the international community during this period? What, in other words, constituted the nationalism and the public performative and symbolic legitimacy of the new dispensation?

THE LEGITIMACY OF LAW

The emerging nationalism of the transition linked not only population and territory but also the law. The Constitution itself – its existence, its contents, its promise, the process of its development and the international esteem in which it was held – was an important part of the nationalism of this period of state formation. As Justice Sachs wrote, law and justice have a 'profound moral-historical dimension'. 'Concepts such as the rule of law, fundamental rights and the independence of the judiciary, occupy distinctive hallowed spaces from which powerfully attractive energies radiate' (Sachs, 2009:57).

This spirit was palpable in relation to the Constitution. For a time at least, the text represented the achievement of the new dispensation.

The legitimacy of the Constitution was largely dependent on the public's perception of and participation in the processes of its development. Although Codesa and the MPNP were held behind closed doors, the CA had a significant public participation programme which, in the words of Philippe-Joseph Salazar (2002:54), 'harnessed the resources of the electronic media not only to source information from the public, but also to publicly reveal their own deliberations and resolutions'. By the time the final draft Constitution was released in May 1996 two million submissions had been received, with views from 120 000 individuals, 500 organisations and nearly 1 300 public meetings, workshops and hearings. Nearly seventy-three per cent of the adult population reported having been reached by one or more media or outreach programme (Salazar, 2002).

Within the negotiation, the new Constitution was also sanctified in law. This is most clear in relation to the Constitutional Principles – the 34 statements settled by the MPNP that underlie many of the terms of the final Constitution. From Codesa's first attempts to draft constitutional principles, they were spoken about as being 'enshrined in and not contradicted by any other provisions of a new Constitution' (COD NA61). A 'Schedule of Constitutional Principles' was included in the first draft of the interim constitution of 21 July 1993 and then adopted by the Negotiating Council. As soon as they were adopted, the language used to refer to them changed, both textually and legally. Until then written in lower case, the Constitutional Principles became capitalised.

When the Constitutional Principles were first challenged, the technical committee suggested that they constituted a solemn pact and the foundation of a social contract. The committee wrote:

> The reason why Constitutional Principles and the key aspects of the Constitution making process should not be amended by legislation during the transition is that these provisions are contained in a solemn pact agreed upon by the parties of the MPNP, and constitute the basis of the future Constitutional state and Constitution making process. Constitutionally, once the MPNP is dissolved, there will be no other body which can change this solemn pact, which must remain binding until the new Constitution has been adopted in accordance with its requirements. (NA NEG 1/3/2/2/14)

There is obviously theological language in this elevation of the frame for the political negotiations. As the online edition of the Oxford English Dictionary puts it, something solemn is '[a]ssociated or connected with religious rites or observances; performed with due ceremony and reverence; having a religious character; sacred'.

Public and parliamentary hearings were told repeatedly that the Constitutional Principles were 'not up for debate' (see, for example, CA F4 1/2/6). Reports from all theme committees were standardised and structured according to the Principles. Each committee had to outline the Principles that applied to its work, the areas of commonality between parties and contentious issues. The contentions were then often resolved in light of an interpretation of the Principles (see, for example, CA 2/1/2/36).

When the IFP took the CA to court to challenge sufficient consensus as a basis for decision-making, the Constitutional Principles were referred to not only as a solemn pact but as sacrosanct. The CA's law advisors expressed the opinion that from 27 April

> these Principles became *sacrosanct* and neither Parliament nor the Constitutional Assembly has the power to change them. No negotiation between the parties, whether by way of international mediation or otherwise can have any effect on the mandate of the Constitutional Assembly as now fixed by the Constitutional Principles. (CA 2/1/2/36, emphasis added)

Enshrined, solemn and sacrosanct – in these ways the underpinnings of the law were themselves declared to be sacred. And in the final Constitution we find something of this in the interpretation clause too. The final statement that 'every court, tribunal or forum must promote the spirit, purport and objects of the Bill of Rights' suggests that the Bill of Rights has a spirit as well as a letter. So, too, does the Constitutional Court, the august body that interprets this spirit.

MANDELA MANIA AND THE TRANSITIONAL EVENTS

It is not only the text that authorised the new dispensation and the political transition. The process of negotiations and the 'miracle' of the political transition were themselves secular authorisations for the new dispensations. The white referendum in 1992, the largely unexpected unbanning of the ANC and other political parties, the steady stream of returning exiles, the opening of Codesa and the removal of some of the racist laws all represented glimmers of a new South Africa. But it was not until the extraordinary first democratic election in 1994 that the new South Africa could appear embodied in a non-racial political community. The now iconic images of miles of queues on voting day confirmed this community.

When Mandela was inaugurated as the country's first black president, a great deal of the symbolism and ritual of the occasion would have needed no religious presence to provide its elevation and its sense of the miraculous.

Mandela was inaugurated at the Union Buildings in Pretoria, until then a bastion of white rule. The military, symbol of apartheid's oppression, expressed its allegiance to the new president in a moving fly-past. Mandela was flanked by his two deputies in a government of national unity, a symbol that nobody would be excluded from the united new South Africa, not even those who had sought to exclude themselves. They were surrounded by heads of state and the world's media, who witnessed and acknowledged the transition and welcomed the country into the 'family of nations'. It was perceived to be a miraculous moment, one that was almost too good to be true. And it was shared by millions, at the Union Buildings and watching on TV, who experienced the promise, achievement and excitement the moment marked.

The following year South Africa hosted the Rugby World Cup, marking the end of sporting sanctions and the return of South Africa to the international community. South Africa not only hosted the event but also won it in an extraordinary final match in what was the heartland of white rugby support. Nelson Mandela was there, wearing a Springbok rugby jersey and cheering on the still mostly white national team.

While the formal entitlements and racial equalities of the new Constitution went some way towards creating a common political community, that community could only be represented to itself and realised in these moments of heightened performance and emotion and through the politics of hope. And Mandela, known affectionately and intimately by his clan name, Madiba, was the centre of a constellation of such emotion and performance.

Much of the creation of a moral community between rulers and ruled was achieved by Mandela through his statesmanship during the transition and in the ways in which he sought to include as wide a range of political actors as possible in the membership of the emerging nation. There were some, of course, who resisted his advances, but many were won over by what came to be called 'Madiba Magic'. It was a very effective strategy. Mandela engaged in a wide range of languages and cultural tropes, from participating in ANC rallies that were recognisably Zulu to taking tea with the aged Betsy Verwoerd, widow of the architect of apartheid.

THE CEREMONIAL PRESENCE OF RELIGION

Many such examples could be given, and they point to the fact that the nationalist foundations of legitimacy of the new South Africa did not make religious presence or content central. But religious leaders and discourses did participate in many events of this early nationalism. From the start, figures of religious and traditional authority were willing participants in the religious sanctioning of moments of political significance.

At the end of 1990 a planning group met to prepare for the first multi-party talks at Codesa and to decide who would chair it. Who would have the dignity, skill, gravitas and neutrality to hold such an event together? At first religious leaders were proposed and Methodist bishop Stanley Mogoba and the Nederduits Gereformeerde Kerk's (Dutch Reformed Church's) Revd Heyns were nominated for the task. But there were complaints about the religious choice, particularly from the PAC, and a concern that non-Christian religious groups would be excluded from the process. The planning committee decided to ask two judges to chair instead, marking a transition that was henceforth to take place under the sign of the law. The two were Chief Justice Michael Corbett and Justice Ismail Mahomed, South Africa's first black Supreme Court judge.

But religious leaders were still felt to be necessary to the occasion. All Codesa's plenary sessions were opened and closed by a multitude of prayers and blessings. The first day, for example, saw Professor Heyns, Rabbi Cyril Harris, Sheikh Nazim Mohammed, Revd Mogoba and Pundit Vedelanker all blessing the gathering (COD NA61). Judge Corbett commended them for infusing 'with richness and dignity' a 'spiritual dimension to an occasion of momentous political and secular significance'.

At Mandela's inauguration a wide range of religious and traditional leaders and healers contributed to the symbolic heightening of the occasion, blessing Mandela and his presidency. In his prayer Tutu spoke of the arrival of the fullness of time, and 'hundreds of traditional healers massed at the Union Buildings to bless the new regime' and 'danced and burnt all the herbs for all South Africans – for Blacks, Whites, Indians and all' (Ashforth, 2000:103).

Another example of such a political rite of passage can be taken from late in the Constitution-writing process. The CA came to the end of its work in May 1996 when it produced a text to be sent to the Constitutional Court for certification and a ceremony was held at Parliament to mark the event. As hundreds of guests stood at the entrance to Parliament, an *imbongi* (praise singer) led Mandela and the others into the National Assembly, where the guests included a range of people considered important to reflect the achievement of national unity and a final Constitution. There were church leaders, imams and religious leaders from all the other faiths. There were non-governmental organisations and business people, the unions and representatives of civil servants and there were traditional leaders and traditional healers.

Nationalist public displays of the apartheid government always included a very visible presence of Reformed Church ministers. The public presence of religion in the transition was, by contrast, always inclusive of a wide range of religious figures. The administrators of the negotiations,

Parliament and the Office of the President all ensured that Muslims, Jews, Christians, Hindus and, more recently, Buddhists and Baha'i, were included in ceremonial functions.

This ceremonial inclusion is not representative of the dominance of Christianity amongst the population. It cannot be doubted that during the transition the political community came to include, in Charles Taylor's (2007:1) terms, 'believers and unbelievers alike', and Christians, Muslims, Hindus and Jews, both legally and socially. The right to religion was granted to all and in law religious affiliation has no impact on the status of citizenship. Both rhetorically and in the ways in which the transition was staged to the public, people of all faiths and none were equally part of, and welcome in, the new South Africa. The ANC itself represented a cosmopolitan and secular religious pluralism and its leaders went out of their way to affirm the membership of religious minorities in the national community.

THE TRUTH AND RECONCILIATION COMMISSION AND CHRISTIANITY AS A RESOURCE FOR NATION-BUILDING

The transition from apartheid to the new dispensation altered the basis of rule in South Africa. By eradicating the racial basis of citizenship and membership of the political community the process of transition sought to constitute a new and, for the first time, truly national political community. Some of the formal elements of this nation-building were addressed in the previous two chapters but they say little of the relationship between the social and political communities of South Africa and the possibility of forging a nation 'united in its diversity'.

After the rending of the 'medieval cloak of religion', nationalism became one of the most important forms by which people were brought into imagined communities. Nationalist movements, events, rhetoric, symbolism and public rituals involve people in a 'common enterprise, calling their attention to their relatedness and joint interests in a compelling way' (Edelman, 1967:16). The development of a South African national public over the course of the transition and the efforts of the new political leadership to consolidate a nation also drew on the resources of Christianity as the pervasive and majority religion in the country. Nowhere was this more apparent than in the processes of reconciliation and transformation.

Salazar (2002:16) has argued that while South Africa's 'new democracy is undoubtedly secular', its 'deliberative world view' was shaped 'in close alliance with a set of religious arguments regarding the nation' – what he terms a 'rhetorical conjunction of sacred and secular'. He argues that the terms of liberation theology popularised by Archbishop Tutu and widely used in his oratory were secularised both in popular discourse and by Mandela.

The idea of 'reconciliation' itself is an idea from St Paul, for example, which Tutu used to rebut the racial divisions of apartheid. It stood against the silencing, banning and arrests of many activists. Liberation theologians called for the 'subjugated to express their experience of oppression as a foundation for transformation' (Doxtader, 2009:74).

The term 'transformation', which was taken up by liberation theologians in the 1980s, was, itself, introduced to the South African lexicon from the concept of *metanoia*, the New Testament Greek word for repentance, which Protestant theologians like Karl Barth interpreted as transformation of heart, mind and action. Another central concept was that of the liberatory present or *kairos*. According to Albert Nolan, a South African Roman Catholic priest, 'The fundamental insight of prophetic theology is the recognition that an *eschaton* or day of reckoning and liberation is near. It is this that turns the present moment into a *kairos*' (Doxtader, 2009:65).

A group of black theologians under the leadership of Chikane met in Soweto in 1985 to challenge the churches about their response to apartheid. The Kairos document they produced in 1986 was a call to action to the churches framed in the language of reconciliation with justice. The idea of South Africa as a 'rainbow nation' came from Tutu's term 'the rainbow people of God', drawing inspiration from both Genesis and Ezekiel. In both biblical sources the rainbow marks God's epiphany and the restoration of the devastated community and its refounding after a period of evil and suffering (Salazar, 2002). Tutu also Christianised the idea of *ubuntu* into a form of generalised but African human compassion which could be contrasted with the divisiveness of apartheid (Marx, 2002).

These discourses remained theological until the 1980s when they were increasingly drawn upon in political rhetoric outside of the churches (Doxtader, 2009). The ANC's Kader Asmal publicly opened the question of amnesty and reconciliation in 1992 (Verdoolaege, 2006) when he set out the challenges of moving from a violent, unjust and divisive apartheid past to a just future; problems that required some sort of reckoning and reconciliation through what he called 'a revival of moral conscience' (Asmal, 1992:11). He argued that this would only be possible through debate, confronting the roots of violence, reconciliation on new terms, confession, justice, the avoidance of revenge and catharsis.

During the MPNP some NP politicians began to seek a blanket amnesty for themselves and their apartheid securocrats. Some in the ANC and all of the PAC, on the other hand, wanted criminal trials for perpetrators of apartheid. 'The amnesty-for-truth exchange of the TRC [Truth and

Reconciliation Commission] was the deal that brought a breakthrough' almost at the end of the MPNP (Verdoolaege, 2006:28).

The interim constitution's preamble refers to the Constitution as a bridge between an unjust past and a future free from injustice. But to span the gulf between past and future requires, it says, a reconciliation of the people and a reconstruction of society. The wording of the postamble was itself designed to be inclusive and to help constitute South Africans, whatever their political past, as members of a single community (Chipkin, 2007). To do this, the postamble avoided asserting a moral dichotomy between apartheid and the struggle.

The past, for example, was said to have generated 'gross violations of human rights', a 'transgression of humanitarian principles in violent conflict' and a legacy of 'hatred, fear, guilt and revenge'. It sought to deal with the past in such a way that it could be both acknowledged and transcended. It did this through a series of dichotomies. The past could now be addressed, it said, on the basis of understanding but not revenge, reparation but not retaliation, *ubuntu* but not victimisation. This was to be achieved via a conditional amnesty for acts, omissions and offences associated with political objectives. The postamble required that the postelection democratic Parliament pass an act to provide a mechanism for this reconciliation and reconstruction.

After the 1994 elections, Parliament debated what became the Promotion of National Unity and Reconciliation Act (No. 34 of 1995). Churches were very involved in these debates (Meiring, 2000). The beginning of the TRC and the completion of the drafting of the final Constitution overlap closely. On 16 April 1996 the first dramatic public hearings of the Human Rights Violations Committee were held. A month later the draft text of the final Constitution was sent to the Constitutional Court for ratification.

In terms of the Act it was Mandela's responsibility to appoint TRC commissioners. He selected Archbishop Tutu as its chair and four of the twelve commissioners were *Baruti* or Christian ministers. Local churches, particularly those affiliated with the SACC, were involved in the TRC in many ways. They provided venues and volunteers who helped to disseminate information about the hearings and who also acted as 'facilitators and spiritual guides' to victims and perpetrators (Meiring, 2000:125).

Piet Meiring, who was a TRC commissioner, writes of a 'TRC liturgy', which was taken from a Service of Dedication and Blessing of Commissioners of the TRC in St George's Cathedral in Cape Town in February 1996. It included hymns, multifaith prayers, the lighting of candles and the presentation of olive branches. 'These elements were repeated at most hearings in many parts of the country' (Meiring, 2000:126).

Hearings were opened and closed with hymns and prayers, and hymns were also used in response to moments of intense emotion and crisis. This custom began when Nomonde Calata, testifying at the first victims' hearing in East London, was overcome with grief in the telling of her husband's murder. After her crying subsided Tutu started singing the Xhosa hymn *Senzeni na* ('What have we done'). Everyone in the hall joined in the singing (Meiring, 2000:126).

But this Christian dominance was not uncontested, including within the TRC. Meiring has written about some of the tensions between those within the Commission who wanted a more secular framing, and Tutu and others who sponsored and enacted a religious rendition of reconciliation.

The first Johannesburg public hearings of the TRC were held at the Central Methodist Church from 26 April to 3 May 1996. The head of the Johannesburg TRC office, Commissioner Fazel Randera, was concerned that the earlier East London hearings had been 'too religious' and sought a more juridical style.

Randera suggested that the TRC follow the example of Parliament, which had decided to have a 'moment of silence' at the beginning of each event – a time for prayer or meditation if people wanted to use it. Tutu agreed to this and, although he appeared at this and all the other hearings in his vestments, with clerical collar and crucifix, he started the proceedings with a moment of silence. But when the first testimony was to get under way, Tutu stopped the proceedings and said, 'No! This is not the way to do it.' Then, as Meiring (2000:124) recounts, 'the Archbishop placed the hearing of the day in the Lord's hands, asking that Jesus Christ, who himself is the Truth, guide us in our quest for truth, that the Holy Spirit of God grant us the wisdom and grace we need'. Where the negotiations had taken place under the sign of the law, the TRC took place under the sign of religion.

The TRC received 31 000 submissions and 7 000 requests for amnesty. In the end it granted amnesty to just 150 people (Salazar, 2002). There were victims' hearings and commissions for amnesty and reparation. There was also a series of 'institutional hearings' that sought to address what the TRC report calls the 'backdrop' or context of 'gross human rights violations'. Institutional hearings covered business and labour, the faith and legal communities, the health sector, media and prisons. In addition, the commissioners initiated a series of what they called special hearings on compulsory military service, children and youth, and women. The greatest attention has been paid to the dramatic victims' hearings, which were televised live in South Africa, condensed into shorter programmes and broadcast nightly during prime time.

There has been considerable criticism of the TRC process as a whole, as well as religion's place in it. It is certainly beyond the scope of this chapter to address these in detail. But some brief comments may contribute to an understanding of the TRC in relation to secularism. Certainly there can be no doubt that Christian elements permeated the models of the TRC and its psychology of reconciliation.

The model for reconciliation was thoroughly Christian in that it was the duty of perpetrators to make a full disclosure of their activities, confess them and repent their actions. Victims, on the other hand, were given a chance to voice their experiences and the impact of those experiences on them and their families; to testify about their suffering. It was hoped they would gain some peace through hearing the truth about what had happened to their loved ones, and a chance to confront their persecutors. The idealised objective of their interaction was forgiveness.

Between confession and forgiveness, reconciliation was to be found. Every step of the process was informed by Christian practice and theology and the doctrine that forgiveness is a Christian calling (Meiring, 2000). Ebrahim Moosa (2000b:114) calls the workings of this model a performance, where 'the actors have already configured the purpose of the play and there is a hope that other participants and viewers will also understand its message'.

Much of the criticism relates to the public pressure on victims to forgive and questions the sincerity of the confessions of perpetrators (Christianse, 2003). Jacques Derrida, for example, criticised this way of instrumentalising forgiveness. Many have also questioned the relationship between individuals reconciling in tense and televised public hearings and a broader social and political process of reconciliation (Van der Walt, 2007). While nobody doubts that there were some powerful individual reconciliations, this clearly did not translate into the 'broader event of national or social reconciliation on which the peace and stability of a future South Africa would come to turn' (Van der Walt, 2007:12).

Significantly, the TRC prosecuted only those who were engaged in illegalities, even under apartheid law, rather than the more widespread injustice that was the law (Sachs, 2009). More than this, the model of individual reconciliation, when applied to a national society, can become what Van der Walt calls an 'offensive clerical moralism' which, he believes, has allowed white South Africans to withdraw from their responsibilities and secure their systematic privilege. 'Clerical moralism' leads to flippant and too easy reconciliation, a false unity under the sign of the rainbow nation.

Christopher Marx is one of many who argue that the TRC paid far too much attention to perpetrators instead of victims. He also argues that the TRC failed to engage with apartheid systematically, dealing instead with 'individual evil'. In doing so, it 'spared the white population from having to confront the system it had supported' (Marx, 2002:51). Instead, black

South Africans were valorised as people with a capacity to forgive, an exemplary spirit of forgiveness, of *ubuntu* (Marx, 2002). In a similar vein, Ivor Chipkin (2007) argues that the TRC failed to produce a South African subject. It produced, instead, an exemplary humanity that was the basis for a dangerous exceptionalism.

Tutu's chairing and theological framing of the TRC were ambiguous in respect of secularisation. Some have argued that the TRC was an affront to secularism, or betrayed it. Marx (2002:58), for example, writes that in the TRC 'the secular order is rejected ... and delegitimized through theocratic notions and concepts. The struggle for the end of apartheid becomes a divine mission in order to restore the order of the world.' But the TRC was not a religious event; it was a case of religious theology and personnel being brought into a nationalist or nation-building project that was quasi-juridical and state sponsored. It attempted to instrumentalise religious conceptions of forgiveness and reconciliation to constitute a national community that could include perpetrators and victims alike. Its goals were political, but, towards these political ends, it drew on a popular and widely shared set of concepts about social relations, evil, forgiveness and the possibility of a shared community. It also drew on the pastoral care of Tutu and other commissioners. TRC discourse combined Christian and human rights elements and the commissioners included non-Christians and people who had notions of a juridical rather than religious format for reconciliation.

The work of the TRC ended when Tutu handed the final report to Mandela in October 1998, though a few of its processes – reparations and the charging of people who were not awarded amnesty – are still ongoing. While the TRC hearings are over, the broader questions of racial and economic reconciliation and the possibility of justice in South Africa remain open. Will the Constitution be the foundation, as it promises, of a future reconciled and more egalitarian society?

6

SECULAR CONSTITUTIONALISM IN SOUTH AFRICA?

Having resisted the bullets and bombs of lead, we now face the bullets and bombs of sugar, and slowly we succumb to their sweetness ... If all power corrupts, the people's power corrupts in a popular way. A lucre continua! ... Now we must display resoluteness in resisting the idea of the inevitability of corruption and the certainty of authoritarianism.
Justice Albie Sachs (1992)

When I was growing up an ungqingili [a gay person] would not have stood in front of me. I would knock him out.
President Jacob Zuma (2006)[1]

South Africa's transition took place well into the rising tide of globalisation, neoliberalism, new forms of religion and a global remobilisation of cultural and ethnic identities. Many have commented on the fact that the South African Constitution is a robustly modernist law formulated at a time when many of the forms of rationality, state, religion and economy that underpin modernism are strained (see, for example, Comaroff and Comaroff, 1999; Garuba and Raditlhalo, 2008; Jacklin and Vale, 2009; Klug, 2000, 2010; Robins, 2008).

How have religion and tradition fared in the postapartheid state? What has happened to relationships between religion, tradition and the African National Congress (ANC) government? How has the right to religion been interpreted? How have its enabling provisions been legislated? Has the ambiguous place of traditional leadership and customary law been resolved? Have the institutions of traditional leadership been consolidated, transformed or limited by the democratic state? What are the consequences of the contrasting places of religion and tradition in law and governance?

These are political and legal questions. They are also closely related to changes in society and the economy. At the time of writing, 20 years have passed since the Constitution came into effect and 22 since the first democratic elections. This is not a very long time for state formation. New processes are constantly emerging. There is no privileged place in the present from which to assess the legacies of the transition, even as there are emerging trends and evident moments of consolidation and crisis. In this sense, all conclusions are provisional.

And many of the elements of postapartheid secularism have yet to be studied. Like much scholarship on religion and politics in South Africa, this book has paid attention to national-level processes and formal relations between politics, law and religious and traditional bodies. Some conclusions can be reached about these things, but the test of secular constitutionalism also lies in the many and diverse sites in which the state and religious and traditional claims engage. There is, as yet, very little academic research into the practical ways in which religious and traditional institutions are engaged in education, local government, social services and culture. As a result, much of the material I draw on for this chapter is journalistic.

AFTER APARTHEID

In the last months of 2015 thousands of university students mobilised across South Africa. Scenes of riot police and teargas so familiar from the anti-apartheid struggle replayed themselves,[2] though this time the protests related to the fulfilment of the promises of the transition. Sons and daughters of the black working and middle classes demanded delivery on the promises made by the ANC when it came to power, taking up the Freedom Charter's aspirations and, more broadly, addressing the rising crisis of confidence in the possibility of delivering on its election promise of 'a better life for all'. In 2016 student protests became increasingly radicalised and violent and were coupled with the widespread use of private security and the presence of the South African Police Services (SAPS) on higher-education campuses.

At the same time, on Facebook and Twitter, white racists were exposed and brought to account for virulent and hateful views aired with seeming impunity. Many online newspapers have had to close their comments section because of the ugliness and bigotry that has been vented there. This is not the politicised formation of the white right from 20 years ago; these are 'private' acts of unreconstructed and widespread racism.

Student and social media protests take place in the context of a decade of much more frequent, widespread and enduring community action against the failure to deliver basic services of housing, water, electricity, sanitation and safety to very poor township-dwellers across the country. The demonstrations express the frustration and disillusionment of ordinary South Africans about corruption, crime, load-shedding (the national electricity provider Eskom's frequent and semi-planned interruptions in electricity supply when there is not enough power on the grid) and ineffective local government.

Community protests have frequently been met with a brutal response from the police. The death of community activist Andries Tatane in a protest in Ficksburg in 2011 and the subsequent acquittal of the police officers who beat him to death mark one extreme of this repressive response to democratic protest. In 2012 at Marikana near Rustenburg, west of Johannesburg, the SAPS opened fire on platinum miners engaged in an illegal strike. One hundred and twelve people were shot and 34 died of their wounds. The massacre recalled the shootings at Sharpeville in 1960 and Soweto in 1976, only this time the political principals were black members of the ANC, in part defending their alliance partner, the National Union of Mineworkers.

The year 2016 began with a series of revelations of state capture by the Gupta family, Indian immigrants who have used their links with the family and close associates of President Zuma to gain access to business opportunities and influence. Evidence is mounting that elements of the ANC have ceded governance decisions to the Gupta brothers, including attempts to appoint and fire the minister of finance.

What do these events say about the first 20 years of South Africa's democracy? And what do they mean for the promises of a Constitution that at last sought to marry law and justice? The political settlement certainly brought hope for the future and an end to many forms of suffering and humiliation, but the record of the postapartheid state in terms of social and economic relief and opportunity for the majority of previously disenfranchised South Africans is very mixed indeed. Despite the ANC's optimistic slogan, the government has not delivered a 'better life for all' and negotiations did not bring an end to racism or white domination of the economy.

NELSON MANDELA – RECONSTRUCTION AND RECONCILIATION

It is possible to identify broad political and economic trends at the macro level in the past 20 years. These are the context and conditions for the ways religion and traditional authority have acted in the public domain. They fall into three periods that roughly correspond to the presidencies of Mandela, Thabo Mbeki and Zuma. First, redistributive Reconstruction and Development Programme (RDP) policies were introduced in conjunction with a somewhat conservative macroeconomic financial policy to address the legacies of apartheid debt.

In 1998 a more neoliberal policy replaced the RDP. Called Growth, Employment and Redistribution (Gear), its prime target was the reduction of national debt and improvements to macroeconomic conditions. While there was a strong rhetorical and pragmatic emphasis on extending basic services in the country, decisions were also made to expose South Africa to global trade and finance after the end of sanctions. Many of South Africa's largest companies divested from South Africa or listed offshore during this time, depriving the country of billions in capital. Some of South Africa's least competitive but most labour-intensive industries were all but gutted by the dropping of trade protection. This was particularly true for the textile industry and agriculture during the transition. No radically redistributive policies or taxes were introduced for previously acquired wealth.

The official unemployment rate went from an already worrying 19.0% in 1995 (Kingdon and Knight, 2005:3) to 25.4% in 2000. By 2003 it had reached 28.2%. Increasing numbers of poor families reported food hunger and insecurity. There is no commonly agreed poverty line in South Africa, which makes comparison difficult. But all measures show that between 1995 and 2000 poor households sank deeper into poverty and the gap between rich and poor widened.

Between 1994 and 1998 between thirty and forty per cent of South Africa's children sometimes went to bed hungry (Altman, Hart and Jacobs, 2009:12). At the same time, moderate macroeconomic growth allowed for increases in spending as the first democratic government attempted to address the extraordinarily unequal spatial and racial distribution of local services, education, health and welfare. There were some symbolic and real gains for the poor in terms of services and the creation of a more open national public sphere with black representation and participation. Policies to give black individuals and businesses access to ownership of the economy were supported. A visible black middle class was fêted as proof of political liberation.

Early on, the ANC established and consolidated its control of the levers of government. In 1994 it won nearly 63.0% of the vote. In 1999 it increased that majority to 66.4%. The National Party broke into two new formations: the New National Party, seeking to distance itself from its apartheid legacy, won only 6.7% and the Democratic Party (DP) won 9.6%.

The tide of HIV infection that was just starting during the transition rapidly became an epidemic as infection rates rose, unchecked by a new government ill-equipped either ideologically or practically for a rapid and early response. 'In 1990, the estimated prevalence of HIV infection was less than 1 percent; by 1998, it had reached 22.8 percent – and as much as 32.5 percent in some parts of KwaZulu-Natal' (Posel, 2008:21). By the turn of the century, somewhere in the region of 5.5 million South Africans were infected with the virus, the largest national infection in the world (Dorrington et al., 2004).

MBEKI AND ECONOMIC AND GOVERNANCE CONSOLIDATION

Mbeki became president in 1999 after the ageing Mandela stepped down after one term. By early 2000 apartheid's internal debts were all but paid off and the recovery of revenue from tax collection was much improved. This provided finance for a programme of expanded spending by the Mbeki presidency, particularly on social grants, which contributed to a reduction in rates of hunger, and on public administration.

Economic growth continued steadily under Mbeki, and increased investor confidence led to a small but steady decrease in the level of unemployment to 22.7% in 2007 (Statistics South Africa, 2015b). Water and electricity services expanded and there was a steady rise in the esteem in which public institutions were held.

These tangible social and economic gains for poor and working-class South Africans paid off at the elections, as did political support for black economic empowerment policies. There was a lower voter turnout in 2004, but the ANC further consolidated its electoral dominance, winning just shy of seventy per cent of the vote. Politics and governance appeared to be normalising. The New National Party fell apart as its members moved either to the ANC, the DP or the right. The liberal DP gained 12.37% and became the official opposition. The Inkatha Freedom Party (IFP) continued to lose support, receiving only 6.97% of the national vote.

But the rapid grasp of the HIV epidemic on South Africa was truly a bitter poison for the new democracy and for the promises of a new society to which the negotiators had looked. The epidemic took hold in part because of Mbeki's AIDS denialism, which confused many, corrupted public debate and held up the roll-out of life-saving medication. Literally hundreds of thousands of lives were lost in the process.

Since the transition was a statist project, with many imagining that a powerful government would deliver both freedom and prosperity, it is ironic that state institutions have turned out to be significant vectors for inequality and poverty. The middle classes have increasingly acquired their services privately and through debt, purchasing private schooling, hospital care and security, while the poor often live with broken schools, policing and healthcare.

Where the late 1990s had been a time of optimism, the mood was changing by 2005. There was a growing impatience with the pace and quality of service delivery in the context of increasing disparities in wealth and opportunity. Corruption and enrichment within the ANC were also becoming more apparent and there was 'a worrisome reversal in trust in virtually all major public institutions, particularly in local government and Parliament, but also in the other two tiers of government' (Roberts, waKivilu and Davids, 2010:5). In the run-up to the 2006 local government elections there were hundreds of protests over local service delivery and the non-provision of housing, roads, toilets and public amenities in townships. The ANC responded with allegations of a third force rather than acknowledging the poor quality of many of its local councillors and the systematic problems of delivery in those areas.

South Africa was also rocked by a series of corruption scandals around senior individuals within the ANC. The credibility of national crime statistics was questioned as it became apparent that police stations were under pressure to underreport major and violent crimes. Even more undermining were the continued revelations of the personal enrichment of senior members of the ANC in the arms deal concluded soon after the transition. Repeatedly foiled attempts to investigate the deal put enormous pressure on the separation of powers and the independent investigative organs of the state. The head of the SAPS and Interpol, Jackie Selebi, was found guilty of fraud and money laundering. South Africa's politics has increasingly been marked by corrupt relations between those in government and the business elite.

The period between the 2004 and 2009 elections was also politically turbulent within the ANC. In May 2005 businessman Schabir Shaik, then Deputy President Zuma's financial advisor, was found guilty of having a 'generally corrupt relationship' with Zuma. In mid-2005 Mbeki announced that Zuma would be relieved of his duties. His dismissal fostered division within the ANC and a backlash against Mbeki, who was already resented for his micromanagement and paranoia.

While the National Prosecuting Authority prevaricated over whether to charge Zuma with fraud and corruption, a charge of rape was brought against him in December 2005. A conviction would have made Zuma ineligible to stand as president, but on 8 May 2006 he was acquitted

(*State v Zuma* 1995(2) SA 642 (CC)). The acquittal opened the way for his continued rise to power, his ambition fuelled by anger and a sense of betrayal. In December 2007 at the ANC's 53rd National Conference, held in Polokwane in Limpopo province, he was elected president of the ANC, defeating an increasingly unpopular Mbeki. A few months later Mbeki was called upon to step down as president and his deputy, Kgalema Motlanthe, became caretaker president until the 2009 elections.

The internal politics of the ANC also produced new challengers to power. After the Polokwane conference that unseated Mbeki, Mosiuoa 'Terror' Lekota, a former ANC Cabinet minister, and Mbhazima Shilowa, a former ANC premier of Gauteng, broke away from the ANC to form a party called the Congress of the People (Cope). Just weeks before the 2009 elections the National Prosecuting Authority decided not to charge Zuma with corruption, leaving him free to stand. The process revealed considerable political interference with organs of the state from both the Zuma and the Mbeki factions of the ANC.

The ANC won the 2009 elections, but for the first time since the transition its following declined. It won only 65.9% of the vote, with breakaway Cope winning 7.42%. The Democratic Alliance (DA, the former DP) won 16.7%, consolidating its status as official opposition.

THE CRACKS WIDEN

The political crisis of 2009 seemed to pass, with Zuma finally becoming president of both the ANC and the country. The subsequent success of South Africa's hosting of the 2010 Soccer World Cup offered a window once again onto a politics of hope. But many of the underlying issues of racism, unemployment, HIV, crime, sexual violence, xenophobia, corruption and inequality did not go away. In addition, South Africa began to feel the consequences of the global economic downturn.

The ANC has repeatedly presented its record in government as an almost unmitigated success and, in some respects, in the first 15 years there were many achievements with regard to the distribution of public goods and services. These gains are particularly visible in the kinds of research that produce multidimensional rather than money-metric poverty measures and consider what policy documents call the social wage – free primary health-care, free education at primary and secondary schools for poor learners, RDP housing and free portions of basic services to households, including small allocations of free water, electricity and sanitation. It was noted in 2013 that 'close to 60 percent of government spending is allocated to the social wage, and expenditure on these services has more than doubled in real terms over the past decade' (Statistics South Africa, 2014:8).

A 2013 study by the University of Cape Town's Southern African Labour and Development Research Unit that compares poverty in a number of domains between 1993 and 2010 (Finn, Leibbrandt and Woolard, 2013) constructed a composite indicator that includes education, health and living standards.

The education indicator takes into account the number of schooling years and attendance rates; health includes child mortality and nutrition; and living standards includes infrastructural access to cooking fuel, sanitation services and water, electricity and housing assets, though each indicator has a very low cut-off point for deprivation. For example, half the population did not have access to piped water to households in 1993 and by 2010 half of those had been connected to bulk water supplies. Using these metrics of access to basic services, the authors state that poverty fell from thirty-seven to only eight per cent, with what they call severe poverty dropping to just over one per cent in 2010 (Finn, Leibbrandt and Woolard, 2013:1).

What such indicators leave out are the subjective and objective measures of quality of life and relative deprivation. They also fail to take into account the fact that even if householders have infrastructure they may not be able to afford consumables such as electricity or water. In addition, service delivery has been uneven, often of poor quality and the source of considerable local corruption and conflict. Housing has been amongst the most difficult areas of delivery. Many of the more than a million houses built in the 12 years between 1993 and 2005 were far from places of employment, poorly serviced and of exceptionally bad quality. The massive investments in formalising township settlements often created spatial poverty traps. By 2004 only thirty-eight per cent of South Africans were satisfied with the performance of their local government or municipality (Roberts, waKivilu and Davids, 2010).

In contrast to the service-delivery approach to poverty research, Statistics South Africa uses self-reported measures of poverty. During a survey for the 2008/09 year, fifty-seven per cent of a representative sample of South Africans identified themselves as poor, saying that they did not have enough income to make ends meet (Statistics South Africa, 2012).

Some of the gains of the 2000s were reversed by the combined impact of the global financial crisis and the ongoing problem of very weak school-level public education. What improvements there were in unemployment rates have been reversed, with unemployment standing at 25.3% in 2010 compared with 22.7% in 2007 (Statistics South Africa, 2015b).

Even where people do have paid work, many jobs are precarious and poorly paid. Though trade unions have been a very important force in the ruling alliance and in South Africa's political life, a relatively small proportion of people employed in the formal sector belong to unions. Of 13.6 million people in formal employment, only 3.7 million are union members.

One of the main contributors to income inequality, even amongst the employed, is the racial differentiation in the levels of skills required by the job, and therefore the levels of remuneration. Sixty-eight per cent of employed white men are in skilled occupations, 34.2% in semi-skilled jobs and only 3.9% in low-skilled occupations. In contrast, the majority of black men with jobs are in semi-skilled (56.3%) or low-skilled (29.9%) work. Only 13.8% are in skilled occupations (Statistics South Africa, 2015b). The wage consequences are huge. And aside from black university gradu- ates, 'at every education level, the absorption rate among black African men is lower than that of men in other population groups' (Statistics South Africa, 2015b:vii). According to data analysed by the Children's Institute, in 2013, thirty-one per cent (5.7 million) of South African children lived in households where no adult was employed.[3] Aside from the dire economic consequences, there is also the hopelessness, humiliation and frustration of life without work.

Even given pro-poor and black economic empowerment policies, inequality has increased since 1994. Martin Wittenberg (2014) argues that although overall mean wages have increased since then, real wages for those at the upper earning end have increased faster. This is partly a result of the depressed earnings of those in informal self-employment, as more and more people turn to this as a livelihood strategy (Wittenberg, 2014). It also mirrors global trends.

The slow pace of delivery on the promises of the transition, coupled with Zuma's record of poor management and integrity, has had an effect on the ANC's electoral performance. The national elections of 2014 had the lowest voter turnout since the transition. The ANC lost support, gain- ing only 62.5% of votes. Cope lost almost all its ground, winning less than 1.0% of the national vote. The DA consolidated its gains, winning 22.3% of the vote.

Internal factions within the ANC again produced a new opposition party. This time, the dismissed head of the ANC Youth League, Julius Malema, registered a new political formation, the Economic Freedom Fighters (EFF), just before the 2014 elections. The party won 6.35% of the national vote in its first election.

What these figures mask is the precipitous decline in ANC support in urban areas, the locations of the growth of the black middle class. In Gauteng the ANC garnered only 54.9% of the vote in 2014 compared to 64.7% in 2009 – a 10.0% drop in just five years in the economic hub of the country. Concern about this is one of the motives for the ANC drawing closer to traditional leaders in rural areas and for the continuation and political importance of social grants.

The majority of South Africans are clearly unhappy with the way things are going. According to 2013 data from the Human Sciences Research Council's (HSRC's) South African Social Attitudes Survey, one of the most reliable public opinion monitors, '[j]ust over half of the population (51%) is unsatisfied with the state of democracy in South Africa, and only 33% were satisfied with the way democracy is working'.[4] These are the lowest recorded levels since the transition.

It is hard to see how the ANC will improve its record of schooling or governance with the current internal dynamics, its economic management paradigm and the global context. The country is experiencing a stagnation of growth that is worrying in contrast to the performance of its Southern African neighbours. South Africa's economy grew at an average of about 3.3% per year from 1995 to 2010 (Pillay et al., 2013), but in 2015 the Business Confidence Index was at its lowest point since 1993 and the International Monetary Fund reduced the country's growth forecast from 2.1% to 1.3% (less than half the global growth rate) for 2016. The growth rate was 1.3% for 2016. IMF projections are 0.3% for 2017 and 0.8% for 2018.[5]

One of the ways the government has responded to falling growth in the aftermath of the 2008 financial crisis is counter-cyclical investment in infrastructure spending. Though creating some employment and bulk infrastructure, this has also massively increased national debt, which rose from twenty-six per cent of GDP in 2008 to forty-seven per cent in 2015. The servicing of debt has become the government's fastest-growing expenditure (Steyn, *Mail & Guardian*, 21 October 2015).

RELIGION AND GOVERNMENT

There has been little evidence of a secular turn since the transition in terms of religious affiliation or adherence. In fact, the most recent HSRC survey reports that an increased eighty per cent of South Africans identify themselves as Christian (Roberts, waKivilu and Davids, 2010). This figure is, however, based on a small sample and it would be wrong to draw firm conclusions about an increased adherence to Christianity. Without a new religion census, it is impossible to accurately track overall trends in religious affiliation.

Having said that, high levels of religious intensity seem plausible. The survey revealed that a little over half the population attends a religious service at least once a week and another twenty-five per cent at least once a month. Even given the likelihood that this is overreported, these are very strong indicators of religious attachment. According to the HSRC, 'three-quarters of the adult population express a resolute faith in the existence of God and claim that "Jesus is the solution to all the world's problems"'. Nine out of ten said they believed in 'the power of prayer' and three-quarters that they prayed at least once a day. 'While trust in many public institutions began to wane in 2005 ... there remained an overwhelming and steadfast confidence in churches and religious organisations' (Roberts, waKivilu and Davids, 2010:11). The institutional assertion of political secularism in South Africa does not appear to have resulted in a reduction in religiosity. In this, South Africa's secularism is similar to that of North America and India.

What *has* changed significantly is the institutional place of religion relative to government. The close and cooperative relationships between the interfaith movement (World Conference on Religion and Peace, or WCRP), mainline Protestants (South African Council of Churches, or SACC) and the ANC during the negotiations continued when Mandela established a Commission for Religious Affairs in 1995. According to its literature, it has a 'spiritual function which includes a chaplaincy', a political function that 'relates spiritual and theological insights to current issues' and a religious function to promote understanding and cooperation with religious bodies.[6]

The SACC offered its support to the new government in many ways. Its 1995 conference captured this relationship in the phrase 'critical solidarity', to denote its desire to be a partner in the South African nation-building project. This solidarity was best expressed in the leadership that members of the SACC provided to the Truth and Reconciliation Commission (TRC).

Institutionally though, the interfaith movement and the SACC weakened considerably after the transition, with many religious leaders withdrawing from the public sphere (Omar, 2002). Others, including senior church leaders, joined the government. Revd Frank Chikane, one-time secretary-general of the SACC, joined the presidency. Father Smangaliso Mkhatshwa, once a member of the Catholic Bishops Conference, was appointed mayor of Tshwane (Pretoria). International financial support received by churches on behalf of the struggle began to be channelled directly to the ANC and government programmes, leaving the ecumenical movements with far fewer resources (Bompani, 2006).

The place where the mainline churches and progressive religionists were most visible was the TRC but, for all its importance, the TRC is only one element of a much more complex story about the public role of religion after apartheid. Even during the TRC the ecumenical churches became more distanced from and critical of elements of government policy. When the Gear macroeconomic policy was introduced in 1998 without consultation with the ruling ANC–Congress of South African Trade Unions (Cosatu)–South African Communist Party alliance or the ANC's civil society supporters (Suttner, 2010), many mainline church leaders felt they had been betrayed (Interview, Chagunda, 2005).

The SACC responded by establishing more formal channels for communication with the government about public policy, not only in direct conversation with the ANC but also in the spaces of Parliament. The SACC created a Public Policy Liaison Office, later called the Parliamentary Office. The following year the Catholic Bishops Conference decided to set up a parallel office after it became clear that the churches differed over the issue of termination of pregnancy (Interview, Pearce, 2005).

In 1997, in an effort to bring the churches back into a closer relationship with the ANC, Mandela convened an interfaith National Religious Leaders Forum (NRLF) to draw religious communities into a common project of nation-building, referring to it as a partnership to bring about transformation. The NRLF acknowledged the separation of religion and state, but not a distance between political and spiritual integrity. A working group met monthly and, in 1998, produced an 'Ubuntu Pledge' and a 'Code of Conduct for Persons in Positions of Responsibility'. The NRLF also helped to conceptualise and launch a Morals Summit in October that year. The following year they drafted a 'Code of Electoral Conduct' in preparation for the April 1999 national elections. It appeared that the close relationships between the ANC, the SACC and the ecumenical movements, now embodied in the NRLF, were to be sustained. But as the ANC consolidated its power and Mbeki took office, this relationship became increasingly antagonistic.

The opening speech of the then secretary-general of the SACC, Dr Molefe Tsele, at the 2001 SACC conference offers some insight into the church's increasing discomfort with its role in providing moral authority to the ANC. Tsele said: 'We must run away from an incestuous co-habitation with government ... To be in alliance with a persecuted political movement is one thing, but to become an ally in government is another' (Tsele, 2001).

He criticised the ANC for seeking to 'instrumentalise the Church' and denounced a government which, he said, 'consorts with their new-found comrades in the World Bank and IMF ... We should refuse to be turned into praise singers of the state,' he said, and 'it is clear that what South Africa needs at this juncture is not a weak or domesticated SACC, but an SACC that has a clear vision of its role as an agent of transformation' (Tsele, 2001). In the rest of his speech he raised concerns about Gear, arms deal corruption and access to HIV and AIDS medication to prevent mother-to-child transmission.

Thabo Mbeki responded angrily. As the newspapers reported at the time, 'President Thabo Mbeki ... joined the chorus of African National Congress criticism of church leaders.' He suggested that the churches had 'abandoned the common struggle against the legacy of apartheid' (Kindra, *Mail & Guardian*, 2 November 2001). The ANC in KwaZulu-Natal (KZN) called Tsele's speech 'satanic and evil' (Kindra, *Mail & Guardian*, 2 November 2001). Caught up in the rhetoric of AIDS denialism, they said that the church was nothing but a sales agent for the pharmaceutical industry.

Tsele was not the only person who felt the ire of the ANC. Archbishop Njongonkulu Ndungane, Desmond Tutu's successor as head of the Anglican Church, was reviled for his outspokenness. This was a new incivility in relations between the churches and the ANC.

In 2001 the disquiet with the situation of 'critical solidarity' was such that the Triennial National Conference, the highest body of the SACC, resolved to adopt an attitude of critical engagement in its dealings with the state and other organs of civil society. Gone was the concept of solidarity. Tutu, now finished with the work of the TRC, became a stronger voice against the government. In 2002, when he received an honorary degree from the University of Pretoria, he used his speech to take on the government over its AIDS policy, its stance on Zimbabwe and on the arms deal.

In November 2004 Tutu, invited to give the Nelson Mandela Annual Lecture, used it as an opportunity to raise concerns about the leadership and direction of the ANC. He was scathing about Mbeki's denialist position on HIV and AIDS and about the fact that many within the ANC seemed unwilling or unable to speak out against him: 'An unthinking, uncritical, kowtowing party line-toeing is fatal to a vibrant democracy. I am concerned to see how many have so easily been seemingly cowed and apparently intimidated to comply' (Tutu quoted in Bompani, 2006:1142).

The president responded with a personal attack on Tutu in the online publication *ANC Today*, a vilification that was widely reported in the press. The chair of the Parliamentary Portfolio Committee on Sport, ANC MP Butana Komphela, went so far as to call Tutu's views 'treasonous' (SACC, 2005). The SACC tried to calm things, calling for a 'culture of open debate without personality characterisation' (SACC, 2004) and the use of 'temperate language'. But clearly, elements within the ANC thought they could no longer afford to allow the SACC or Tutu to be the voice of South Africa's moral conscience.

Mbeki's team mounted a dual strategy of undermining and co-opting the SACC, which succeeded in taking some of the edge off their antagonistic relationship. The inner-circle religious working group Mbeki formed was intended, William Gumede (2005:369) contends, to draw 'critical clerics away from rebellious ANC allies and closer to the Mbeki camp'. Mbeki also used his speech opening the 2004 SACC conference to take a swipe at the council, saying that it should not be 'content merely to criticize or approve what others are striving to achieve'.[7] Referring to the ANC's landslide 2004 election victory, Mbeki described the millions of SACC members as 'the same millions who, only two and a half months ago, voted us into government'. Continuing in a rather patronising tone, he suggested that the SACC should 'identify itself with the national agenda I have sought to explain'.

Delegates at the conference took this criticism to heart, framing the nature of the organisation's relationship with the state in much less political terms and in the technical language of development. The new relationship was to be characterised by what it termed 'church-state development cooperation'. The conference mandated its national executive committee to 'research and define models of cooperation between Churches and Governments' and to 'negotiate a new partnership for community development'. The resolution states that 'such a model of cooperation shall seek in combining the resources of the Government with the networks and capacities of the Churches, to establish equity, good governance and the realisation of the Millennium Development Goals (MDGs) in order to benefit the poorest and alleviate poverty' (SACC, 2004).

As the ANC entered a period of deepening crisis after 2006, particularly in relation to its own integrity and leadership battles, it increased the visibility and intensity of its relationships with religious bodies once again. While it may have contained the critical voice of the SACC, it could no longer rely on the council's members to provide open support for new policies. This was particularly true for the ANC faction emerging under the leadership of Zuma.

In 2006, for example, Tutu publicly urged Zuma to drop out of the party's presidential succession race. By 2009 both parties were reporting 'frank and robust' discussions.[8] The SACC president at the time, Tinyiko Maluleke, was reported as saying that the SACC wanted to be 'free to differ' with the ANC, 'When we agree with them, it should not be because they tell us to' (Mataboge, *Mail & Guardian*, 18 September 2009b). The SACC accused the ANC of marginalising it because it refused to 'cosy up' to the party (Mataboge, *Mail & Guardian*, 18 September 2009b). More specifically, the SACC intervened, unsuccessfully, to try to broker a deal internal to the ANC in which Mbeki would step down at the end of his term rather than being recalled. They were also viewed by some to be too closely aligned with the breakaway Cope, whose parliamentary head, Revd Mvume Dandala, was a previous president of the council. So too, however, was Frank Chikane, Mbeki's head of the Office of the President.

In 2008 Ray McCauley, head of the Rhema Church, together with an embattled Zuma, announced the creation of a new body to be called the National Interfaith Leadership Council (NILC). It was to become one of the vehicles for an increasingly close relationship between the ANC and the Rhema Church. According to one government source quoted in the *Mail & Guardian* (Mataboge, 18 September 2009b), the charismatic churches should be rewarded because they had mobilised people to vote for Zuma and the NILC was more representative and supportive of informal churches. Zuma called for a new language and logic of relations with religious groups (West, 2010).

Two of McCauley's closest colleagues, Dr Carl Niehaus and Revd Ron Steele, sat on the NILC's working committee. Niehaus was later appointed head of the ANC's communications division, an appointment he had to relinquish when a trail of fraud and indebtedness was exposed by the press. Composed of 20 religious leaders, NILC included four ANC MPs, including Ebrahim Rasool, then Western Cape premier, and Dr Mathole Motshekga, previous chief whip of the ANC and previous ANC premier of Gauteng.

Rhema's 30th anniversary celebrations were attended by Zuma's wife MaNtuli as well as by the then minister of social development, Edna Molewa. The NILC has been known to use ANC parliamentary facilities to communicate with the media, and there is an increasing overlap between the ANC and socially conservative religionists.

Rhema gave Zuma an exclusive platform during his election campaign. Zuma attended a megachurch service in Rustenburg in March 2009 where he was given a chance to speak from the pulpit. Standing with bowed head, McCauley and his attending ministers prayed for and blessed Zuma. About 50 members of the congregation walked out in protest (Shoba, *Business Day*, 17 March 2009). Vusi Mona, Rhema spokesperson at the time, defended the church's actions. Shortly afterwards Mona was appointed to Zuma's presidential communications team, following in Niehaus's footsteps.

In September 2011 the NRLF and the NILC were officially merged into a new National Interfaith Council of South Africa. McCauley and Roman Catholic Archbishop Buti Thlagale were elected to co-chair the body. National Interfaith Council of South Africa has the spirit of the NILC, although it is also more conspicuously aligned with traditional leaders and revisionist versions of Africanist spiritualism. It is dominated by Dr Motshekga, founding director of the Kara Heritage Institute, which educates communities about indigenous cultural heritage and African tradition. The two bodies share offices in Pretoria.

A lawyer by training, Motshekga now lectures on the psychic history of African spirituality. He is also a member of the Institute of Traditional

Leadership and a legal advisor to the National House of Traditional Leaders of South Africa and the National Coalition of Traditional Leaders. Increasingly, the link between charismatic Christianity, traditional authority and the ANC is being forged in an antiliberal alliance.

It was not only to the Rhema Church that Zuma turned for legitimacy and moral standing in his political battles. He made public appearances at many smaller Pentecostal and Zionist churches. In February 2007, for example, Bishop Steven Zondo's Rivers of Living Waters Ministry held a prayer meeting for Zuma in Everton in Gauteng. There Zuma said that the ANC really needed the church and its prayers in this period. Then, with Gospel music star Solly Moholo, Zuma sang his hallmark electioneering song, *Mshini Wam* (Bring me my machine gun), and four bishops put their hands on him and prayed for him. He then put on the red coat worn by male members of the church. The prayer meeting was followed by a fundraising 'business lunch' in aid of the church and the Friends of Jacob Zuma Trust, a group established to raise funds to meet the costs of Zuma's legal battles.

In May 2007 Bishop Ben Mthethwa declared Zuma an 'honorary pastor' of a Charismatic independent church at Ntuzuma, north of Durban. In his talk there, Zuma is reported to have urged churches to work closely with government 'in order to transform society' (*News24*, 6 May 2007). Speaking of his ordination, Zuma called it 'a symbol that has been decided on by the church, that we should work together ... This is, in a sense, to arm me in my work as one of the leaders, that we could jointly lead the people together' (*News24*, 6 May 2007). The Full Gospel Church later distanced itself from the ordination, maintaining that although it had taken place at its venue, the ceremony had been performed by another church (*Mail & Guardian*, 8 May 2007).

Zuma's campaign was marked by more than just this visible support from church leaders. He also drew on a popular messianic lexicon. At a rally in Khayelitsha outside Cape Town in May 2008, he said, 'Even God expects us to rule this country because we are the only organisation which was blessed by pastors when it was formed. It is even blessed in heaven. That is why we will rule until Jesus comes back' (Dube, *The Citizen*, 6 May 2008). In June 2009 Zuma said, 'The ANC will rule until the Son of Man comes.' When the SACC general secretary, Eddie Makue, criticised this statement, the Friends of Jacob Zuma Trust responded that the SACC was trying to 'privatise Jesus and turn Christianity into a cult' (Mabena, *The Times*, 22 June 2009; Ncana, *The Times*, 24 June 2009).

Zuma was not the only person to claim divine sanction. The Free State's powerful ANC premier, Ace Magashule, suggested that Zuma was like Jesus; that he was being 'crucified like Christ'. Yvonne Phosa, a senior ANC leader in Mpumalanga, expressed similar sentiments at a rally at Elukwatini the week before the 2009 elections, after local priests had prayed for an ANC electoral victory, saying that the ANC 'had the wisdom of Christ and the stick of Moses' (Mkhabela, *Sunday Times*, 19 April 2009).

'As we emerge from the Easter, we are sprinkling the blood of Jesus Christ into the body and soul of the ANC,' she said. 'If you go with Jesus Christ, nothing is impossible ... Now, He is with the ANC' (Mkhabela, *Sunday Times*, 19 April 2009). On 4 April 2009, the day Zuma heard that the corruption charges against him were to be dropped, he visited the powerful Shembe Church in KZN. There he wore the white robes of purity of that congregation. The caption of a front-page image of this visit in the *Sunday Times* the next day read 'white as snow'.

Mobilising traditional and religious tropes, Zuma appeared as a positively messianic figure; a black Jesus. Both he and the ANC played up to this image of a charismatic and religious man (Suttner, 2010:53). While this dimension of Zuma's leadership rather faded from view after he won the ANC presidency in 2007 and the national elections in 2009, it returns in moments of crisis. In October 2013 at the Evangelical Presbyterian Church in Guyani, for example, Zuma said that those who insult leaders in positions of authority will be cursed (Moloto, *IOL*, 7 October 2013). Before the 2014 national elections, Zuma again toured churches where he preached, was prayed for and hands were laid on him.

It was not only the ANC that sought to garner support through its proximity to the church. Cope, the first ANC breakaway political party, appointed Methodist minister Dandala as its parliamentary head. Dandala immediately resigned all his positions in the church. Although Phillip Dexter, then Cope's head of communications, suggested to the media, 'He [has] committed himself to defend the secular nature of our democracy' (Dexter, *Mail & Guardian*, 3–8 April 2009), the link between Dandala's religious leadership and his political promise was central to Cope's strategy. Dexter called Dandala a man of 'unassailable integrity' who would take a strong stance on 'clean governance' (Mataboge, *Mail & Guardian*, 27 February–5 March 2009a). The ANC denounced what it saw as Cope's strategy to woo the religious vote. In a fine piece of biblical banter, Zuma said Cope was like Jesus's donkey, and the ANC, by inference, was like Jesus (West, 2010:8).

There can be no doubt that Christianity was politicised in the run-up to the 2009 and 2014 elections. During these campaigns Zuma appeared to promise churches the possibility of amending the Constitution to allow for the death penalty, corporal punishment and an end to abortion and gay marriage. Although careful not to be seen to support these demands directly, he suggested that the time had come for 'open debate' about them. In September 2009 (Rossouw, *Mail & Guardian*, 11 September 2009), six months after the elections, McCauley announced that the Rhema Church wanted to revisit laws legalising abortion and same-sex marriage. At that point Zuma made it clear that the Constitution could not be changed on these matters and the debate was thereby curtailed.

While the ecumenical WCRP and the mainline Protestant SACC won over a version of moralising Pentecostalism in the constitutional negotiations, Pentecostal Christians' views are far more representative of national mores about social and sexual morality. Judith Stacey and Tey Meadow (2009) refer to a 1995 survey that showed that forty-four per cent were against gay rights in the Constitution and sixty-eight per cent opposed gay people being allowed to adopt children. An HSRC survey conducted in 2003 revealed that seventy-five per cent were in favour of capital punishment, seventy-four per cent thought abortion wrong and seventy-eight per cent thought that gay sex was always wrong (Pillay, Roberts and Rule, 2006:36).

During the transition period 'moral values' that dealt with sexual and familial morality did not seem to affect voting behaviour (Pillay, Roberts and Rule, 2006). The ANC garnered substantial support despite its strong counter-majoritarian stance on issues of termination of pregnancy, pornography and the protection of the right to non-normative sexual orientation. In contrast, parties like the African Christian Democratic Party, which did mobilise on this basis, received very little support.

But with the muting of the voice of 'prophetic' Christianity in the postapartheid period and the person of Zuma as president, new charismatic Christian leaders have mobilised around populist social issues that have the potential to politicise the gap between policy and the views and experiences of many South Africans.

Demographically, these forms of religiosity are far more numerous than their mainline church opposition and they are all the stronger because they have a great deal of affinity with claims to tradition and culture articulated by traditional leaders. It is only in this context and in the midst of now acknowledged problems of corruption and 'tenderpreneurship' that the ANC's increasing attention to discourses of morality, culture and tradition can be understood.

TRADITIONAL LEADERSHIP, CUSTOM AND GOVERNANCE

The Constitution articulates contrasting frameworks for religion and tradition. Put simply, traditional leaders were institutionally included in the state but their grounds for legitimacy were rhetorically and performatively excluded during negotiations. Religion was institutionally excluded from the state but was rhetorically and performatively included in the project of nation-building, particularly through a political theology of reconciliation. Religion's place was clearly articulated. The legal articulation of custom, customary law and traditional authority, on the other hand, was ambiguous, confused and unfinished.

ADDRESSING TRADITIONAL LEADERSHIP IN POLICY

Throughout the negotiations, elements of the ANC sought to simultaneously include, discipline and transform the institution of traditional leadership. For their part, traditional leaders sought to secure their place *qua* traditional leaders locally, within the ANC and in national legislation. The tension among these various interests continued unresolved after 1996. Neither the interim nor the final Constitution repealed apartheid or homeland legislation on chieftainship. As a result, from 1994 until 2003 tribal and regional authorities continued to exist largely as they had in the homelands, but without coherent legislative authority (Williams, 2009). Writing about Sekhukhuneland in 2000, Barbara Oomen (2005:38) could say that 'almost all the institutional arrangements that singled out the former homelands as separate spheres of rule, largely under chiefly jurisdiction, were still in place'.

After the transition the state's financial support for traditional leaders increased dramatically. 'It was estimated in 1999 that … paying the salaries of traditional leaders (excluding headmen and representatives of the national and provincial houses) cost the South African government R577 million a year, of which R18 million went to the Zulu King alone' (Oomen, 2005:56). As of April 2007 kings and paramount chiefs were paid an annual salary of R545 066 and the approximately 800 chiefs received R130 830 each per annum. In addition, chairs and deputy chairs of the national and provincial houses of traditional leaders were paid salaries on a par with senior administrative positions in the state.[9]

A review in 2014 again substantially increased payments for all levels of traditional leadership. Salaries for headmen and traditional leaders went to R80 000 and R190 000 respectively. In the higher echelons increases were biggest, with the chair of the National House earning R730 000. The Congress of Traditional Leaders of South Africa (Contralesa) is pushing for the country's ten certified kings to earn the same as the president (Govender, *Times LIVE*, 14 July 2014). In 2014 the royal household of the Zulu king received R51.3 million for its upkeep from the province of KZN and the National Treasury.

Soon after the transition a commission was established to certify the validity of the claims to traditional standing, particularly of senior leaders. Called the Nhlapo Commission, it finished its preliminary work in

2011. Even then a further 1 332 disputes were moved to the now defunct Department of Traditional Affairs.

Alongside this institutional support for traditional leadership, democratic local government was installed in areas of traditional authorities, with rural municipalities established after 1996. At least initially, many of their elected councillors came from the South African National Civics Organisation, a body deeply opposed to the institution of traditional leadership (Ntsebeza, 2006). They were mandated to perform duties previously performed by traditional leaders, including liaising with local and national government, organising state-led development and allocating land. Between 1995 and 2000 many of these municipalities were consolidated into bigger administrative units and, in the process, the boundaries of some traditional authorities were swallowed up in new municipal structures (Ntsebeza, 2006).

In 1997 the Eastern Cape legislature tried to divest traditional authorities of development functions and give them to elected councillors. Nationally, Derek Hanekom, the first ANC minister of land affairs, proposed a Land Rights Bill that would have taken over control of land allocation and tenure from chiefs. Hanekom was reviled by Contralesa and his proposed Land Rights Bill was withdrawn. In 1999 he was replaced by Thoko Didiza, whom Oomen calls 'an Africanist minister'. She shelved the Bill and announced that 'African structures of governance should be respected' (Oomen, 2005:75). Since then there has been a steady stream of Africanist political principals with oversight over rural governance and traditional affairs.

The tensions came to the fore during the preparations for the 2000 local government elections, just as they had before the 1995 elections. A new Municipal Systems Act (No. 32 of 2000) was passed in which traditional leaders were allocated no local government administrative functions at all and were only given ex-officio representation on municipal councils. The nature and extent of this representation became highly contested.

The first draft of the Act provided for a maximum of ten per cent representation of traditional leaders on municipal councils. This would mean that in some areas not all traditional leaders would have standing. Contralesa mobilised to boycott the local government elections. Mandela stepped in to press for resolution and the traditional leaders only agreed to let the elections go ahead after a meeting with Mbeki, where he promised postelection reforms. Contralesa then unsuccessfully pushed to have municipalities completely abolished in former homeland areas in favour of traditional authorities as the providers of local government (Ntsebeza, 2006). The elections were postponed to the end of 2000 to allow time for a resolution of the impasse. To settle it, amendments allowed the significant concession of twenty per cent representation on local councils.

After the elections the ANC released a statement of intent promising that the 'government would amend the Constitution so that the powers of local government and traditional leaders were more clearly defined; but [it] never sought the passage of the amendment' (Williams, 2009:197). It did, however, amend the Municipal Structures Act (No. 117 of 1998) for a second time to include new roles for traditional leaders. Some of these related to local government, including the delegation of municipal functions, collecting and spending traditional taxes and convening meetings of community members. An early draft of these amendments also included a long list of religious or ceremonial functions. Among these were the facilitation of 'the gathering of fire-wood', 'to coordinate first fruit ceremonies', 'to co-ordinate rain making ceremonies' and 'to attend to matters related to witchcraft and divination' (Muriaas, 2002:121). The traditional leaders called these 'an insult to their intelligence, decorum and good faith' (Oomen, 2005:67). These functions were removed by the time the amendment came before Parliament.

Traditional leaders gained the upper hand in these exchanges in the context of weak local government administration. Official discourse and policy processes increasingly acknowledged their de facto local government powers. The 2002 draft White Paper on the Traditional Leadership Governance and Framework Act acknowledged the institution's 'potential to transform and contribute enormously towards the restoration of the moral fibre of our society, and in the reconstruction and development of the country' (Williams, 2009:193). The language of moral regeneration and social fabric started to be shared by religious and traditional leaders in the early 2000s.

Two major pieces of legislation then consolidated the powers of traditional leaders in terms of their previous apartheid roles. The first was the Traditional Leadership and Governance Framework Act (No. 41 of 2003). The objects of the Act highlight the task of transforming traditional structures in order to move towards greater democratic representation. It required that at least one-third of the members of the traditional councils be women. It also 'formally links chieftaincy with local government institutions and its development goals' in a way that had been rejected by the ANC until that point (Williams, 2009:191). Patekile Holomisa claimed that once the Act came into effect, 'we should be able to proudly proclaim the country as a republic of the United Kingdoms of South Africa' (Williams, 2009:191).

The following year the Communal Land Rights Act (No. 11 of 2004) (CLARA) was passed. As scholars have noted, despite ostensibly seeking to 'provide legal security of tenure', CLARA restored all the powers of traditional leaders granted under the 1951 Black Authorities Act and gave traditional councils the power to take over the administration of land currently managed under a number of other regimes.

CLARA would have given traditional councils the power to administer and allocate all land in rural areas by automatically acting as land administration committees. It was the first time that traditional leaders and Contralesa wholeheartedly endorsed a Bill dealing with rural administration (Ntsebeza, 2006). Four communities that manage their land under indigenous law but not under the authority of traditional councils challenged CLARA in the High Court in 2006 on both procedural and substantive grounds. This is an important distinction often overlooked by chiefs who are active in the new constitutionally instituted bodies of traditional leadership: there are many situations in which custom or tradition guides practice without any involvement by chiefs. The customary does not necessarily require traditional authority.

The court ruled sections of CLARA unconstitutional and therefore passed the case on to the Constitutional Court. While the Constitutional Court was investigating the matter the minister filed an affidavit to say that CLARA needed to be reviewed and would either be repealed *in toto* or drastically amended. In a judgment by Justice Sandile Ngcobo, and with the concurrence of the entire court, CLARA was ruled 'invalid in its entirety' on procedural grounds (Case CCT 100/09 [2010] ZACC 10).

In 2008, while CLARA was under dispute, the Justice Department tabled a Traditional Courts Bill in Parliament. Traditional courts still functioned under a combination of the Union's 1927 Bantu Administration Act and the transitional provisions 18 years after the end of apartheid. But in attempting to legislate for traditional courts anew, the Bill sought to entrench the apartheid jurisdictions of traditional authorities.

Contralesa's Mwelo Nonkonyana, spokesperson for the Cape Delegation of Traditional Leaders during the negotiations, was the sponsor and architect of the Bill, which would give traditional leaders the power to 'sentence offenders to forced labour and to strip people of their customary entitlements to land, water and community membership. It [would] also give the findings of traditional courts the same weight as those of magistrate's courts' (Joubert, *Mail & Guardian*, 16 May 2008).

In a heated debate in Parliament, women's and rural advocates pointed out that the Bill had been workshopped by traditional leaders but not with rural communities. Cosatu, the Legal Resources Centre, the Commission on Gender Equality and a range of others contested the Bill on the grounds that it would give sweeping and unaccountable powers to traditional leaders over rural South Africans. Estimates of the number of people living under traditional authorities in rural areas range between 14 million and 22 million. Given these debates, the Portfolio Committee on Justice was unable to recommend the Bill before its parliamentary deadline, so the 1927 Act remains on the books.

RURAL GOVERNANCE AND TRADITIONAL LEADERSHIP

Municipal or third-tier government in postapartheid South Africa is generally weak. Effective rural municipalities have been particularly difficult to establish and their problems are acute. Local councillors in rural areas have performed extremely poorly. Lungisile Ntsebeza (2006:278) argues that rural dwellers 'generally lost confidence in rural councillors and local government between 1994 and 2000'. One reason is that legislation and policy on the roles and functions of traditional leaders and elected officials were often contradictory, vague and unclear (Goodenough, 2002). In this context, and with little budget or policy attention to rural development, elected officials were not able to appropriate the tasks of local government from traditional leaders.

As Fred Hendricks and Ntsebeza (1999) put it, the longer this tension existed, the more it was exploited by traditional leaders. Robin Turner (2014:31), writing about the North West province, for example, says 'traditional leaders exert substantial – albeit ill-defined and contested – authority within the boundaries of their so-called traditional communities, presiding over meetings, resolving disputes, interpreting customary law, allocating communal land, mediating between external actors and their subjects and granting or withholding support for development initiatives'.

There are two main arguments against traditional authority in contemporary debates (Hagg and Kanyane, 2013). The first is that traditional leadership is not appropriate in a constitutional democracy. This position is best captured in the title of Ntsebeza's influential 2006 book, *Democracy Compromised*. He and others question the legitimacy of chiefs controlling land under communal tender, point out gender discrimination in customary law and problematise the lack of separation of powers between legislation and adjudication in customary courts. Many of these issues have been taken up by advocacy groups for rural women as well as rural communities that have, ironically, come under the control of traditional authorities where they weren't governed by chiefs under apartheid. They basically refute the claim by chiefs that they are the sole legitimate arbiters of custom and culture.

The second critique raises accusations of self-enrichment and corruption that undermine the possibilities of rural development (Hagg and Kanyane, 2013). The dangers of unaccountable judicial powers were highlighted when AbaThembu King Sabata Dalindyebo was found guilty of arson, kidnapping, defeating the ends of justice, assault with the intent to do grievous bodily harm and culpable homicide – charges that arose from the rulings of his courts. The king imposed punishments including fines of R1 200, six cows, being stripped naked and beaten with a *sjambok* (by the king) and a beating by community members that resulted in a boy's death (*The Sun*, 7 December 2009).

King Dalindyebo, a political hot potato, was, at one time, an uMkhonto weSizwe soldier in exile. After leaving the ANC he became a prominent member of the DA and an opposition party MP for the Eastern Cape. After he was found guilty of these crimes he was suspended from the DA. He is also a catalyst for the question of whether a king is to be treated like other citizens and whether justice under customary law – in this case a flawed justice – can be adjudicated by civil or constitutional law. The Constitution is unequivocal on this, but public opinion is greatly divided and traditional leaders are themselves highly vocal.

A wide range of political and traditional personages have come to King Dalindyebo's defence and paid their respects. After finally running out of options for appeal, the king was incarcerated late in 2015. Almost immediately he started a hunger strike. The EFF's Malema personally rushed to visit him, saying from outside the hospital, 'we have never seen such humiliation. We thought that the humiliation of our traditional leaders ended with colonial times and the apartheid regime' (Thamm, *Daily Maverick*, 13 January 2016). Holomisa argued that King Dalindyebo should be treated as a judicial officer whose decision was overturned, rather than as criminally liable (Thamm, *Daily Maverick*, 13 January 2016).

It is clear that chiefs act with varying degrees of accountability and integrity, and the conditions for communities under traditional authority vary considerably. Turner, for example, studied four traditional authorities within 100 kilometres of each other in North West – the areas of Lekgophung, Molatedi, Pitsedisulejang and Supingstad – and describes the very different ways in which the four chiefs acted in their roles.

The then chief of Lekgophung was described as leading through consultation and cooperation, though some also found this largely uneducated man weak and ineffectual. His approach left much room for other civic-based organisations to take the initiative for local development (Turner, 2014). Molatedi's king, who was described as much more proactive in development efforts, was able to negotiate effectively with local government and development initiatives, including getting concessions on a game reserve. Turner calls his style 'directive developmentalism' (2014:37), although when consulting with community members he sometimes overrode their decisions. The Supingstad chief, who is very involved in national-level traditional leadership processes and representation, had been powerful in the Bophuthatswana government and, although he was widely held to be a skilled and influential man, many believe he has not served his local chieftainship well. He is often absent and has failed to take up development possibilities for the community. Turner (2014:38) describes his leadership as 'authoritarian neglect'. In Pitsedisulejang there has been a series of contestations based on ethnic membership and disputes within the royal family and about territorial boundaries.

Turner (2014:48) concludes that what she calls 'citizen-subjects' involve themselves in a wide range of attempts at community development. Some do so with the help of traditional authorities and some despite them or in active opposition. Where they oppose the chief, the reason given is often that he is not acting in accordance with the customary, and community members often use customary means and resources to make that claim. Turner (2014:48) highlights 'the need for greater state responsiveness to citizen-subjects for democratising traditional leadership reforms' exactly because of this variability of practice.

It is clear that there is a wide range of relationships between people living in rural areas and chiefs and chieftainship. The HSRC reports quite high levels of trust in traditional leaders, a finding that was consistent from 2005 to 2010. Gerard Hagg and Barwa Kanyane (2013:145) report that between forty-eight and fifty per cent trust or strongly trust their traditional leaders, in contrast to between twenty-four and thirty-one per cent who distrust or strongly distrust them. They continue: 'interestingly, few opponents to traditional leaders want to have the institution completely abolished, as their emphasis is on re-democratisation of the institution and limitation of its powers' (Hagg and Kanyane, 2013:146). They also write that 'few opponents contest the role of traditional leaders in areas that do not directly impact on socioeconomic development, such as the preservation of culture and customary ceremonies' (2013:146).

Areas under traditional authority are among the poorest and least developed in the country. What Statistics South Africa calls tribal areas are the poorest settlement types by money-metrics. A 2009 survey showed that nearly eighty per cent of rural individuals were poor. They lived on less than R577 per person per month, the upper poverty line that was supposed to reflect access to adequate nutrition and basic services at that time. In contrast, the highest number of those who self-identified as poor were concentrated in peri-urban and urban informal settlements where life is more expensive and precarious (Statistics South Africa, 2012).

J. Michael Williams (2009:195) describes attempts to resolve the role of traditional leadership under democracy as an ongoing struggle, taking place over a variety of different policy issues, between chieftaincy and the state over the nature of chieftaincy's authority. With each successive policy, traditional leaders have resisted attempts to limit their authority and instead sought to further entrench themselves into a post-apartheid order.

Attempts to legislate local government and traditional courts have struggled with the tensions between the de facto powers of traditional leaders and constitutional imperatives towards democratic government.

Recognition within the state has provided traditional leaders with jobs, budgets, cars, administrative roles, renewed powers and sometimes legitimacy. This is in contrast to religious institutions, which are excluded from exactly these kinds of benefits. But the cost of inclusion within the state is the strict legal subordination to other values of the Constitution, such as democracy and gender equality.

THE CUSTOMARY IN POLITICS

Customary law, which relates to a wide range of cultural practices and not only to the legitimacy of traditional leaders, has become entangled between an articulation of a patriarchal social structure and gender equality. In this entanglement lies a battle for control between state lawyers and legal non-governmental organisations, traditional leaders, gender activists, individuals and communities who organise themselves according to dynamic 'living customary law' and versions of the customary idealised and claimed by traditional leaders.

The area of succession has been fraught and there are increasing numbers of women traditional leaders. In 2002 Cheryl Goodenough (2002) reported that at least eleven women chiefs were recognised by the then Department of Traditional Affairs in KZN. These appointments were made by royal houses in the context of legislative change and the Constitution. But formal representations by traditional leaders, Contralesa included, have largely opposed changes to the customary law of succession that would legislate this (Tebbe, 2008) and have been overruled repeatedly.

In a 2007 court case the right of a woman to succeed to chieftainship was upheld when it was contested on the grounds that it infringed customary law. In what is known as the *Shilubana* case (CCT 03/07 [2007] ZACC 14), the Constitutional Court ruled that women could be appointed traditional leaders in their own right and not only as regents. In 2004 the rule of male primogeniture, both for traditional leaders and for black succession more generally, was struck down by the Constitutional Court in the *Bhe* case (CCT 40/03; CCT 50/03.0). The court ruled that this 'fundamental element of African customary law infringed unconstitutionally on the rights of women' (Stacey and Meadow, 2009:12).

The early phases of postapartheid rule pushed to use law to transform both practice and public opinion in a wide range of areas, including the customary. But as the institutions of state have been unable to enforce the kinds of relations idealised in law, a socially conservative discourse of moral regeneration has become prominent within some religious and traditional groups. The ANC, contrary to many of its stances in the negotiations, has allied itself with this increasingly visible conservatism as a defence against criticisms of the morality – sexual and financial – of its leaders.

An example of this is the use of customary tropes by ANC leaders within party politics and in their engagements with the public. As Oomen (2005:12) points out, many African leaders have been able to derive additional legitimacy from their association with 'that other traditional, moral and political order' which would enable them to get 'around their own administrative weakness and the physical and emotional distance from their populations'. In contrast to Mbeki's extremely distanced articulation of the African subject and its renaissance, Zuma's appeal is his ability to be 'one of the people'. He has managed to string together a range of claims of the underdog, a 'chain of equivalences' between being black, Zulu and victimised (Laclau, 2005). Zuma mobilised a version of rural Zulu masculinity in his defence in the rape trial, where he performed as 'a tribal elder-cum-liberation struggle icon', as Robins (2008:189) puts it.

MARRIAGE

Marriage is an arena of potential competition between the state and other institutions and values that seek to regulate the terms of sexual intimacy and social reproduction. It is therefore a fruitful area in which to examine relationships between society, law and the state. The family has become a major site of governance as well as religious reassertion and anxiety about society (Casanova, 1994; Hunter, 2011; White, 2010, 2012, 2015). It is also the focus of strong public opinion and religious and cultural mobilisation.

The right to freedom of religion, belief and opinion contained in the Constitution includes an enabling provision relating to marriage and family law. The Bill of Rights states: '15(1) Everyone has the right to freedom of conscience, religion, thought, belief and opinion.' After a section dealing with state institutions, it goes on to add: '15(3)(a) This section does not prevent legislation recognising (i) marriages concluded under any tradition, or a system of religious, personal or family law; or (ii) systems of personal or family law under any tradition, or adhered to by persons professing a particular religion.' Such legislation 'must be consistent with this section and the other provisions of the Constitution'.

The legislature has attempted to institute the Constitution's dual imperative of recognising religious and traditional systems of family law and marriage on the one hand, and equality on the basis of gender and sexuality on the other. It is important not to automatically conflate religious leadership and socially conservative perspectives in South Africa. Some influential progressive Christians and Muslims have looked to the Constitution as an opportunity for the transformation of religion in terms of gender and racial equality.

As Davis (2011:59) notes, religious communities have been among South Africa's most progressive *and* most conservative forces. But it is true that social progressives are a minority, and women are largely absent from leadership roles in religious and traditional institutions. Nor is the ANC without its own patent contradictions. By no means all ANC members support equality on the basis of gender or sexuality in their political actions or their personal opinions, families and sexual relationships.

For feminists, the issue of Muslim and customary marriages posed twin challenges at the dawn of democracy. On the one hand, because of non-recognition in law, women who married under these regimes were not protected by the state and had no guarantee of their rights in terms of these regimes (Amien and Leatt, 2014). It was up to local traditional leaders or *ulama*, for example, to rule on men's obligations to wives and ex-wives in terms of maintenance, divorce and custody. These only have social sanction and are often arbitrated in deeply patriarchal settings.

The state did not, in other words, provide the means of enforcement such as orders, fines or imprisonment for the breach of marriage contracts made under customary or Muslim law. For this reason it was imperative for many women that such marriages be recognised. There is also a very important dignity matter when it comes to the non-legitimation of marriages. During apartheid, women married under these regimes were considered mistresses and their children illegitimate. This had to change.

For feminists, the other part of the equation was that the content of these marriage contracts discriminated against women and, at least potentially, contradicted the equality principles of the Constitution. To petition to recognise them therefore required that they also be changed and brought in line with the gender equality provisions. This rather tricky balance of recognition and reformulation became the object of the development of new marriage legislation.

Customary marriages

The new government got to work on customary marriages almost immediately after the Constitution came into effect. In 1997 the South African Law Commission (SALC) proposed a draft Bill to recognise customary marriages. It led with the suggestion that certain rules should apply to marriages of all kinds: the consent of both parties, a minimal age of consent, legal equivalence between the parties to a marriage and some standard terms of divorce.

It also argued that 'in certain areas, spouses should be free to follow their cultural preferences as guaranteed in sections 30 and 31 of the 1996 Constitution' – the rights to language and culture and the rights of cultural, religious and linguistic communities (Henrard, 2002:214). The SALC therefore proposed legislation that would recognise both polygamous and monogamous customary marriages, but altered the terms of the marriage contract in such a way that it would strengthen women's legal entitlements.

The proposals were widely debated. They went to the then newly established national and provincial houses of traditional leaders, which were extremely critical of them. The Commission on Gender Equality organised a consultation process with rural women where the question of polygamy was constantly raised. Reports in the black press tended to present the proposal as the 'redemption of black culture' after it was distorted under colonialism and apartheid (Yarbrough, 2005:12). White liberal reportage, on the other hand, saw customary law only as an apartheid exploitation of black culture and, together with some women's groups, sought an end to polygamy.

After a period of consultation the then Department of Justice and Constitutional Development pushed the Bill through Parliament with its ANC majority and the Recognition of Customary Marriages Act (RCMA) (No. 120 of 1998) was passed. The RCMA recognised all customary marriages, both monogamous and polygamous, in existence at the time it was passed. It also recognised future polygamous marriages.

The question of how to deal with polygamy was central. As Cheryl Gillwald, then deputy minister of justice and constitutional development, said in her keynote address at the launch of the RCMA in November 2000: 'The main reasons ... for not imposing a ban on polygamy are that such a ban would be almost impossible to enforce and that the popularity of the practice seems to be waning' (Available on request from the Department of Justice). Despite this, Debbie Budlender, Ntabaleng Chobokoane and Sandile Simelane (2004:12) calculated that 'the relatively high percentage of 7.2% of married women' reported that their husbands were party to polygamous unions. Statistics from KZN, where polygamy rates are highest, show that 'polygamous marriages constitute 12% of marriages in women and 14% in men in 2006' (Hosegood, McGrath and Moultrie, 2009:292). It is much more prevalent among older people and does indeed appear to be on the decline, as do marriage rates in general.

Equality in the RCMA does not mean that male and female partners have the same rights. Role differentiation was maintained in law, for example, in that women were not granted the right to have more than one husband. Substantial rather than formal equality was recognised in accommodating the structures of customary marriage. To this extent, customary marriages under the RCMA continue earlier practices and codification. But the Act also changes fundamentally the substance of customary marriage by incorporating many elements of civil law (Himonga, 2005). In particular, new marriages conducted under the RCMA are automatically made in community of property, asserting women's rights to an equal share of the marital estate. If a man wants to take a second or further wife he is legally obliged to apply to the courts to show that he will be able to support this new spouse. One aspect of such an application is the consent of the first wife to his taking another partner.

Ilobolo (bride wealth) is not a necessary condition for a customary marriage under the RCMA. This is very striking, since *lobola* is one of the most widely practised and normative dimensions of marriage in both urban and rural black culture in South Africa (Hunter, 2011). In fact, the difficulty of raising *lobola* in conditions of widespread unemployment is one of the main reasons for the decline in marriage rates of the poor.

There also appears to be a widespread failure to implement the terms of this law in the sanctioning of customary marriages, though the workings of changes to customary marriage are difficult to ascertain. According to Statistics South Africa, between 14 000 and 18 000 marriages were registered each year between 2003 and 2008. This does not reflect the number of weddings that took place, since less than ten per cent of them were registered in the year of the marriage, partly because customary marriages from before 1998 may now be registered. Some may be decades old. The low rate of registration is contrary to the Act, which requires the spouses to register a new customary marriage within 12 months (s4(3) of the RCMA). The compilers of the report also did not have access to the marital status of the parties at the time of marriage and therefore could not state how many of the marriages were polygamous.

It appears likely that the passage of this Act has not much altered the way in which people marry, except that it legalises polygamy. Having cleared the backlog of registering earlier customary marriages, current marriage rates in terms of the Act are very low. According to a Statistics South Africa (2015a) report, the number of customary marriages fluctuated between

2003 and 2007 and since then there has been a consistent decline. In 2013 only 3 498 customary marriages were registered, most (68.5%) of which took place in KZN.

Civil marriages

During apartheid the Marriage Act (No. 25 of 1961) only provided for Christian and Jewish marriage officers (Budlender, Chobokoane and Simelane, 2004). The SALC set about reviewing all marriage legislation in 1999. This led to revisions to the Marriage Act, which now allows for the registration of Hindu, Muslim and other marriage officers. In this sense civil marriages were made more inclusive and religiously neutral and marriages under civil contract can now take place in a variety of locations, and not only churches and synagogues. While some Muslims, Hindus and others marry in terms of the Marriage Act, there remains a strong social sanction against Muslims in particular using civil law to arrange their marriage contracts, though there is evidence this may be changing (Amien and Leatt, 2014).

Data reveal that in 2013, 53.4% of civil marriages were conducted by a magistrate or someone in the Department of Home Affairs. This gives no indication of whether religious or traditional ceremonies were also held. In contrast, 30.1% of ceremonies were conducted by religious officiants registered as marriage officers. The status of the marriage officer in the remaining 16.5% of marriages was unrecorded (Statistics South Africa, 2015a). It is impossible to tell from the data collected by the Department of Home Affairs how many of the religious marriages were Christian, Jewish, Muslim, Hindu or within another tradition.

Muslim marriages

Despite the specific inclusion of the enabling clause in the Constitution, Muslim marriages are still not recognised in South Africa. The history of the attempts to have Muslim law recognised predates the constitutional negotiations. Apartheid state president, John Vorster, was petitioned to introduce Muslim Personal Law (MPL) in 1975, but failed to respond. In 1987 the apartheid SALC invited comments on matters of MPL as a result of a Private Member's Bill introduced in the Tricameral House of Delegates. This initiative was largely spurned by the Muslim community, which rightly suspected that the offer of recognition was made to legitimate the Tricameral Parliament (Moosa, 2001).

The enabling clause in the 1993 interim constitution, therefore, set a new process in motion. In response to the petition to the Multiparty

Negotiations Process, the ANC facilitated the establishment of an MPL Board under the auspices of the SALC in 1994 (Moosa, 2001). The board's task was to seek a way of legislating for MPL, including marriage law. It looked at the possibility of new legislation which would, in effect, have codified aspects of MPL. But it was marred by internal friction from the start, and it disbanded when conservative *ulama* withdrew after tensions with progressive Muslims and women representatives (Amien, 2006).

Irrevocable disagreements emerged between some Muslim clergy on the one hand and, on the other, human rights and women's rights groups who were allied to a small minority of progressive Muslim *ulama* and academics. The conservative *ulama* refused to consent to a codification that would have provided for equal or nearly equal benefits for male and female partners in a marriage contract, on the grounds that it would be in opposition to the dictates of the Qur'an.

A long list of provisions under Islamic law would, according to feminist legal scholars such as Amien, Sloth-Nielson and O'Sullivan, simply never pass the requirement of equality on the grounds of gender (Amien, 2006; O'Sullivan and Murray, 2005; Sloth-Nielsen and Van Heerden, 2003). The conservative *ulama* wished to petition the Constitutional Assembly to 'exempt Muslim family law legislation from the human rights provisions of the new Constitution' (Moosa, 2001:129). This was the same stance as that taken by traditional leaders during the negotiations with respect to customary law, a stance that was not successful.

The issue fell into abeyance until the SALC established a new project committee at the beginning of 1999 to investigate the legislative options for Muslim marriages. This shrank the terms of reference of the earlier board, which had sought to address a full recognition of MPL (Tayob, 2005). The focus was reduced to marriage and succession and the committee was more widely representative of Muslim rather than Islamic opinion. A public nomination process resulted in the inclusion of Muslim men and women from the judiciary, legal profession, academia and various *ulama* bodies (Amien and Leatt, 2014).

In July 2000 the committee circulated an Issue Paper and, after amendments had been made, a Discussion Paper was published in December 2001 (SALRC, 2003). It garnered widespread interest and 113 written submissions were received from a wide range of 'Muslim religious organisations, gender and cultural groups as well as individuals' (SALRC, 2003:14). The final report, published in 2003, contained draft legislation to be taken forward by the Department of Justice (Amien and Leatt, 2014).

Despite producing a potential legal resolution between Shari'a and gender equality, the report was not acted upon. According to Waheeda Amien and Dhammamegha Leatt (2014:522), 'even though there was significant consensus on the 2003 MMB (Muslim Marriages Bill) it languished in the Ministry amidst the perhaps more urgent task of rewriting almost every piece of legislation on the books. Still, it is unclear why they did not push for its enactment. The Department of Justice failed to table the Bill'.

While legislative development has stalled, a number of cases have paved the way for the recognition of marriages conducted under MPL by enforcing obligations through the civil courts. In *Ryland v Edros* (1997) the Cape High Court enforced a contractual relationship established under MPL. In the case of *Amod v Multilateral Motor Vehicle Accident Fund* (1998), a woman married under Islamic law successfully claimed compensation after the death of her spouse. This, too, resulted in a civil court recognising the validity of a Muslim marriage contract (Henrard, 2002). These cases overturned 'a long line of decisions by South African courts in the colonial and apartheid era that women married by Muslim rites were akin to concubines and did not qualify as legally married spouses' (Sachs, 2009:159).

While neither addressed the broader recognition of Muslim marriages as such, these and other cases put pressure on the courts and legislature to address the issue. In 2010 the SALC submitted an amended version of the Bill to Cabinet, which subsequently approved it, opening the way for it to be tabled in Parliament, but this has yet to happen (Amien and Leatt, 2014). Those *ulama* that supported the MMB in 2003 have withdrawn support for this newer version, apparently drafted without consultation. It is not clear what process, if any, will bring this Bill to fruition to legalise Muslim marriages.

Same-sex marriages

Same-sex marriage received official sanction at the ANC's 1997 policy conference on the back of the inclusion of sexual orientation as grounds for equality in the Bill of Rights. The SALC, when it reviewed marriage legislation in 1999, also recommended that same-sex marriage be recognised but this aspect of the report was ignored in the revisions to the Marriage Act. In the meantime, gay rights groups mobilised to take a range of discriminatory measures to court. These cases resulted in the decriminalisation of sodomy, the assertion of equal pension benefits and joint adoption rights. The Department of Home Affairs, then headed by the IFP's Buthelezi, appealed every one of these court decisions and lost each appeal on the grounds of non-discrimination on the basis of sexual orientation in the equality clause.

In 2002 *Fourie v Minister of Home Affairs*, a case that took up the specifics of the recognition of gay marriage, worked its way from the High Court to the Supreme Court of Appeal and eventually to the Constitutional Court in 2005 (ZACC 1). The Constitutional Court acknowledged that there was unfair discrimination against same-sex couples in marriage legislation and ruled that this was unconstitutional. It did not, however, rule that the Marriage Act should simply be amended to allow for same-sex marriage.

Acknowledging the problem of popular support for such issues, it passed the onus back to the legislature (Sachs, 2009), giving Parliament one year to pass new legislation that allowed same-sex couples to 'enjoy the same rights and benefits as married heterosexuals' (Cock, 2007:9). If they failed to do this, the court ruled, the Marriage Act must automatically be amended to include a gender-neutral 'spouse' where it had stated husband and wife. The ANC was put in a corner.

The court's ruling caused huge controversy. The ANC produced a draft Civil Unions Bill and Parliament opened it up for public comment. Vociferous public and parliamentary debate took place and no fewer than 5 822 petitions, as well as a 'considerable amount [sic] of submissions', were received. Lines were drawn between gay rights activists and church and traditional leaders' groups. As Steven Robins (2008:186) puts it:

> While political, religious and traditional leaders vigorously attacked the Bill at these hearings, citing homosexuality as 'unAfrican', 'immoral' and 'sinful', gay activists from numerous organisations in turn registered their anger at what they perceived to constitute homophobia, hate speech and the violation of their constitutional rights as citizens.

In fact, Christian civil society's response was unevenly divided. A formation that called itself The Marriage Alliance, including Doctors for Life and a range of evangelical churches, found the proposal completely contrary to their faith and their readings of the Bible. Many of their arguments came directly from US advocacy material against gay marriage. The right to sexual orientation was pitted against the right to religion in this position.

In contrast, the mainline ecumenical response represented by the SACC acknowledged the human rights framework and the secularity of the state and left the decision to the state. But the SACC, too, expressed a concern that religious marriage officers would be forced to solemnise gay marriages in opposition to the doctrines of their faith, their ecclesiastical autonomy and individual conscience.

In a dramatic last minute argument in Parliament, ANC MPs were instructed in an impassioned speech by Mosiuoa Lekota to vote for the Civil Unions Bill:

> Our approach as the ANC is informed by respect for human rights and opposition to any form of discrimination. In its discussion the NEC [National Executive Committee] noted that some matters of this kind

can occasion discomfort amongst members of our movement and the rest of society. However we agreed that in the final analysis, respect for human rights entails recognising diversity and also ensuring that we always take into account the sensitivities of our society.

Despite this formal rhetoric, then Deputy President Zuma is reported to have said that gay marriages are 'a disgrace to the nation and to God' (Robins, 2008:186). He also made the statement that opens this chapter, about his childhood perspective on gay people. He later apologised. The ANC members voted *en bloc* and the Civil Unions Act (No. 17 of 2006) was passed just before the deadline set by the Constitutional Court.

As the then minister of home affairs, Nosiviwe Mapisa-Nqakula, wrote in a statement widely placed in the media: 'The right of ministers of religion not to conduct a marriage contrary to the dogma of his or her religion remains. The Civil Union [Act] allows a marriage officer to object to solemnising civil unions on grounds of conscience' (*Cape Times*, 20 October 2006:9). The situation is similar to that of the Termination of Pregnancy Act (No. 92 of 1996), which upholds civil servants' freedom of conscience, religion and belief. Magistrates and other marriage officers employed by the state are not compelled to solemnise civil unions if to do so goes against their conscience, religion and belief (Sachs, 2009).

The take-up of same-sex marriage under the Civil Unions Act has been slow, particularly because of the difficulty of finding registered and willing marriage officers. In 2013, 993 civil unions were registered, an increase from the 760 in 2009 and 888 in 2010. By far the greatest numbers of gay marriages are conducted in urban areas: seventy-four per cent of them took place in either Gauteng or the Western Cape in 2013 (Statistics South Africa, 2015a).

There is a productive comparison to be made across these forms of marriage contract and the legal, political and popular deliberations around their recognition. They reveal the consequences of differences in institutional position and legal entitlement between religious and traditional bodies and help to explain some of the different outcomes in legislative processes. Comparing Muslim and customary marriage reveals some of the consequences of secular versus non-secular institutional relationships with the state and in law.

Many of the issues that drafters faced in reconciling the terms of religious and traditional marriages on the one hand and substantive gender equality on the other are shared between customary law and MPL. They include polygamy, grounds for divorce, rules of succession, custody, inheritance, division of marital estates at divorce, age of consent and women's legal standing in marriage contracts.

The legislation drafted for customary and Muslim marriages treats these issues in very similar ways, with one core component of civil law that prioritises equality and another that provides for gender differentiation according to religion and tradition. There are other similarities too. Women married under customary and Muslim rites have historically been prejudiced by the non-recognition of those marriage contracts. Men claiming authority over their traditions – *ulama* and traditional leaders – contested the authority of the state to transform these traditions. And in both cases an alliance of progressive religionists and traditionalists contested patriarchal authority in the name of the transformation of religion and tradition through gender equality. Both law-making processes began in the early years of democracy and therefore under similar national political conditions.

How then to explain the very different outcomes? Customary marriages are recognised, while Muslim marriages are still operating outside the ambit of state law 20 years later. I would argue that the difference is a direct result of the secular and non-secular relations between the state and religious and traditional bodies. The institutions of traditional leadership and customary law are part of the state and its law and for this reason are uniquely subject to legislative development and therefore to the equality provisions. They do not have autonomy from the state; in fact, they are employed by the state. The state is within its rights and under a positive obligation to intervene in customary law in ways consistent with the Constitution. Customary law was codified by colonial administrators, legislated for by apartheid administrators and now, again, has been codified in legislation in the RCMA. There is the right to custom, but it is subordinated to other aspects of the Constitution.

What then of MPL as well as the expressed Christian interests in the issues of gay marriage? The ideas of religious autonomy, conscience and a separation of powers between civil and religious domains have been central to the development of secularism. These ideas were defended by the ANC and religious groups during the negotiations. The constitutional right to religion includes the right to the integrity of conscience. Religious organisations as institutions of civil society have the right to autonomous ecclesiastical and theological control, and religious groups sought separation from the state exactly so that their ecclesiastical and theological control could remain autonomous. They claim a singular authority to interpret sacred text.

There is, in other words, a wide remit for religious autonomy and a conscience-based exemption from general law. The Constitutional Court in particular has 'emphasised the duty of the state to accommodate, where reasonably possible, exemption for religious believers from general law' (Sachs, 2009:119). This exemption has limits, but it is also taken very seriously. In the judgment in *Christian Education South Africa v Minister of Education* (9 BHRC 53, para 55) in 2000, for example, on the issue of religiously motivated use of corporal punishment, the Constitutional Court had this to say:

> ... believers cannot claim an automatic right to be exempted by their beliefs from the law of the land. At the same time, the state should, wherever reasonably possible, seek to avoid putting believers into extremely painful and intensely burdensome choices of either being true to their faith or else respectful of the law.

In that case corporal punishment was banned at school, but not within the homes of Christians, effectively delineating a private religious sphere.

An exception to the general law is built into the Civil Unions Act, which allows churches to choose whether or not they sanction gay marriage. Exemption from general law also gives marriage officers employed by the state the right to refuse to marry couples of the same sex. A similar conscientious objection provision is included in the Termination of Pregnancy Act (De Freitas, 2011).

When it came to developing customary marriage legislation, lawmakers followed due process, took comments into account, framed a compromise and then acted against the wishes of the majority of traditional leaders in passing the RCMA. When it came to developing Muslim marriage legislation, they began the same way. They formed a consultative body, followed due process, took comments into account and then framed a compromise. They did not, however, act against the wishes of those Muslims, particularly the *ulama*, who claimed interpretive authority and who were opposed to the compromise. Instead, they acknowledged the autonomy of Islam and the Muslim community in deciding on this matter. They gave cognisance to the idea of the sacred authority of the Qur'an and were unwilling to codify elements of scripture in opposition to its claimed authoritative interpretation.

As long as a social practice or institution does not seek the authorisation of the state, as long as nobody takes the practice to court and as long as an organisation can claim to be a religion with a domain of autonomy through conscience or sacred authority, the state has not legislated religious practices to bring them in line with equality provisions. But the moment a practice or institution falls under the rubric of legislation, equality becomes an issue. The ordination of women in the church, for example, is a matter of ecclesiastical and theological autonomy. Unless someone takes it to court, and perhaps even then, the state is unlikely to intervene. On the other hand, the access of women to chieftainship, for example, has been both proactively legislated and contested in court.

The examples of marriage legislation also point to the different avenues open for the legislation of majoritarian and counter-majoritarian demands. Demands for equality that are in opposition to public opinion have been taken up through the courts. This is most clear in the advancement of the equal rights of gay and lesbian people. Sachs has argued that this is exactly where the unelected nature of the judiciary is most useful:

> It is precisely in situations where political leaders may have difficulty withstanding constitutionally undue populist pressure, and where human dignity is most at risk, that it becomes an advantage that judges are not accountable to the electorate. (2009:213)

The Constitutional Court put enormous political pressure on the ANC at a time when it sought to defend itself against claims of immorality and corruption. It is clear that the executive branch of the ANC had to override the 'popular' will represented in the views of MPs in order to support the Civil Union Act. The question of Muslim marriages, on the other hand, which affects a small minority (some 1.5% of the population), has been dealt with in specially established forums. The state has not yet been willing to intervene to force a resolution in favour of one or another position.

There is something deeply ironic in the contrast between the considerable legislative attention paid to marriage in postapartheid South Africa and the empirically low levels of marriage and high levels of divorce. It is clear that contestations over family norms, economic conditions and the politicisation of social morality go closely together. In South Africa this is inextricably linked with almost unprecedented levels of sexual and domestic violence and child rape outside of a situation of civil war. And it is tied to an HIV epidemic that has affected millions of young adults and the family structures they might have supported.

The reasons for this are largely tied to economic conditions after apartheid. Poverty and inequality have had a profound impact on social reproduction. There has been a long, slow decline in marriage rates since the 1980s. All statistical accounts show that there was a sharp drop in new marriages after the financial crisis and rates of marriage have not risen again. Getting married is an expensive business, particularly for the majority of South Africans for whom *lobola* payments are necessary to the proper constitution of kinship between families.

POLITICAL OR PUBLIC RELIGION?

The state under the ANC government has consolidated with respect to religion. There is no evidence of the emergence of a 'political religion' in South Africa, a religious movement that would seek to wrest government power away from the ANC or the parliamentary process. But there is certainly evidence of a 'public religion' that seeks to contest the terms of social life and alter the ways in which political powers interpret the Constitution.

The democratic government succeeded early in co-opting public religious presence through the TRC and the occupation of visible roles in government by struggle church leaders. In addition, the ANC founded what it called a moral regeneration movement that sought to appropriate moral authority. As the mainline churches have become increasingly critical of the government and its weak delivery, its corruption, economic policy and internal dynamics, the ANC, particularly under Zuma's leadership, has needed moral legitimacy and Pentecostal and evangelical church groupings have sought a closer alliance with the ANC in order to win moral majoritarian public demands. Zuma and his supporters have breached the secular separation of church and state at times of crisis and elections.

South Africa's political culture is not saturated with an ideology of secularism or a public critique of religion. While secularism may have played a role in the negotiations it is not deeply embedded in the political culture of the ANC or other parties. And because nothing in the Constitution states as a matter of principle that South Africa is a secular country, this concept has not become vernacularised in the same way as many other elements of the Constitution. If anything, Zuma's time as president has modelled a mildly non-secular political theology. It remains to be seen what happens after he leaves office.

The distinction between religious and customary, cultural or 'African' practices has had widespread political, legal and distributive consequences in South Africa and, in retaining this distinction, democratic South Africa has continued some of its earlier forms of governance. The distinction between religion and culture that was fundamental to the 'civilising' and indirect rule policies of colonialism and apartheid has remained largely unchallenged in the process of democratic transition.

During the negotiations and since, modernist aspirations within the ANC have simply not been strong enough to discipline and curtail traditional leadership or customary law. Not secularised or autonomised in the process of state formation, the chiefs were given a significant place within the state. From 1994 until about 2002 the ANC made repeated attempts to limit the powers of traditional leaders in legislation and policy. Each attempt failed, as customary institutions were neither replaced nor curtailed by alternative democratic structures and traditional leaders mobilised against potential legislative change. The de facto powers of traditional authorities at local level were recognised in a series of Acts in 2003 and 2004.

The price of the inclusion of traditional leadership and customary law in the state and its legislation is, however, an absolute legislative subordination to the equality principle, one that does not provide for institutional autonomy or an argument of conscience. The postapartheid years have witnessed repeated and highly contested legislative and juridical interventions in customary law, particularly with respect to gender equality. But these issues are only part of the broader question of custom. The cultural and ethnic nationalism that ANC-aligned traditional leaders disavowed during the negotiations experienced something of a revival in the latter half of the first decade of the new century. In parallel with the mobilisation of majoritarian concerns articulated in a discourse of sexual morality, traditional tropes have also been used by the ANC in its time of crisis. The pressures on the ANC towards the end of the decade, and the personality and power base of President Zuma, saw a revitalisation not only of degrees of ethnic nationalism but also of the performance of a traditional cultural and religious world within the state and, in some cases, sponsored by the state.

While the institutional and legal places of religion and tradition are in opposition in the Constitution, there are increasing areas of rhetorical and performative convergence. Both traditional and religious leaders articulate a version of idealised patriarchal social stability and promise a set of social mechanisms for the rehabilitation of a social fabric. Since this is clearly beyond the capacity of the state or the economy, elements within the institutions of the state are once again looking towards autochthonous culture as an ally to rule. The ANC in crisis, and under the leadership of Zuma, has drawn on a more labile, performative and populist rendition of religion and culture. Both the social and legitimacy concerns have provided religious and traditional leaders with new avenues of influence outside the policy and legislative processes.

On the whole, postapartheid South Africa is secular in relation to world religions. Secular institutional relationships have been established and secular political foundations and nationalism have been created. There is little evidence of a form of political religion that would attempt to contest the leadership of the state or its institutions. But there is increasing pressure on the secularity of the relationship between the ANC and religious groups in the context of a weak articulation of secularism as an explicit political ideology. This pressure is also closely related to the ambiguities of a counter-majoritarian Constitution in areas of social and sexual morality.

There has been a rise of 'public religion' in South Africa since 1994, a religious presence that appears to be growing in strength, numbers and avenues of access to government. Driven by increasingly transnational Pentecostal charismatic mobilisation around 'biblical' and 'family' values, it is also fuelled by social crisis and repeated moral panic over events that reveal the extraordinary social suffering in South Africa. This is a context for an increasingly strong assertion of a conservative social agenda.

In contrast, the attempts during the negotiations to both recognise and curtail traditional leadership have largely failed and have introduced significant legal and governance ambivalence that has been exacerbated by weak and underresourced rural government. Repeated attempts to legislate a reduction in the roles of local chiefs have failed; until recently they have simply been acknowledged. But this inclusion in the state has also required a complete legislative subordination to the equality provisions of the Constitution. In this, idealised patriarchal and customary worlds that also articulate a socially conservative agenda are increasingly put in opposition to a strong constitutional assertion of gender equality.

It is clear that South Africa is involved in a halted and stuttering transition. Activists from student and community movements and the EFF now actively criticise the legacy of Mandela and the negotiations. They say that the ANC gave away too much; that it made compromises that undermined the possibility of freedom. They say that the second turn of the revolution that would lead to economic freedom and real justice is only now on the horizon. They chastise their parents for their lack of anger and for not holding the beneficiaries and perpetrators of apartheid to account.

Will the Constitution hold through the second turning of political change? A Constitution forged in the shadow of homelands war and white supremacist politics will now be tested under the anvils of inequality, racism and the decline of the ANC.

Conclusion

In this book I have defined political secularism as the development of a normative account of the place of religion in politics and society and a series of disciplinary interventions that seek to secure that religion is put and kept in that place.

This definition, which offers a basis for the comparative analysis of secularism across the world, includes interlocking elements derived from a range of historical and contemporary forms of secularism. The first element is a configuration of relationships between religious and state bodies through which religious institutions are excluded from the exercise of state power. The second concerns the foundations of political authority. While secular regimes may appropriate religious language and rituals, they are basically authorised by some mode of representation of the will of the people, mediated by parties, constitutions or elections.

Examining political secularism outside the transatlantic world, and beyond the historical trajectory of Christianity, reveals three moves in the establishment of this form of governance. The first, and often least visible to political analysis, is the *differentiation* of the religious from the political. The second involves the *separation* of religion and politics as institutions as well as forms of thought and practice. The third concerns the forms of *relationship* once they have been differentiated and separated. Political secularism is not, therefore, the absence of religion. Instead, it is a range of quite specific forms of relationships such that religion does not contest political power.

This theory of political secularism has been used in this book to track and analyse the negotiations through the 1980s and 1990s that led South Africa from apartheid to a secular democratic dispensation through a process of constitution-making. I have found this a useful way of understanding the operations and ideals of political and religious actors and the historical contingencies of the political power of religion during this transition.

My hope is that this understanding of secularism provides a way of analysing the often complex power and authority negotiations in contemporary postcolonial government. It can also help to identify conditions for the continuation of political secularism – the capacities of contemporary states to mobilise ideological, administrative and institutional means to frame and discipline religion and to govern on secular terms.

THE FUTURE OF POLITICAL SECULARISM

South Africa and the making of its Constitution has been used as a case study to decentre debates about political secularism that shuttle between North American and European scholarship. I hope that this general framing can be of use in other contexts, particularly in understanding situations where Christianity is not the only or main religious interlocutor and where politics takes place in the long shadows of colonialism and imperialism.

There are at least three grounds on which the future of political secularism will be contested. The first is the capacity, power and ambition of late modern states. The second is the public and political aspirations of emerging religious movements, institutions and theologies. And the third is the fate of the differentiation between politics and religion, both in philosophy and in the context of religious traditions.

I would like to suggest that much of what is currently at stake in secularism is being confounded at the point of differentiation. What constitutes politics is shifting and what constitutes religion is shifting and we cannot assume a naturalised distinction between them. We are in the field of the theologico-political.

The work of differentiation is not only becoming more visible though the analysis of Muslim and other non-Christian engagements with secularism; its problematisation is also increasingly part of critical and social theory. Despite the predominance of explicitly atheist critical thought there has been a marked 'return' of religion as an object of inspiration and a source of texts to the horizons of philosophy. Slavoj Žižek may be the most prominent of these, but he is not the only post-Christian thinker. There are also significant reiterations of Jewish tradition, most notably by Emanuel Levinas, Jacques Derrida and, more recently, Judith Butler, who all mine the seams of negative or apophatic theology.

In their work we find a renewal of languages of transcendence in metaphorical and allegorical registers of trace and difference. Wendy Brown (2001:143) asks: 'What must be exhausted in certain strains of secular progressive thought for quasi-theological figures conventionally opposed to such thought, and deposed by it, to be made to seem valuable, perhaps even essential?' Her answer is that such language provides an alternative to sociological narrative, an historical consciousness that is not dependent on 'discredited narratives of systematicity, periodicity, laws of development, or a bounded coherent past and present' (Brown, 2001:143). There is much still to be examined in the affinities between the pressure on a differentiation between religion and politics and the many ways in which religion is clearly returning to public and political life.

Aside from contesting a founding differentiation, there is also the question of the force and authority required to separate religion and politics institutionally and ideologically. This concerns the relative strength, strategies and ambitions of the state and religion in any place and time. I hope to have shown that political secularism is not about an absence of religion; it is a balance of power between state and religion that gives and assumes the considerable capacity of states to intervene and impose discipline.

Political secularism is a form of rule closely tied to the national state and there can be no doubt that massive trans- and subnational forces are altering the capacities of the national state. Corporate and financial capital permeates borders at every turn. Whether this is a race to the bottom between governments competing for investment or state capture by parasitic industries, both undermine the capacity of governments.

Transnational processes also permeate wide areas of political and cultural life that relate to governance. Health threats and pharmaceuticals, international non-governmental organisations, fascism, neoliberal aesthetics and subjectivities, terror strategies and identitarian politics engage with states in every area of the globe. New media technologies create new publics and new forms of sociability. Very little of this can be brought under the rubric of state-led governmentality.

And of course many of the transnational movements are religious. There is a constitution of the Muslim *umma* in light of the impact of many of these forces in the Middle East. This, in turn, affects forms of Islam in India, Indonesia and elsewhere. There are increasing links between right-wing Buddhist groups across South East Asia. And powerful Christian-right preachers seek to influence social and political ideals in Africa and the Americas.

In light of weakening states, transnational and subnational forces may strengthen and provide what national governments cannot: security, basic infrastructure, social care and belonging. Sometimes these are religious and sometimes they are not. Where the state is corrupt and unjust or just plain ineffective, it may well be that religious institutions and ideas are more capable, powerful or compelling.

Both logically and historically, the possibility of political secularism depends on the capacity of states to mobilise ideological, administrative and institutional mechanisms to frame and discipline religion and offer the conditions for good and meaningful lives. Both logically and empirically its sustainability also depends on the forms and ambitions of religion that are present within each nation-state, their subnational and transnational links, and how willing and able they are to contest or approve of the place they have been allocated in law.

SOUTH AFRICA

The political negotiations of the 1990s settled a new regime of relationships between politics and religion in both its institutional configuration and its legal foundation. Law is the bearer of political secularism and the institutions of the state are its guarantor.

Relations between the state and Christianity were fundamentally altered and all religions are now accorded equal legal recognition. This goes hand in hand with strong constitutional protections against discrimination on the grounds of religion; the individual right to religion, belief and conscience; and rights for religious institutions to a degree of autonomy and self-determination. Christianity was excluded from the legal foundations of the new Constitution, its founding provisions and modes of interpretation.

The negotiations produced a normative account of the place of religion in the state and society. To do so, they excluded some Pentecostal-charismatic and Islamic imaginaries of the place of religion. They countered the demands of those religious formations that contest liberal humanism. And they did this with the support of the most significant public religious groupings. But ecumenical mainline Protestants and interfaith bodies are not that representative of the views of most South Africans about the place of religion or the necessity for a religiously informed public morality. The future of this contradiction looms increasingly large.

There remains an extraordinary ambivalence about the status, locus, form and presence of things African in law and political culture. The long conversation of colonialism has continued into the postapartheid present. The differentiating operations of secular modernity have not been fully applied to traditional authority.

Markers of religion, politics and culture are deeply and jointly tied to the institution of traditional authority and the institutionalisation of customary law. Traditional leaders were not differentiated from politics. The institution of traditional leadership has not been separated from the exercise of political power. Once again, the institution of traditional leadership has been taken into the state. A fundamental ambiguity has been introduced into the democratic dispensation that will continue to be very difficult to arbitrate.

THE SOUTH AFRICAN CONSTITUTION

In many respects, the Constitution has been the most important nexus for the politics of transition in South Africa. It is fundamental to the ways in which a 'new' South Africa was envisaged in the transition and the way in which all sorts of fault lines, anxieties and uncertainties were resolved or postponed.

The Constitution is also increasingly contested in practice and as an overarching idea to guide governance in the face of poverty and widespread injustice. Many civil society groupings seek to defend the Constitution as a mode of progressive politics and a way of holding political power to account. Others hold that the Constitution is so fundamentally flawed it can offer nothing to a search for justice in the country.

Criticism of the Constitution is growing, along with a tendency to represent it as the product of a few powerful men like Nelson Mandela and Frederik W. de Klerk wrapped in high-level negotiations. Perhaps believing something of the rainbow myth of the peaceful transition, many critics of the Constitution forget the context of those negotiations: the extraordinary levels of violence and the battle for territorial unity against successionist claims from the white right and some homeland leaders. The negotiations were far more fragile, violent and ambivalent than they seem to be remembered by the political public.

I hope that this book has offered a more careful and fine-grained story of the Constitution-making process, with its often surprising alliances and about-turns. As one of the anonymous reviewers of the manuscript wrote: 'This is not just politics as the search for power, or the politics of big men, or institutional rationalism but a thoroughly human affair with its attendant messiness, idealism, complexities and ambiguities.' Amidst very high stakes, the Constitution was indeed a way of resolving or postponing tensions, setting limits to their resolution and therefore shaping the future.

Many of the negotiators changed their positions, made compromises, fought for advantage with limited options and related principles to real outcomes. The Constitution was the result of all sorts of institutional, personal, legal and political motives. Its use by government, civil society and religious and traditional bodies is still open. Remembering a broader agency in making the Constitution might also offer a more nuanced and institutional view of the state we are now in and the power we have to influence it. The book of the Constitution is not yet finished.

Notes

CHAPTER 1

1   See 'Letter Concerning Toleration' http://oll.libertyfund.org/titles/locke-the-works-vol-5-four-letters-concerning-toleration (accessed 15 May 2017).

CHAPTER 2

1   Translation from the *New International Version* Bible.
2   See 'Native Policy in Africa' https://archive.org/stream/africaandsomewor027995mbp/africaandsomewor027995mbp_djvu.txt (accessed 9 May 2017).
3   See South African History Archive http://www.saha.org.za/ (accessed 9 May 2017).
4   See 'Cottesloe Consultation: The Report of the Consultation among South African Member Churches of the World Council of Churches 7-14 December 1960 at Cottesloe, Johannesburg' http://psimg.jstor.org/fsi/img/pdf/t0/10.5555/al.sff.document.ydlwcc2079_final.pdf (accessed 15 May 2017).

CHAPTER 3

1   Published in the *Argus* newspaper on 1 February 1991.
2   The IFP participated in Codesa but Buthelezi refused to be present because of the perceived snub of the Zulu monarch as well as of his government.
3   All data presented here are from the 1996 and 2001 census data, available from www.statssa.gov.za (accessed 9 May 2017). Calculations were done by the author using simple descriptive statistical techniques.
4   WCRP affiliates included progressive and moderate members from across the major world religions. Hindu members included Arya Prathindi Sabha, the Ramakrishna Society, South African Hindu Dharma Studies, South African Hindu Maha Sabha, the South African Hindu Students Association, Veda Dharma Sabha and the South African Tamil Federation. The Baha'i were represented by their national body, the National Spiritual Assembly

of Baha'is. The Buddhist Dharma Centre, Pretoria Buddhist Group and Buddhist Institute of South Africa affiliated to WCRP. South African Judaism was represented by the Jewish Board of Deputies, Jews for Social Justice, the South African Union for Progressive Judaism and the Union of Orthodox Synagogues. Muslim members included the Call of Islam, Central Islamic Trust, the Islamic Council of South Africa and the Muslim Judicial Council. Christian groups included the South African Council of Churches, the South African Catholic Bishops' Conference and the Institute for Contextual Theology. There was even some representation by AICs through the Council of African Independent Churches as well as the Federal Council of Spiritual African Indigenous Churches.

5   WCRP Newsletter, Volume One, Issue One. 1988. Source: SAHA O4.3.

6   WCRP Newsletter, Volume One, Issue One. 1988. Source: SAHA O4.3.

7   WCRP Newsletter, 'Interfaith', 1990. Source: SAHA O4.3.

8   The Ecumenical Monitoring Programme in South Africa (EMPSA) was sponsored jointly by the Johannesburg offices of the SACC and the Pretoria offices of the South African Catholic Bishops' Conference (NA NEG 1/5/7).

9   *Ulama*, which literally means 'learned ones', refers to a body of Muslim clergy which usually includes men trained in the seminaries of the Middle East, the Indian-Pakistani subcontinent and locally (Moosa, 2001:125).

CHAPTER 4

1   Set out in the document 'Robben Islanders Take a Frank and Critical Look at the Political Situation in Natal – the Way Forward'. Discussed in Sandra Klopper (1996).

2   Khoshi Mothiba from the Lebowa delegation, for example: 'The only King we have is in the Bible, the rest are Magoshi in Lebowa.' And later: 'It is only because of colonisation of some of the Chiefs by white people who came to this country that they started giving – I mean trying to classify our Magoshi according to different categories. We have indunas, we have Magoshis, we have Paramount Chiefs, then we have Kings. All that terminology has been created by the white man' (COD NA61 Volume 103/2).

3   See 'Ready to Govern: ANC policy guidelines for a democratic South Africa' http://www.anc.org.za/docs/pol/1992/readyto.html (accessed 15 May 2017).

4   In a letter dated 4 March 1993 Contralesa expressed its concern that homeland administrations had been appointed to constitute delegations. It suggested that it or the MPNP or the Organisation of African Unity would be more appropriate. Two days later the congress sent a memorandum which stated: 'Contralesa as an organisation submits that it has a right to be granted full participatory status in the MPNP planning conference, and any other structure where the role of Traditional Leaders is to be discussed' (NA NEG 1/2/1/1).

5   Memorandum of Agreement for Reconciliation and peace between the Inkatha Freedom Party/KwaZulu Government and the African National Congress and the South African Government/National Party. Source: Constitution of the Republic of South Africa Act (No. 200 of 1993).

CHAPTER 5

1   Neither the WCPCC nor the National Archives has a copy of the submission or a transcript of the meeting. I have relied on minutes of the meeting for the content of the discussions.

2   Anti-communist party supported by Ian Smith and the apartheid government.

3   See, for example, Contralesa's claim that hereditary leaders ran 'transparent and accountable systems of government'. In 'On the Constitutional Role of Traditional Leaders', 13 February 1995 (CA 2/3/1/6/11).

4   *Ex Parte: Chairperson of the Constitutional Assembly; In Re Certification of the Constitution of the Republic of South Africa, 1996.* Handed down 6 September 1996 (1996(4) SA 744 (CC); 1996(10) BCLR 1253 (CC)).

CHAPTER 6

1   Then Deputy President Jacob Zuma to a large crowd at Heritage Day celebrations in September 2006 in KwaZulu-Natal. After a great deal of pressure from gay rights organisations, which accused him of acting against the Constitution, he later apologised (Robins, 2008).

2   For details of some of these events, see *The Daily Vox* articles from October 2015 onwards. Available at www.thedailyvox.co.za (accessed 9 May 2017).

3   This analysis is available at www.childrencount.org.za/indicator. php?id=2&indicator=52 (accessed 9 May 2017).

4   See 'Trends in Satisfaction with Democracy in South Africa' http://www.hsrc. ac.za/en/media-briefs/sasas/trends-democracy-satisfaction (accessed 8 May 2017).

5   See 'A Shifting Global Economic Landscape' https://www.imf.org/external/ pubs/ft/weo/2017/update/01/ (accessed 15 May 2017).

6   See 'The ANC and Religion' http://www.anc.org.za/content/anc-and-religion (accessed 16 May 2017).

7   Mbeki's address to the South African Council of Churches, SACC Triennial Conference, 2004, Cedar Park Hotel, Johannesburg.

8   See, for example, the joint statement 2009 http://www.anc.org.za/content/ joint-statement-anc-commission-religious-affairs-and-sacc (accessed 15 May 2017).

9   Proclamation No. 48, 2007: Determination of Salaries and Allowances of Traditional Leaders, Members of the National and Provincial Houses of Traditional Leaders. Government Gazette, 14 December 2007.

Appendix 1   Postamble to the interim constitution

CHAPTER 15 OF THE CONSTITUTION OF THE REPUBLIC OF SOUTH AFRICA, ACT NO. 82 OF 1993

National Unity and Reconciliation

This constitution provides a historic bridge between the past of a deeply divided society characterised by strife, conflict, untold suffering and injustice, and a future founded on the recognition of human rights, democracy and peaceful co-existence and development opportunities for all South Africans, irrespective of colour, race, class, belief or sex. The pursuit of national unity, the well-being of all South African citizens and peace require reconciliation between the people of South Africa and the reconstruction of society.

The adoption of this Constitution lays the secure foundation for the people of South Africa to transcend the divisions and strife of the past, which generated gross violations of human rights, the transgression of humanitarian principles in violent conflicts and a legacy of hatred, fear, guilt and revenge.

These can now be addressed on the basis that there is a need for understanding but not for vengeance, a need for reparation but not for retaliation, a need for ubuntu but not for victimisation.

In order to advance such reconciliation and reconstruction, amnesty shall be granted in respect of acts, omissions and offences associated with political objectives and committed in the course of the conflicts of the past. To this end, Parliament under this Constitution shall adopt a law determining a firm cut-off date, which shall be a date after 8 October 1990 and before 6 December 1993, and providing for the mechanisms, criteria and procedures, including tribunals, if any, through which such amnesty shall be dealt with at any time after the law has been passed.

With this Constitution and these commitments we, the people of South Africa, open a new chapter in the history of our country.

Nkosi sikelel' iAfrika. God seën Suid-Afrika.

Morena boloka sechaba sa heso. May God bless our country.

Mudzimu fhatutshedza Afrika. Hosi katekisa Afrika.

Appendix 2 Excerpts from the final constitution

CONSTITUTION OF THE REPUBLIC OF SOUTH AFRICA,
ACT NO. 108 OF 1996

Preamble

We, the people of South Africa,
Recognise the injustices of our past;
Honour those who suffered for justice and freedom in our land;
Respect those who have worked to build and develop our country; and
Believe that South Africa belongs to all who live in it, united in our diversity.
We therefore, through our freely elected representatives, adopt this Constitution as the supreme law of the Republic so as to –

Heal the divisions of the past and establish a society based on democratic values, social justice and fundamental human rights;

Lay the foundations for a democratic and open society in which government is based on the will of the people and every citizen is equally protected by law;

Improve the quality of life for all citizens and free the potential of each person; and

Build a united and democratic South Africa able to take its rightful place as a sovereign state in the family of nations.

May God protect our people.
Nkosi Sikelel' iAfrika. Morena boloka setjhaba sa heso.
God seën Suid-Afrika. God bless South Africa.
Mudzimu fhatutshedza Afurika. Hosi katekisa Afrika.

CHAPTER I: FOUNDING PROVISIONS

Republic of South Africa

1.   The Republic of South Africa is one, sovereign, democratic state founded on the following values:
      a.   Human dignity, the achievement of equality and the advancement of human rights and freedoms.
      b.   Non-racialism and non-sexism.
      c.   Supremacy of the constitution and the rule of law.
      d.   Universal adult suffrage, a national common voters' roll, regular elections and a multi-party system of democratic government, to ensure accountability, responsiveness and openness.

CHAPTER 2: BILL OF RIGHTS

Equality

9.   (1)   Everyone is equal before the law and has the right to equal protection and benefit of the law.
      [...]
      (3)   The state may not unfairly discriminate directly or indirectly against anyone on one or more grounds, including race, gender, sex, pregnancy, marital status, ethnic or social origin, colour, sexual orientation, age, disability, religion, conscience, belief, culture, language and birth.
      (4)   No person may unfairly discriminate directly or indirectly against anyone on one or more grounds in terms of subsection (3).

Interpretation of Bill of Rights

39.   (1)   When interpreting the Bill of Rights, a court, tribunal or forum –
      (a)   must promote the values that underlie an open and democratic society based on human dignity, equality and freedom;
      (b)   must consider international law; and
      (c)   may consider foreign law.
      (2)   When interpreting any legislation, and when developing the common law or customary law, every court, tribunal or forum must promote the spirit, purport and objects of the Bill of Rights.

Freedom of Religion, Belief and Opinion

15. (1) Everyone has the right to freedom of conscience, religion, thought, belief and opinion.

    (2) Religious observances may be conducted at state or state-aided institutions, provided that –

        (a) those observances follow rules made by the appropriate public authorities;

        (b) they are conducted on an equitable basis; and

        (c) attendance at them is free and voluntary.

    (3) (a) This section does not prevent legislation recognising –

            (i) marriages concluded under any tradition, or a system of religious, personal or family law; or

            (ii) systems of personal or family law under any tradition, or adhered to by persons professing a particular religion.

        (b) Recognition in terms of paragraph (a) must be consistent with this section and the other provisions of the Constitution.

Language and Culture

30. Everyone has the right to use the language and to participate in the cultural life of their choice, but no one exercising these rights may do so in a manner inconsistent with any provision of the Bill of Rights.

Cultural, Religious and Linguistic Communities

31. (1) Persons belonging to a cultural, religious or linguistic community may not be denied the right, with other members of that community –

        (a) to enjoy their culture, practise their religion and use their language; and

        (b) to form, join and maintain cultural, religious and linguistic associations and other organs of civil society.

    (2) The rights in subsection (1) may not be exercised in a manner inconsistent with any provision of the Bill of Rights.

CHAPTER 6: PROVINCES

Provincial Legislatures

Legislative Authority of Provinces

104.   (1)   The legislative authority of a province is vested in its provincial legislature, and confers on the provincial legislature the power –
        (a)   to pass a constitution for its province or to amend any constitution passed by it in terms of section 142 and 143;
        (b)   to pass legislation for its province with regard to –
            (i)   any matter with a functional area listed in Schedule 4;
            (ii)   any matter with a functional area listed in Schedule 5;
        [...]

Schedule 4 includes 'Functional Areas of Concurrent National and Provincial Legislative Competence,' which includes 'cultural matters,' 'indigenous law and customary law subject to Chapter 12 of the Constitution' and 'traditional leadership subject to Chapter 12 of the Constitution.'

Schedule 5 includes 'Functional Areas of Exclusive Provincial Legislative Competence,' which includes 'Provincial cultural matters.'

Provincial Constitutions

Contents of Provincial Constitutions

143.   (1)   A provincial constitution, or constitutional amendment, must not be inconsistent with this Constitution, but may provide for –
        [...]

        (b)   the institution, role, authority and status of traditional monarch, where applicable.

CHAPTER 7: LOCAL GOVERNMENT

There is no specific mention of traditional leadership or traditional authorities in the Local Government Chapter.

Objects of local government

152.   (1)   The objects of local government are –
        (a)   to provide democratic and accountable government for local communities;
        [...]

CHAPTER 9: STATE INSTITUTIONS SUPPORTING CONSTITUTIONAL DEMOCRACY

Commission for the Promotion and Protection of the Rights of Cultural, Religious and Linguistic Communities

Functions of Commission

185. (1) The primary objects of the Commission for the Promotion and Protection of the Rights of Cultural, Religious and Linguistic Communities are –

    (a) to promote respect for the rights of cultural, religious and linguistic communities;

    (b) to promote and develop peace, friendship, humanity, tolerance and national unity among cultural, religious and linguistic communities, on the basis of equality, non-discrimination and free association; and

    (c) to recommend the establishment or recognition, in accordance with national legislation, of a cultural or other council or councils for a community or communities in South Africa.

    (2) The Commission has the power, as regulated by national legislation, necessary to achieve its primary objects, including the power to monitor, investigate, research, educate, lobby, advise and report on issues concerning the rights of cultural, religious and linguistic communities.

    (3) The Commission may report any matter which falls within its powers and functions to the Human Rights Commission for investigation.

    (4) The Commission has the additional powers and functions prescribed by national legislation.

Composition of the Commission

186. (1) The number of members of the Commission for the Promotion and Protection of the Rights of Cultural, Religious and Linguistic Communities and their appointment and terms of office must be prescribed by national legislation.

    (2) The composition of the Commission must –

    (a) be broadly representative of the main cultural, religious and linguistic communities in South Africa; and

    (b) broadly reflect the gender composition of South Africa.

CHAPTER 12: TRADITIONAL LEADERS

Recognition

211. (1) The institution, status and role of traditional leadership, according to customary law, are recognised, subject to the Constitution.

(2) A traditional authority that observes a system of customary law may function subject to any applicable legislation and customs, which includes amendments to, or repeal of, that legislation or those customs.

(3) The courts must apply customary law when that law is applicable, subject to the Constitution and any legislation that specifically deals with customary law.

Role of traditional leaders

212. (1) National legislation may provide for a role for traditional leadership as an institution at local level on matters affecting local communities.

(2) To deal with matters relating to traditional leadership, the role of traditional leaders, customary law and the customs of communities observing a system of customary law –

(a) national or provincial legislation may provide for the establishment of houses of traditional leaders; and

(b) national legislation may establish a council of traditional leaders.

SCHEDULE 6: TRANSITIONAL ARRANGEMENTS

Courts

16. (1) Every court, including courts of traditional leaders, existing when the new Constitution took effect, continues to function and to exercise jurisdiction in terms of the legislation applicable to it, and anyone holding office as a judicial officer continues to hold such office in terms of the legislation applicable to that office [...]

A note on archival sources

The negotiations left a trail of documents lodged in archival collections across South Africa. They include minutes; media statements and submissions from political parties, civil society organisations and individuals; verbatim transcriptions of negotiating meetings; draft constitutional texts; legal opinions and technical reports.

Papers from the Convention for a Democratic South Africa (Codesa) of 1991 to 1992 and the Multiparty Negotiations Process of 1993 are housed at the National Archives in Tshwane. After the 1994 elections both houses of the new Parliament together formed the Constitutional Assembly (CA) to draft the final Constitution. Although the CA was housed at Parliament, it also subsequently lodged its papers at the National Archives. While these archives are remarkably complete, I was able to access some missing party submissions in a donation of personal papers from Hugh Corder that is housed at the Special Collections library at the University of Cape Town (UCT).

Research for this book drew on some 900 primary documents from the negotiations' archives. It would be too much to give full reference details for each of these sources. The aim here is to give enough information for serious researchers to access these materials themselves from the National Archives and other sources. They are referenced by codes that denote the archive collection, followed by file numbers as they are organised in that collection and, where appropriate, their date.

The codes are:

CA – Constitutional Assembly collection
COD – Codesa Archive, National Archives
NA – National Archives
NEG – Multiparty Negotiations collection, National Archives
Corder – Hugh Corder Collection, UCT

Bibliography

Ackerman, B. (1997). The Rise of World Constitutionalism. *Virginia Law Review*, 83(4), pp. 771–797.

Adam, H. and Moodley, K. (1993). *The negotiated revolution: society and politics in post-apartheid South Africa*. Johannesburg: Jonathan Ball Publishers.

Agamben, G. (2005). *State of exception*. Chicago, IL: University of Chicago Press.

Ali, T. (2002). *The clash of fundamentalisms: crusades, jihads and modernity*. London: Verso.

Altman, M., Hart, T. and Jacobs, P. (2009). *Food security in South Africa*. Cape Town: HSRC Press.

Amien, W. (2006). Overcoming the Conflict between the Right to Freedom of Religion and Women's Rights to Equality: A South African Case Study of Muslim Marriages. *Human Rights Quarterly*, 28, pp. 729–754.

Amien, W. and Leatt, D.A. (2014). Legislating Religious Freedom: An Example of Muslim Marriages in South Africa. *Maryland Journal of International Law*, 29(1), pp. 505–547.

Anderson, B. (1991). *Imagined communities: reflections on the origin and spread of nationalism*. 2nd ed. London: Verso.

Arendt, H. (1958). *The human condition*. 2nd ed. Chicago and London: University of Chicago Press.

Aries, P. (1975). *Western attitudes towards death*. Baltimore, MD: Johns Hopkins University Press.

Asad, T. (1993). *Genealogies of religion: discipline and reasons of power in Christianity and Islam*. Baltimore, MD: Johns Hopkins University Press.

Asad, T. (1999). Religion, nation-state, secularism. In: P. van der Veer and H. Lehman, ed., *Nation and religion: perspectives on Europe and Asia*. Princeton, NJ: Princeton University Press.

Asad, T. (2003). *Formations of the secular: Christianity, Islam, modernity*. Stanford, CA: Stanford University Press.

Ashforth, A. (2000). *Madumo: a man bewitched*. Cape Town: David Philip.

Ashforth, A. (2005). *Witchcraft, violence and democracy in South Africa*. Chicago, IL: University of Chicago Press.

Asmal, K. (1992). Sins of apartheid cannot be ignored. In: E. Doxtader and P.-J. Salazar, ed., *Truth & reconciliation in South Africa: the fundamental documents*. Cape Town: Institute for Justice and Reconciliation.

Atkinson, D. (1994). Insuring the future? The bill of rights. In: S. Friedman and D. Atkinson, ed., *The small miracle: South Africa's negotiated settlement.* Johannesburg: Ravan Press.

Balcomb, A. (2004). From Apartheid to the New Dispensation: Evangelicals and the Democratisation of South Africa. *Journal of Religion in Africa,* 34(1–2), pp. 5–38.

Balcomb, A. (2008). From apartheid to the new dispensation: evangelicals and the democratisation of South Africa. In: T. Ranger, ed., *Evangelical Christianity and democracy in Africa.* Oxford: Oxford University Press.

Barnes, C. and De Klerk, E. (2002). *South Africa's Multi-Party Constitutional Negotiation Process.* [Online] Available at: www.c-r.org/our-work/accord/public-participation/south-africa.htm [Accessed 17 May 2007].

Baudrillard, J. (1983). *In the shadow of the silent majorities; or, the end of the social and other essays.* Translated by P. Foss, J. Johnston and P. Patton. New York: Semiotext(e).

Beinart, W. (2001). *Twentieth-century South Africa.* New ed. Oxford: Oxford University Press.

Bellah, R. and Hammond, P. (1980). *Varieties of civil religion.* San Francisco, CA: Harper & Row.

Bennett, T.W. (2004). *Customary law in South Africa.* Cape Town: Juta.

Benyon, J. (1980). *Proconsul and paramountcy in South Africa: the high commission, British supremacy and the sub-continent 1806–1910.* Pietermaritzburg: University of Natal Press.

Bhargava, R. (2006). *Multiple Secularisms and Multiple Secular States.* Spoke Four Workshop, Munk Centre for International Studies, Toronto.

Blumenberg, H. (1966). The legitimacy of the modern age. In: R.M. Wallace, trans., T. McCarthy, ed., *Studies in contemporary German social thought.* Cambridge, MA: MIT Press.

Bompani, B. (2006). 'Mandela Mania': Mainline Churches in Post-Apartheid South Africa. *Third World Quarterly,* 27(6), pp. 1137–1149.

Brown, W. (2001). *Politics out of history.* Princeton and Oxford: Princeton University Press.

Budlender, D., Chobokoane, N. and Simelane, S. (2004). Marriage Patterns in South Africa: Methodological and Substantive Issues. *Southern African Journal of Demography,* 9(1), pp. 1–25.

Burleigh, M. (2006). *Sacred causes: religion and politics from the European dictators to Al Qaeda.* London: Harper Perennial.

Cachalia, A., Cheadle, H., Davis, D., Haysom, N., Maduna, P. and Marcus, G. (1994). *Fundamental rights in the new constitution: an overview of the new constitution and a commentary on chapter 3 on fundamental rights.* Johannesburg: CALS and Juta & Co.

Cape Times (2006). Civil Union Bill is about equality for all in our country. 20 October, p. 9.

Campbell, C. (1987). *The romantic ethic and the spirit of modern consumerism.* Oxford: Basil Blackwell.

Casanova, J. (1994). *Public religions in the modern world.* Chicago, IL: University of Chicago Press.

Casanova, J. (2007). Immigration and the new religious pluralism: a European Union/United States comparison. In: T. Banchoff, ed., *Democracy and the new religious pluralism*. Oxford: Oxford University Press.

Cassidy, M. (1995). *A witness for ever: the dawning of democracy in South Africa, stories behind the story*. London: Hodder & Stoughton.

Chatterjee, P. (2006). Fasting for Bin Laden: the politics of secularization in contemporary India. In: D. Scott and C. Hirshkind, ed., *Powers of the secular modern: Talal Asad and his interlocutors*. Stanford, CA: Stanford University Press.

Chidester, D. (1992). *Shots in the streets: violence and religion in South Africa, contemporary South African debates*. Cape Town: Oxford University Press.

Chidester, D. (1996). *Savage systems: colonialism and comparative religion in Southern Africa*. Cape Town: University of Cape Town Press.

Chipkin, I. (2007). *Do South Africans exist? Nationalism, democracy and the identity of 'the people'*. Johannesburg: Wits University Press.

Chipkin, I. and Leatt, A. (2011). Religion and Revival in Post-Apartheid South Africa. *Focus*, 62, pp. 39–46.

Christianse, Y. (2003). Passing away: the unspeakable (losses) of postapartheid South Africa. In: D.L. Eng and D. Kazanjian, ed., *Loss: the politics of mourning*. Berkeley, CA: University of California Press.

Cochrane, J.R. (1987). *Servants of power: the role of English-speaking churches 1903–1930*. Johannesburg: Ravan Press.

Cock, J. (2003). Engendering Gay and Lesbian Rights: The Equality Clause in the South African Constitution. *Women's Studies International Forum*, 26(1), pp. 35–45.

Cock, J. (2007). *More than a 'Grammatical Construction'? Same-sex Marriage and the South African LGBT Movement*. Paper presented to the Department of Sociology, University of the Witwatersrand.

Comaroff, J. and Comaroff, J.L. (1991). *Of revelation and revolution: Christianity, colonialism and consciousness in South Africa*, vol. 1. Chicago, IL: University of Chicago Press.

Comaroff, J.L. and Comaroff, J. (1997). *Of revelation and revolution: the dialectics of modernity on a South African frontier*, vol. 2. Chicago and London: University of Chicago Press.

Comaroff, J. and Comaroff, J.L. (1999). Occult Economies and the Violence of Abstraction: Notes from the South African Postcolony. *American Ethnologist*, 26(2), pp. 279–303.

Comaroff, J. and Comaroff, J.L. (2004). The Struggle between the Constitution and 'Things African'. *The Wiser Review*, 1, p. 6.

Comaroff, J.L. and Comaroff, J. (2008). Ethnicity. In: N. Shepherd and S. Robins, ed., *New South African keywords*. Johannesburg: Jacana.

Costa, A.A. (2000). Chieftaincy and Civilisation: African Structures of Government and Colonial Administration in South Africa. *African Studies*, 59(1), pp. 13–43.

Darwin, C.R. (1859). *On the origin of species by means of natural selection, or the preservation of favoured races in the struggle for life*. London: John Murray.

Davies, H. and Shepherd, R.H.W. (1954). *South African missions 1800–1950*. London: Thomas Nelson and Sons.

Davis, F. (2011). 'Doing God' and Policy: In Search of Social Capital and Innovation. *Focus*, 62, pp. 54–59.

De Freitas, S.A. (2011). Freedom of Conscience, Medical Practitioners and Abortion in South Africa. *International Journal for Religious Freedom*, 4(1), pp. 75–85.

De Vries, H. and Sullivan, L.E. ed., (2006). *Political theologies: public religions in a post-secular world*. New York: Fordham University Press.

Delius, P. (1996). *A lion amongst the cattle: reconstruction and resistance in the Northern Transvaal*. Johannesburg: Ravan Press.

Derrida, J. (2002). Faith and knowledge: the two sources of 'religion' at the limits of reason alone. In: G. Anidjar, ed., *Acts of religion: Jacques Derrida*. New York and London: Routledge.

Dexter, P. (2009). Comment: of politicians, priests and prostitutes. *Mail & Guardian*, 3–8 April.

Dorrington, R., Bradshaw, D., Johnson, L. and Budlender, D. (2004). *The demographic impact of HIV/AIDS in South Africa: national indicators for 2004*. Cape Town: South African Medical Research Council.

Doxtader, E. (2009). *With faith in the works of words: the beginnings of reconciliation in South Africa, 1985–1995*. Cape Town: David Philip.

Du Plessis, L. (1994). A background to drafting the chapter on fundamental rights. In: B. de Villiers, ed., *Birth of a constitution*. Cape Town: Juta & Co.

Dube, M. (2008). Zuma's God talk condemned. *The Citizen*, 6 May.

Ebrahim, H. (1998). *The soul of a nation: constitution making in South Africa*. Cape Town: Oxford University Press.

Edelman, M. (1967). *The symbolic uses of politics*. Chicago and London: University of Illinois Press.

Elazar, D.J. (1994). Form of state: federal, unitary, or ... In: B. de Villiers, ed., *Birth of a constitution*. Cape Town: Juta & Co.

Ellis, S. and Ter Haar, G. (2004). *Worlds of power: religious thought and political practice in Africa*. Johannesburg: Wits University Press.

Fields, K.E. (1982). Political Contingencies of Witchcraft in Colonial Central Africa: Culture and the State in Marxist Theory. *Canadian Journal of African Studies*, 16(3), pp. 567–593.

Finn, A., Leibbrandt, M. and Woolard, I. (2013). *What Happened to Multidimensional Poverty in South Africa between 1993 and 2010?* A Southern African Labour and Development Research Unit Working Paper No. 99. Cape Town: SALDRU, University of Cape Town.

Foucault, M. (1965). *Madness and civilisation: a history of insanity in the age of reason*. Translated by R. Howard. New York: Vintage Books.

Foucault, M. (1976). *The will to knowledge: the history of sexuality*, vol. 1. Translated by R. Hurley. London: Penguin Books.

Foucault, M. (1977). *Discipline and punish*. Translated by A. Sheridan. New York: Penguin Books.

Foucault, M. (1985). *The use of pleasure: the history of sexuality*, vol. 2. Translated by R. Hurley. New York: Vintage Books.

Foucault, M. (1986). *The care of the self: the history of sexuality*, vol. 3. Translated by R. Hurley. New York: Vintage Books.

Foucault, M. (1991). Governmentality. In: G. Burchell, C. Gordon and P. Miller, ed., *The Foucault effect: studies in governmentality*. Chicago, IL: University of Chicago Press.

Foucault, M. (1997). Society must be defended. In: M. Bertani and A. Fontana, ed., *Lectures at the College de France, 1975–1976*. New York: Picador.

Friedman, S. ed., (1993). *The long journey: South Africa's quest for a negotiated settlement*. Johannesburg: Ravan Press.

Froise, M. ed., (1986). *South African Christian handbook 1986/87*. Florida, South Africa: World Vision of Southern Africa.

Froise, M. ed., (1996). *South African Christian handbook 1996/7*. Welkom, South Africa: Christian Info.

Garuba, H. and Raditlhalo, S. (2008). Culture. In: N. Shepherd and S. Robins, ed., *The new South African keywords*. Johannesburg: Jacana.

Gauchet, M. (1997). *The disenchantment of the world: a political history of religion*. Translated by O. Burge. T. Pavel and M. Lilla, ed., Princeton, NJ: Princeton University Press.

Geschiere, P. (2006). Witchcraft and the limits of the law: Cameroon and South Africa. In: J. Comaroff and J.L. Comaroff ed., *Law and disorder in the postcolony*. Chicago and London: University of Chicago Press.

Geuss, R. (2008). *Philosophy and real politics*. Princeton, NJ: Princeton University Press.

Giliomee, H. (1988). The eastern frontier, 1770–1812. In: R. Elphick and H. Giliomee, ed., *The shaping of South African society, 1652–1840*. Middletown, CT: Wesleyan University Press.

Gill, A. (2008). *The political origins of religious liberty*. Cambridge: Cambridge University Press.

Gill, A. and Keshavarzian, A. (1999). State Building and Religious Resources: An Institutional Theory of Church-State Relations in Iran and Mexico. *Politics & Society*, 27(3), pp. 431–465.

Gloppen, S. (1997). *South Africa: the battle over the constitution*. Dartmouth: Ashgate.

Goodenough, C. (2002). *Traditional leaders: a KwaZulu-Natal study 1991 to 2001*. Durban: Independent Projects Trust.

Goodhew, D. (2000). Growth and Decline in South Africa's Churches, 1960–1991. *Journal of Religion in Africa*, 23(3), pp. 344–369.

Govender, P. (2014). SA's ten kings want the same salary as Zuma. *Times LIVE*, 14 July. [Online] Available at: http://www.timeslive.co.za/politics/2014/07/14/SAs-ten-kings-want-the-same-salary-as-Zuma [Accessed 15 May 2017].

Gumede, W.M. (2005). *Thabo Mbeki and the battle for the soul of the ANC*. Cape Town: Zebra Press.

Gunner, L. ed., (2004). *The man of heaven and the beautiful ones of God: Isaiah Shembe and the Nazareth Church*. Pietermaritzburg: University of KwaZulu-Natal Press.

Habermas, J. (2002). *Religion and rationality: essays on reason, God and modernity*. Cambridge, MA: MIT Press.

Habermas, J. (2006). On the relations between the secular liberal state and religion. In H. de Vries, L.E. Sullivan, ed., *Political theologies: public religions in a post-secular world*. New York: Fordham University Press.

Hagg, G. and Kanyane, M.H. (2013). Traditional institutions of governance: legitimate partners in governance or democracy compromised? In: U. Pillay, G. Hagg, F. Nyamnjoh and J.D. Jansen, ed., *State of the nation: South Africa 2012-2013: addressing inequality and poverty*. Cape Town: HSRC Press.

Harber, A. and Ludman, B. ed., (1994). *A-Z of South African politics: the essential handbook*. London: Penguin Books.

Harris, R. (1999). *Lourdes: body and spirit in the secular age*. London: Penguin Books.

Harris, S. (2006). *The end of faith: religion, terror and the future of reason*. London: The Free Press.

Haynes, J. (1996). *Religion and politics in Africa*. Nairobi and London: East African Educational Publishers and Zed Books.

Hendricks, F. and Ntsebeza, L. (1999). Chiefs and Rural Local Government in Post-Apartheid South Africa. *African Journal of Political Science*, 4(1), pp. 99–126.

Henrard, K. (2001). The Accommodation of Religious Diversity in South Africa against the Background of the Centrality of the Equality Principle in the New Constitutional Dispensation. *Journal of African Law*, 45(1), pp. 51–72.

Henrard, K. (2002). *Minority protection in post-apartheid South Africa: human rights, minority rights and self-determination*. Westport, CT: Praeger.

Herzfeld, M. (1992). *The social production of indifference: exploring the symbolic roots of Western bureaucracy*. Chicago and London: University of Chicago Press.

Himonga, C. (2005). The Advancement of African Women's Rights in the First Decade of Democracy in South Africa: The Reform of the Customary Law of Marriage and Succession. *Acta Juridica*, 2005, pp. 82–107.

Hobbes, T. (2006[1651]). *Leviathan*. Ed. C.A. Gaskin. New York: Dover Publications.

Hosegood, V., McGrath, N. and Moultrie, T. (2009). Dispensing with Marriage: Marital and Partnership Trends in Rural KwaZulu-Natal, South Africa, 2000–2006. *Demographic Research*, 20(13), pp. 279–312.

Hunter, M. (2011). Beneath the 'Zunami': Jacob Zuma and the Gendered Politics of Social Reproduction in South Africa. *Antipode*, 43(4), pp. 1102–1126.

Huntington, S. (2002). *The clash of civilisations and the remaking of world order*. New York: Free Press.

Hyslop, J. (1995). The Prophet Van Rensburg's Vision of Nelson Mandela: White Popular Religious Culture and Responses to Democratisation. *Social Dynamics*, 21(2), pp. 23–55.

Jacklin, H. and Vale, P. ed., (2009). *Re-imagining the social in South Africa: critique, theory and post-apartheid society*. Durban: University of KwaZulu-Natal Press.

Jäger, C. (2007). Is critique secular? Thoughts on enchantment and reflexivity. In: *Is critique secular?* Critical Theory Initiative, Townsend Centre for the Humanities. Berkeley, CA: University of California.

Joubert, P. (2008). Back to the dark days. *Mail & Guardian*, 16 May.

Keddie, N.R. (1997). Secularism and the State: Towards Clarity and Global Comparison. *New Left Review*, I(226), pp. 21–40.

Kindra, J. (2001). Unholy battle between ANC and churches. *Mail & Guardian*, 2 November.

Kingdon, G. and Knight, J. (2005). *Unemployment in South Africa, 1995–2003: causes, problems and policies*. Oxford University Centre for the Study of African Economies and Department of Economics.

Klaaren, J. (2000). Post-apartheid citizenship in South Africa. In: A. Aleinikoff, ed., *From migrants to citizens: membership in a changing world*. Washington, DC: Brookings Institute Press.

Klopper, S. (1996). 'He is my King, but he is also my child': Inkatha, the African National Congress and the Struggle for Control over Zulu Cultural Symbols. *Oxford Art Journal*, 19(1), pp. 53–66.

Klug, H. (2000). *Constituting democracy: law, globalism and South Africa's political reconstruction*. Cambridge: Cambridge University Press.

Klug, H. (2010). The constitution of South Africa: a contextual analysis. In: P. Leyland and A. Harding, ed., *Constitutional systems of the world*. Oxford: Hart Publishing.

Laclau, E. (2005). *On populist reason*. London: Verso.

Lawrence, R. (1994). From Soweto to Codesa. In: S. Friedman and D. Atkinson, ed., *The small miracle: South Africa's negotiated settlement*. Johannesburg: Ravan Press.

Leatt, A. (2008). Faithfully Secular: Secularism and South African Political Life. *Journal for the Study of Religion*, 20(2), pp. 29–44.

Lefort, C. (1988). *Democracy and political theory*. Cambridge: Polity Press.

Lefort, C. (2006). The permanence of the theological-political. In: H. de Vries and L.E. Sullivan, ed., *Political theologies*. New York: Fordham University Press.

Legassick, M. (1980). The frontier tradition in South African historiography. In: S. Marks and A. Atmore, ed., *Economy and society in pre-industrial South Africa*. London: Longman.

Lilla, M. (2007). *The stillborn God: religion, politics and the modern West*. New York: Vintage Books.

Lodge, T. (1983). *Black politics in South Africa since 1945*. Johannesburg: Ravan Press.

Lopez, D.S. Jr. (1998). Belief. In: M.C. Taylor, ed., *Critical terms for religious studies*. Chicago, IL: University of Chicago Press.

Mabena, K. (2009). ANC until 'Jesus comes'. *The Times*, 22 June.

Machiavelli, N. (2009). *The prince*. Translated by T. Parks. London: Penguin Classics.

Madan, T.N. (1987). Secularism in its place. *The Journal of Asian Studies*, 46(4), pp. 747–759.

Magubane, B.M. (1996). *The making of a racist state: British imperialism and the Union of South Africa, 1875–1910*. Trenton, NJ and Asmara, Eritrea: Africa World Press.

Mahmood, S. (2005). *Politics of piety: the Islamic revival and the feminist subject*. Princeton, NJ: Princeton University Press.

Mail & Guardian (2007). Zuma's no pastor of ours, says church. [Online] Available at: https://mg.co.za/article/2007-05-08-zumas-no-pastor-of-ours-says-church [Accessed 16 May 2017].

Mamdani, M. (2004). *Good Muslim, bad Muslim: America, the Cold War, and the roots of terror*. Johannesburg: Jacana Media.

Marks, S. (1986). *The ambiguities of dependence: race, class and nationalism in twentieth century South Africa*. Johannesburg: Ravan Press.

Martens, J. (2006). The impact of theories of civilization and savagery on native policy in colonial Natal. In: T. Lyons and G. Pye, ed., *Africa on a global stage.* Trenton, NJ: Africa World Press.

Marx, C. (2002). Ubu and Ubuntu: On the Dialectics of Apartheid and Nation Building. *Politikon,* 29(1), pp. 49–69.

Masondo, S. (2011). African Traditional Religion in the Face of Secularism in South Africa. *Focus,* 62, pp. 32–38.

Masuzawa, T. (2005). *The invention of world religions. Or, how European universalism was preserved in the language of pluralism.* Chicago and London: University of Chicago Press.

Mataboge, M. (2009a). Sleepless nights on his knees. *Mail & Guardian,* 1 March. [Online] Available at: https://mg.co.za/article/2009-03-01-sleepless-nights-on-his-knees [Accessed 18 May 2017].

Mataboge, M. (2009b). Why ANC dumped council of churches. *Mail & Guardian,* 18 September. [Online] Available at: https://mg.co.za/article/2009-09-18-why-anc-dumped-council-of-churches [Accessed 18 May 2017].

Mbembe, A. (2001). *On the postcolony.* Berkeley, CA: University of California Press.

McCafferty, C. and Hammond, P. (2001). *The pink agenda: sexual revolution in South Africa and the ruin of the family.* Cape Town: Christian Liberty Books.

McClendon, T. (2004). The Man who would be *Inkosi*: Civilising Missions in Shepstone's Early Career. *Journal of Southern African Studies,* 30(2), pp. 339–358.

Mead, S. (1965). *The nation with the soul of a church.* New York: W.W. Norton.

Meiring, P. (2000). The *Baruti* versus the lawyers: the role of religion in the TRC process. In: C. Villa-Vicencio and W. Verwoerd, ed., *Looking back, reaching forward: reflections on the Truth and Reconciliation Commission of South Africa.* Cape Town: University of Cape Town Press.

Mill, J.S. (2002[1859]). *On liberty.* P. Negri, ed. New York: Dover Publications.

Mkhabela, M. (2009). Be like Jesus' disciples for ANC. *Sunday Times,* 19 April.

Moloto, M. (2013). Zuma invokes wrath of God. *IOL,* 7 October. [Online] Available at: http://www.iol.co.za/news/politics/zuma-invokes-wrath-of-god-1587841 [Accessed 18 May 2017].

Moodie, T.D. (1975). *The rise of Afrikanerdom: power, apartheid and the Afrikaner civil religion.* Berkeley, CA: University of California Press.

Moosa, E. (2000a). Tensions in legal and religious values in the 1996 South African constitution. In: J.R. Cochrane and B. Klein, ed., *Sameness and difference: problems and potentials in South African civil society.* Washington, DC: Council for Research in Values and Philosophy.

Moosa, E. (2000b). Truth and reconciliation as performance: spectres of Eucharistic redemption. In: C. Villa-Vicencio and W. Verwoerd, ed., *Looking back, looking forward: reflections on the Truth and Reconciliation Commission of South Africa.* Cape Town: University of Cape Town Press.

Moosa, E. (2001). Shaping Muslim law in South Africa: future and prospects. In: W. Scharf and D. Nina, ed., *The other law: non-state ordering in South Africa.* Cape Town: Juta.

Mouffe, C. (2000). *The democratic paradox.* London: Verso.

Mouffe, C. (2005). *On the political.* London and New York: Routledge.

Muriaas, R.L. (2002). 'Two bulls in a kraal': recognising cultural difference in post-apartheid South Africa. PhD thesis. Department of Comparative Politics, University of Bergen.

Nandy, A. (1983). The intimate enemy: loss and recovery of self under colonialism. Delhi: Oxford University Press.

Nandy, A. (1988). The Twilight of Certitudes: Secularism, Hindu Nationalism and Other Masks of Deculturation. Postcolonial Studies, 1(3), pp. 283–298.

Nandy, A. (2002). Time warps: silent and evasive pasts in Indian politics and religion. New Brunswick, NJ: Rutgers University Press.

Ncana, N. (2009). Church is privatising Jesus. The Times, 24 June.

Ndeltyana, M. ed., (2008). African Intellectuals in the 19th and early 20th century South Africa. Cape Town: HSRC Press.

News24 (2007). 'Pastor' Zuma calls for unity. 6 May. [Online] Available at: http://www.news24.com/SouthAfrica/News/Pastor-Zuma-calls-for-unity-20070505 [Accessed 15 May 2017].

Nina, D. and Scharf, W. (2001). Introduction: the other law? In: W. Scharf and D. Nina, ed., The other law: non-state ordering in South Africa. Cape Town: Juta.

Ntsebeza, L. (2006). Democracy compromised: chiefs and the politics of land in South Africa. Cape Town: HSRC Press.

O'Malley, P. (1996). 16 Oct 1996: Holomisa, Patekile. [Online] Available at: https://www.nelsonmandela.org/omalley/index.php/site/q/03lv00017/04lv003 44/05lv00965/06lv01042.htm [Accessed 20 December 2010].

Omar, A.R. (2002). Muslims and Religious Pluralism in Post-Apartheid South Africa. Journal of Muslim Minority Affairs, 22(1), pp. 1–6.

Oomen, B. (2005). Chiefs in South Africa: law, power & culture in the post-apartheid era. Oxford, Pietermaritzburg and New York: James Currey and University of KwaZulu-Natal Press.

O'Sullivan, M. and Murray, C. (2005). Brooms Sweeping Oceans? Women's Rights in South Africa's First Decade of Democracy. Acta Juridica, 2005(1), pp. 1–41.

Penn, N. (2005). The forgotten frontier: colonist and Khoisan on the Cape's northern frontier in the 18th century. Athens, OH: Ohio University Press.

Pillay, U., Roberts, B. and Rule, S. (2006). South African social attitudes: changing times, diverse voices. Cape Town: HSRC Press.

Pillay, U., Hagg, G., Nyamnjoh, F. and Jansen, J.D. ed., (2013). State of the nation: South Africa 2012–2013: addressing inequality and poverty. Cape Town: HSRC Press.

Posel, D. (2008). AIDS. In: N. Shepherd and S. Robins, ed., New South African keywords. Johannesburg: Jacana.

Posel, D. (2011). The apartheid project, 1948–1970. In: B. Nasson, A. Mager and R. Ross, ed., The Cambridge history of South Africa. Cambridge: Cambridge University Press.

Ranger, T. (1983). The invention of tradition in colonial Africa. In: E. Hobsbawm and T. Ranger, ed., The invention of tradition. Cambridge: Cambridge University Press.

Ranger, T. (1993). The invention of tradition revisited: the case of colonial Africa. In: T. Ranger and O. Vaughan, ed., Legitimacy and the state in twentieth-century Africa. London: Macmillan.

Ritchken, E. (1995). *Leadership and conflict in Bushbuckridge: struggles to define moral economies within the context of rapidly transforming political economies (1978–1990)*. PhD thesis. Department of Political Science, University of the Witwatersrand, Johannesburg.

Roberts, B., waKivilu, M. and Davids, Y.D. ed., (2010). *South African social attitudes 2nd report: reflections on the age of hope*. Cape Town: HSRC Press.

Robins, S. (2008). Rights. In: N. Shepherd and S. Robins, ed., *New South African keywords*. Johannesburg: Jacana.

Rorty, R. (2003). Religion in the Public Sphere: a Reconsideration. *Journal of Religious Ethics*, 31(1), pp. 141–149.

Rossouw, M. (2009). Pastor Ray: ANC at Prayer? Faith group plans to challenge Constitution. *Mail & Guardian*, 11 September.

SACC (South African Council of Churches) (2004). *SACC Statement on Archbishop Tutu's Mandela Lecture*. 29 November. [Online] Available at: http://www.sacc.org.za/news04/tutulect.html [Accessed 10 September 2005].

SACC (2005). SACC asks ANC to act against Komphela. 2 March. [Online] Available at: http://www.sacc.org.za/news05/komphela.html [Accessed 10 September 2005].

Sachs, A. (1990). *Protecting human rights in a new South Africa: contemporary South African debates*. Cape Town: Oxford University Press.

Sachs, A. (1992). *Perfectibility and corruptibility: preparing ourselves for power*. Inaugural lecture, University of Cape Town.

Sachs, A. (2009). *The strange alchemy of life and law*. Oxford: Oxford University Press.

Salazar, P.-J. (2002). *An African Athens: rhetoric and the shaping of democracy in South Africa*. Mahwah, NJ: Lawrence Erlbaum Associates.

SALRC (South African Law Reform Commission) (2003). Project 59, *Islamic Marriages and Related Matters Report*. [Online] Available at: http://www.justice.gov.za/salrc/reports/r_prj59_2003jul.pdf [Accessed 9 May 2017].

Schmitt, C. (1985). *Political theology: four chapters on the concept of sovereignty*. Translated by G. Schwab. Cambridge, MA and London: MIT Press.

Schmitt, C. (2007). *The concept of the political*. Translated by G. Schwab. Chicago and London: University of Chicago Press.

Shaw, M. (1994). The bloody backdrop: negotiating violence. In: S. Friedman and D. Atkinson, ed., *The small miracle: South Africa's negotiated settlement*. Johannesburg: Ravan Press.

Shoba, S. (2009). Voters are also churchgoers. *Business Day*, 17 March.

Sloth-Nielsen, J. and Van Heerden, B. (2003). The Constitutional Family: Developments in South African Family Law Jurisprudence under the 1996 Constitution. *International Journal of Law, Policy and the Family*, 17(2), pp. 121–146.

Smart, J.J.C. (2013). Atheism and agnosticism. In: E.N. Zalta, ed., *The Stanford encyclopaedia of philosophy*. [Online] Available at: http://plato.stanford.edu/archives/spr2013/entries/atheism-agnosticism [Accessed 9 May 2017].

South African Law Commission (1989). *Working Paper 25: Project 58: Group and Human Rights*. Government Publications.

Sparks, A.H. (1994). *Tomorrow is another country: the inside story of South Africa's negotiated revolution*. Sandton: Struik.

Spitz, R. and Chaskalson, M. ed., (2000). *The politics of transition: a hidden history of South Africa's negotiated settlement*. Johannesburg: Wits University Press.

Stacey, J. and Meadow, T. (2009). New Slants on the Slippery Slope: The Politics of Polygamy and Gay Family Rights in South Africa and the United States. *Politics & Society*, 37(2), pp. 167–202.

Statistics South Africa (2012). *Subjective Poverty in South Africa: Findings of the Living Conditions Survey, 2008/2009*. Pretoria: Statistics South Africa.

Statistics South Africa (2014). *Poverty Trends in South Africa: An examination of Absolute Poverty between 2006 and 2011*. Pretoria: Statistics South Africa.

Statistics South Africa (2015a). *Marriages and Divorces, 2013*. Statistical Release P0307. Pretoria: Statistics South Africa.

Statistics South Africa (2015b). *Quarterly Labour Force Survey, Quarter 3: 2015*. Statistical Release P0211. Pretoria: Statistics South Africa.

Statistics South Africa (2015c). *Gross Domestic Product. Third Quarter 2015*. Statistical Release P0441. Pretoria: Statistics South Africa.

Steyn, L. (2015). Budget speech: Tough times ahead, says finance minister. *Mail & Guardian*, 21 October. [Online] Available at: https://mg.co.za/article/2015-10-21-tough-times-ahead-says-finance-minister [Accessed 15 May 2017].

Streek, B. and Wicksteed, R. (1981). *Render unto Kaiser: a Transkei dossier*. Johannesburg: Ravan Press.

Sullivan, W.F. (2002). Neutralising Religion: or, what is the Opposite of 'Faith-Based'? *History of Religions*, 41(4), pp. 369–390.

Sullivan, W.F. (2005). *The impossibility of religious freedom*. Princeton, NJ: Princeton University Press.

Sundkler, B.G. (1948). *Bantu prophets in South Africa*. London: Lutterworth Press.

Suttner, R. (2010). The Zuma Era: its Historical Context and the Future. *African Historical Review*, 41(2), pp. 28–59.

Taylor, C. (2007). *A secular age*. Cambridge, MA: The Bellknap Press of Harvard University Press.

Tayob, A. (1995). Islamic resurgence in South Africa: the Muslim Youth Movement. In: D. Chidester, ed., *Religion in southern Africa*. Cape Town: University of Cape Town Press.

Tayob, A. (2005). The Struggle over Muslim Personal Law in a Rights-Based Constitution: A South African Case Study. *Recht Van de Islam*, 22, pp. 1–16.

Tayob, A. (2008). Islamic Politics in South Africa: between Identity and Utopia. *South African Historical Journal*, 60(4), pp. 583–599.

Tayob, A. (2009). *Religion in modern Islamic discourse*. London: Hurst & Company.

Tebbe, N. (2008). Inheritance and Disinheritance: African Customary Law and Constitutional Rights. *The Journal of Religion*, 88, pp. 466–496.

Thamm, M. (2016). A royal conundrum: King Dalinyebo and the traditional leaders hot potato. *Daily Maverick*, 13 January. [Online] Available at: www.dailymaverick.co.za/article/2016-01-13-a-royal-conundrum-king-dalindyebo-and-the-traditional-leaders-hot-potato/#.WFtV53dh28U [Accessed 18 May 2017].

The Sun (2009). It's jail for Thembu King. 7 December.

Theron, P.F. (2008). From Moral Authority to Insignificant Minority: the Precarious State of the Dutch Reformed Church in South Africa. *Journal of Reformed Theology*, 2, pp. 228–239.

Tsele, M. (2001). *General Secretary's report to the 2nd Triennial national conference of the South African Council of Churches.* [Online] Available at: www. sacc.org.za [Accessed 9 May 2017].

Turner, R.L. (2014). Traditional, Democratic, Accountable? Navigating Citizen-Subjection in Rural South Africa. *Africa Spectrum,* 49(1), pp. 27–54.

Vail, L., ed. (1991). *The creation of tribalism in southern Africa.* Berkeley and Los Angeles, CA: University of California Press.

Van der Vyver, J.D. (1999). Constitutional Perspective of Church–State Relations in South Africa. *Brigham Young University Law Review,* 1999(2), pp. 635–673.

Van der Walt, J. (2007). The time of reconciliation. In: W. le Roux and K. van Marle, ed., *Post-apartheid fragments: law, politics and critique.* Pretoria: University of South Africa Press.

Van der Westhuizen, C. (2007). *White power & the rise and fall of the National Party.* Cape Town: Zebra Press.

Vattimo, G. (2005). The age of interpretation. In: S. Zabala, ed., *The future of religion.* New York: Columbia University Press.

Verdoolaege, A. (2006). The Debate on Truth and Reconciliation: a Survey of Literature on the South African Truth and Reconciliation Commission. *Journal of Language and Politics,* 5(1), pp. 15–35.

Villa-Vicencio, C. and Verwoerd, W. ed., (2000). *Looking back, looking forward: reflections on the Truth and Reconciliation Commission of South Africa.* Cape Town: University of Cape Town Press.

Waldmeir, P. (1997). *Anatomy of a miracle: the end of apartheid and the birth of a new South Africa.* London: Penguin Books.

Walshe, P. (1997). Christianity and the anti-apartheid struggle: the prophetic voice within divided churches. In: R. Elphick and R. Davenport, ed., *Christianity in South Africa: a political, social and cultural history.* Oxford and Cape Town: James Currey and David Philip.

Weber, M. (1978). *Economy and society: an outline of interpretive sociology,* vol. 1. G. Roth and C. Wittich, ed. Berkeley, CA: University of California Press.

Weber, M. (2004). *The vocation lectures: science as a vocation, politics as a vocation.* Translated by R. Livingstone. D.S. Owen and T.B. Strong, ed. Cambridge, MA: Hackett Publishing Company.

Welsh, D. (1972). The Cultural Dimension of Apartheid. *African Affairs,* 71(282), pp. 35–53.

West, G. (2010). Jesus, Jacob and the New Jerusalem: Religion in the Public Realm between Polokwane and the Presidency. *Journal for the Study of Religion,* 23(1), pp. 43–70.

White, H. (2010). Outside the Dwelling of Culture: Estrangement and Difference in Postcolonial Zululand. *Anthropological Quarterly,* 83(3), pp. 497–549.

White, H. (2012). A Post-Fordist Ethnicity: Insecurity, Authority, and Identity in South Africa. *Anthropological Quarterly,* 85(2), pp. 397–428.

White, H. (2015). Custom, Normativity and Authority in South Africa. *Journal of Southern African Studies,* 41(5), pp. 1–13.

Williams, J.M. (2009). Legislating 'Tradition' in South Africa. *Journal of Southern African Studies,* 35(1), pp. 191–209.

Wilson, M. (1971). *Religion and the transformation of society: a study in social change in Africa.* Cambridge: Cambridge University Press.

Wittenberg, M. (2014). *Wages and Wage Inequality in South Africa 1994–2011: The Evidence from Household Survey Data.* Southern Africa Labour and Development Research Unit Working Paper No. 135 and DataFirst Technical Paper 26. Cape Town: SALDRU, University of Cape Town.

World Council of Churches (1960). *Cottesloe Consultation: The Report of the Consultation among South African Member Churches of the World Council of Churches.* Johannesburg: The Cottesloe Consultation.

Yarbrough, M.W. (2005). *We thee wed: marriage, law, culture and subjectivity in post-apartheid South Africa.* Yale University, Comparative Research Workshop.

Young, C. (2004). The End of the Post-colonial State in Africa? Reflections on Changing African Political Dynamics. *African Affairs*, 103, pp. 223–249.

Zîzêk, S. (2000). *The fragile absolute: or, why is the Christian legacy worth fighting for?* London and New York: Verso.

Zîzêk, S. (2002). *On belief.* London and New York: Routledge.

INTERVIEWS AND PERSONAL COMMUNICATION

Interview, Hugh Corder, Professor of Public Law, University of Cape Town, 8 April 2008.

Pers. comm., Justice Albie Sachs, Constitutional Court Judge, Cape Town, 12 May 2011.

Interview, Chance Chagunda, South African Catholic Bishops Conference Parliamentary Liaison Officer, Cape Town, 28 September 2005.

Interview, Father Peter-John Pearce, Head of the South African Bishops Conference Parliamentary Liaison Office, Cape Town, 29 June 2005.

Index

Printed and bound by CPI Group (UK) Ltd, Croydon, CR0 4YY

09/06/2025

14685821-0002